James Baldwin Brown

The Soul's Exodus and Pilgrimage

James Baldwin Brown

The Soul's Exodus and Pilgrimage

ISBN/EAN: 9783337290702

Printed in Europe, USA, Canada, Australia, Japan

Cover: Foto ©Thomas Meinert / pixelio.de

More available books at **www.hansebooks.com**

THE SOUL'S EXODUS

AND

PILGRIMAGE.

BY

JAMES BALDWIN BROWN, B.A.,

MINISTER OF CLAYLAND'S CHAPEL, CLAPHAM ROAD, LONDON.

"THE WAY OF THE WILDERNESS."—EXODUS XIII. 18.

SECOND EDITION.

LONDON:

SMITH, ELDER AND CO., 65, CORNHILL.

M.DCCC.LXII.

TO

THE DEAR

COMPANION

AND

GOOD ANGEL

OF MY

PILGRIMAGE,

I INSCRIBE

THESE.

J. B. B.

CONTENTS.

CONTENTS.

PREFACE TO THE SECOND EDITION.

In sending forth a second edition of " *The Soul's Exodus and Pilgrimage*," I should be ungrateful indeed, if I did not express my very warm sense of the cordiality with which it has been noticed by the critics of the press, and received by the public at large; if I may form an estimate from the fact that a new edition has been called for so soon.

There is but one point in the criticisms which have fallen under my notice which seems to me to need a word of explanation. A friendly critic mixes with many warm encomiums a complaint that I have omitted all reference to the Passover in connection with the Exodus. He is right in supposing that the omission was purposed. What the Passover seemed to mean to the Israelites that night, is one thing; what it means to us, who can look at it in the light of God's sub-

sequent revelations of Himself, is another. I
could not have referred to it in its place without
entering on a discussion of theological tenets
which would have been premature ; which would
not only have interrupted the moral continuity
of the narrative, but would have anticipated the
period in the history of the education of the
people, when these truths were formally presented to their minds by the Lord. It seems
to me much more true to the method of the
Book of Exodus to deal with these portions of
the subject as I have done, as a whole, in connection with that which gives to them their full
significance—the Dispensation of the Law.

With this one explanation of a matter wherein
my method might, without explanation, be easily
misunderstood, I send forth this new edition of
my book, with an earnest hope that God may
make it the means of arousing some who are
"in captivity" to attempt the Exodus, and of
helping them to bear themselves Christianly
through the pilgrimage of life.

April 4th, 1862.

PREFACE.

*To the Members of the Congregation
of Clayland's Chapel.*

My dear Friends,

It is to you first, and through you to a
wider congregation, that I offer these thoughts
on a Soul's Exodus and Pilgrimage, as illustrated by that way of the wilderness through
which of old God led His sons. You are fully
familiar with my conviction, that we have been
in some danger of slighting the instruction and
influence which the records of the Old Dispensation are capable of affording to us, and which
unfold to us the way of God for nearly two thousand years in the education of mankind. I believe
that every man, in a measure, repeats in his own
experience the experience of the race; that in
a sense we all live through the stages through
which the world has lived; and that the records
of God's methods with the world in any age of
its history, have not merely speculative but prac-

tical and personal bearings on us all. And I think, too, that, on a wider scale, it will help us not a little to understand the revelation which God has given to us in His Son, if we trace back His course of preparation for the fulness of times, His education of the world for the light and freedom which it now enjoys. Those will see most in Christ, and will comprehend best what "the adoption of a son" may mean, who trace most reverently the steps by which God unfolded the revelation, and educated men to receive all the fulness which it contains.

I confess that I hear with a strange shrinking of spirit, the notions about the Old Testament which some of the more advanced even of our orthodox teachers and writers put forth, as though the less we studied it the better; as though it were the record of some palæozoic age of human development, cut off utterly from any vital communion with us—belonging, in fact, to a period and stage of human culture and intelligence which we, in our enlightened age, do right to scorn. Unhappy the nation where childhood is not beautiful, and is lightly esteemed. And unhappy the Church which has no eye of reverence to bend on the childhood of humanity—which feels itself far removed from those perplexities and perils with which adolescence is

familiar, and regards the record of them as meet
pabulum for weaklings, and such as love to dote
about the past. We are all of us too much
children to be able to despise the history of
God's education of the world's childhood; nor
can I afford to close my Old Testament, while
the Christian repeats so constantly the experience, sufferings, and sins of the old Jewish
world.

I think that there is a growing reaction
against that tendency to depreciate the old,
which is so characteristic of all radical schools,
political, intellectual, and Christian. I think
that Mr. Maurice's " *Prophets and Kings of the
Old Testament*" did much to promote the reaction
in the province with which we have here to do.
I remember reading it many years ago with deep
interest, and being led by it to consider more
thoughtfully, whether I had fairly appreciated
the significance of the Old Testament in relation
to the New. I have always endeavoured to study
the Old Testament in the light which the New
sheds upon it, being fully convinced—in spite of
a marvellous argument to the contrary in some
"Strictures" upon my "*Divine Life in Man*"—
that that which is typical must be essentially
smaller and narrower than the thing typified, and
cannot therefore explain it, but must be explained

by it, while it reflects a rich light upon it, as revealing the method in which the way for it was prepared by God.

If there be any part of the Old Testament which is of the widest and grandest human interest, surely it is the way of the wilderness, which I have taken as the text of this present book. It is human from beginning to end. It is this universal human interest which I have endeavoured to elicit; that it is there,—that I do not put it into, but draw it out of the narrative,— I hope my book will show. We have here a complete inspired history of a great human progress. The education of a people who had been bondmen, to be the freemen of God, and His elect ministers to the world; a ministry which the nation refused, but which such men as Daniel and, in a far higher form, St. Paul, fulfilled. I am sure, then, that we must have here a complete picture of a human pilgrimage from the bondage into which sin has sunk us, to the freeman's home for which God is seeking to educate us by His Gospel. I am sure that a whole Christian philosophy of life is here, looking back upon it in the light of the great principle of the Apostle, that the angel who was with the Church in the wilderness, was the Lord who is " God with us."

But I have not attempted to present any-thing like a complete philosophy of life in these pages. Many may feel disposed to complain of the absence of formal symmetry in the treatment of the subject, of the stations omitted, and of the want of a blending of the picture of our human pilgrimage into one harmonious whole. I should plead guilty to the charge without shame. I have not attempted to interpret every-thing, because I do not understand everything. I have not attempted to make a complete methodical picture of man's pilgrimage on this basis, because I am sure that such a picture would be the more incomplete for the very appearance of completeness which it might wear. I do not comprehend God's whole thought about man and man's life. I see here a little and there a little, assured that what is most essential is brought out by our heavenly Teacher into the clearest daylight. What I see, I have set down, but I have not attempted to dogmatize where I do not see, under the idea of making my book on our pilgrimage more complete.

I can fancy, too, that some may complain of an uncertainty of utterance as to the precise spiritual character of the nation, and what God intends it spiritually to illustrate. Now, I speak of the glory of the dispensation, and now, of its darkness; now, of the people as God's chosen ones—His sons beloved, cherished, and elect to Canaan—and now, as faithless, slavish, denounced and disowned by Him. I can only answer, that I find this formal inconsistency in the Book, and that I have tried to be faithful to it; and that such uncertainties and apparent inconsistencies must inhere, in any faithful attempt to set forth the truth of Divine things within the range of our comprehension; that St. Paul's writings are full of them; that I should distrust deeply the man who should profess his ability to clear up all difficulties, and explain precisely what God means by every act and word; and finally, that to those who will look honestly, the counterpart of these inconsistencies and uncertainties, and in some measure the key to them, is within.

I have spoken of the Jewish dispensation as having its own essential glory. With St. Paul's words before me, I could do no otherwise. In 2 Cor. iii. he says distinctly, that it was glorious; no prison-house for bondmen, but a training-school for sons. I have endeavoured to recall that glory, while showing how in the glory that excelleth, it is not abolished, but absorbed, and thus more nobly lost.

It will be seen that this is mainly a book of experience. I have not sought to unfold doc-

trines; not because I undervalue their importance, but because they are among the things
which are most surely believed in our churches;
and the great need amongst us is to have them
married to life. I have assumed, without
lengthened proof, that the Jehovah of the Old
Testament is the "Emmanuel" of the New;
and that, as St. Stephen testifies, the Spirit of
the Lord who strove against their sins, and
educated their souls, was the Holy Ghost. I
have adopted the thoughts and phraseology
of the New Testament, as matter of course;
believing that in doing so I am doing precisely
what a believing Israelite would have delighted
to do, had he enjoyed our fuller knowledge of
the things of God—the fact of the Incarnation,
and the mission of the Holy Ghost, the Comforter
and Quickener of men.

My readers will see that I avail myself of the
works of Oriental travellers for the purpose of
illustrating the scenery of the wilderness way.
I had published the syllabus of the series of
Discourses which I now give to the public, and
had preached some of the earlier ones, before
Dr. Stanley's masterly work on "*Sinai and Palestine*" appeared. I read it with intense interest,
and was delighted to find how amply his descriptions confirmed the views, which I had been led

to entertain as to the fitness of the wilderness of Sinai to be the scene of the education of a noble race. I know how hard it is to bring a fresh eye to bear on scenes oft described, and about which a stereotyped impression is abroad. This rare merit attaches to Dr. Stanley's work. It is evidently a fresh and faithful record of the impressions of a man whose eye may be trusted, and is invaluable to those who, like myself, endeavour to comprehend and set forth the reasons why by that way God led His sons.

And now, my dear friends, I commend my book to your thoughtful perusal, and myself to your sympathies and prayers. I never cease to give thanks for the cordial sympathy and co-operation which, for fifteen years, you have afforded to me ; and for the zeal—never more conspicuous than at present, with which you sustain my efforts to instruct, comfort, help, and bless the poor of the neighbourhood, to whom we, in common with other Christian congregations, are set to be as " the salt of the earth," and " the light of the world."

150, *Albany Street, Regent's Park,*
    December 3rd, 1861.

THE SOUL'S EXODUS

AND

PILGRIMAGE.

—◦◇◦—

Sermon i.

The Land of Egypt: the House of Bondage.

Exodus xx. 2.

EGYPT stands foremost among the countries of
the elder pagan world. Egypt is, in truth, the
mother of paganism, the fruitful parent of idolatries, the nurse of pagan civilization, of pagan
literature, politics, and art; and therefore the
fitting representative in the language of Scripture
of that "world" out of which, in all ages, God
calls His sons.

Let us first study the physical aspects of the
country. The plains of the Nile, the Euphrates,
the Ganges, the Hoang-ho, bear indisputable marks
of having been the earliest settled homes of the
human race. In these vast valleys, under the fos-

1

tering warmth of an almost tropical sun, agriculture was at once simple and productive; bodies of men could be nourished readily, and society—using the word in a popular sense, the aggregation of masses of men around common centres—became easily possible. The soil of these alluvial plains is of the richest, and is cheaply renewed by inundation. Egypt has never been manured for four thousand years, and is as fruitful now as in the days of Sesostris. The means of communication, moreover, are in such countries easy and rapid; and the apparatus of a complicated social system can be set up with less toil and cost than in those varied and temperate regions which are fitted to develop the higher faculties of man, and to be the home of civilization at a more advanced era of its history. The early settlers in the valleys of Mesopotamia and Egypt attained very rapidly to an advanced stage of social and political development. While the Hebrew patriarchs were still feeding their flocks on the wolds of Canaan, and struggling with the inhabitants for no greater matter than a well, Egypt had a settled and complicated polity, castes of labourers, soldiers, and priests, a hierarchy, a court of great ceremonial pomp, and commercial relations with the most distant nations of the world.

At an equally early period Mesopotamia became

the seat of a powerful and splendid monarchy, whose earliest records are being disinterred from the sand-hills which, like the monasteries of the middle ages, guard treasures of which they little know the worth. These records show the exceeding rapidity of the growth of civilization under the propitious circumstances at which we have glanced. If, as has been suggested, the name Peleg, Gen. x. 25 (division), marks the period of the canalization of Mesopotamia, it shows what rapid progress had been made in that region in the time of the great-grandson of Shem.*

But such civilization is not fruitful in true progress. Though rich, it is stagnant, like the climate and the land. In such wealthy regions, where nature is so lavish and her smile is to be had for asking, man misses the stimulus to action, and that play of his nobler qualities and passions which the more thrifty temperament of nature in a colder climate and more broken country secures. If you want to see man in his individual manhood, full-grown, free, noble, and productive of his highest works, you must seek the colder and more varied European Continent. If you want to see men living in herds, springing up and perishing like the crops of summer fruits, preserving unchanged characteristics of form, feature, and

---

* *Proceedings of the Royal Geographical Society.* 1856.

habit, without progress, without regress, through
thousands of years, you must go to the basins of
the Euphrates, the Ganges, and the Nile.   The
fellah of Egypt lives still, uncomplaining and
hopeless, the life of his oppressed forefathers in
the days of the Pharaohs, while the whole Western
world has been in rapid progress, and has left all
ancient landmarks, even the loftiest, hull-down in
her wake.

Of the four regions which dispute the palm of
antiquity and contend for the name of Mother of
Civilization, Egypt stands first in interest and
importance, as the wisest, the most developed,
and, above all, the most influential on the civilization of Europe and the fortunes of mankind.
From Egypt were carried the seeds which, received into the generous soil of the Greek nature,
bore as their fruit the completest form of pagan
society; and in Egypt was nursed and educated
that intellect, which, receiving a diviner wisdom
from on high, gave birth to the social and national
institutions which have unfolded out of their
bosom the Christian Church. Thus the two great
streams of human progress had their starting-
point from Egypt; which became, though for different reasons, the classic ground of the pagan
and Christian worlds.

Egypt is, in point of physical features, the

strangest country upon earth. It consists simply of a long narrow valley, with the Delta formed by the deposits of its river where it issues into the sea, of the length of about five hundred miles, and an average breadth of not more than seven. The cultivable land, from Syene to the commencement of the Delta, is simply a narrow slip of fertile soil, hemmed in by a belt of stony or sandy plain, reaching to the foot of the mountain chains which enclose it, and sometimes press closely on the river on either hand. The productive area, from Syene to the sea, may be estimated liberally at seven thousand square miles. In the time of the Pharaohs, it is said to have contained 7,000,000 of inhabitants; but the statement is a vague one, and, there is reason to think, somewhat exaggerated. Sir Gardner Wilkinson estimates the present population at 1,500,000. It is a country in which rain seldom falls, but the dews are copious. The land, as every child knows, is irrigated by the periodical overflowing of the river; which begins to rise at the time of the summer solstice, overflows the belt of cultivable land on its borders, and during its hundred days' dominion amply enriches the soil. The height of a fair average inundation is about forty feet at the Cataracts, thirty-six feet at Thebes, twenty-five feet at Cairo, and four feet at the mouth of the river. A height of only twenty-three feet or twenty-four feet at Cairo, near which the Nilometer is situated, is followed by famine; a height of twenty-seven feet lays the whole country waste. The rains in April and May in the highlands of Central Africa are supposed to be the cause of this marvellous phenomenon, on which depends, and has depended for ages, the very existence of millions of the human family, and, in ancient times, the fate of the world's most splendid empire; and yet, though lawless storms are the feeders of this river of Egypt, so strong and sure is the hand of the Creator, so delicate the balances in which He holds the adjustments of nature, that the Nile has continued to rise and fall within the prescribed limits, with rare exceptions, for, at any rate, four thousand years. The cultivation of the soil is most easy. The plough is hardly required; it serves chiefly as a harrow. In the sculptures, the sower precedes the ploughshare, which is a slight instrument, and managed by a single hand. At the same time, the rise of the river was watched with intense anxiety, and the cultivation of the country was matter of extreme difficulty, in the years when the required height was not attained. With what joy does Moses contemplate the physical features of the Promised

Land :—"For the land, whither thou goest in to possess it, is not as the land of Egypt from whence ye came out, where thou sowedst thy seed, and wateredst it with thy foot, as a garden of herbs : but the land, whither ye go to possess it, is a land of hills and valleys, and drinketh water of the rain of heaven : a land which the Lord thy God careth for : the eyes of the Lord thy God are always upon it, from the beginning of the year even unto the end of the year."— *Deut.* xi., 10—12.

Eyes wearied with the monotony of Egyptian scenery, hearts sick of the monotony of Egyptian life, revelled in the prospect of a land of rich natural beauty—of brooks, purling through green meadows nestled in the bosom of the hills, of mountains, springs, and foamy torrents, and all the brilliant variety of a highland country. Egypt is a monotone. · Her part has been a monotone in the great choral hymn of the progress of the ages. Her unfathomable sphynx expresses, as perfectly as human art can express it, the mystery of the life of man. And Egypt is as far from the solution of it now, as when Moses led forth his shepherd tribes to seek, amid the awful desolations of Sinai, the solution from the lips of God. I do not know whether it has ever struck you, as you look into the faces of the Egyptian images at

the Museum or the Crystal Palace, that they are
full of wonder and awe—as children amazed at a
mystery which holds them in its spells, rather
than as men of intellect and resolution, who see
the mystery, but are minded to explore it or die.
The Apollo looks out with open face into the universe. Beauty in the Venus of Milo reigns. The
masterpieces of Greek art hold up their heads
with defiant or conquering strength and courage :
you see that the men who carved those images
are men who will invent, discover, and explore
all domains where man's foot may tread ; they
have in them the principle of progress—they
will grow, create, and leave a glorious legacy to
the Future. The Egyptian figures, on the other
hand, are full of intellect ; but it is beaten,
baffled, oppressed by the mystery which oppresses
the world. The men who wrought those images
will not strive to wring out the secret from nature.
Nature will master them ; they will bow down,
and worship abjectly what they cannot explore.
Every beast and reptile, every blade of grass, will
re-present the mystery, and seem to them full of
God. And such was actually their history. Their
sphynx looked out with calm, unintelligent, un-
aspiring wonder over the prolific land on whose
borders it stood sentinel—beautiful in the serenity
of its despair : and thus the people looked with

idolatrous awe and reverence at the teeming
fertility of the soil and of every living thing in
Egypt; and they bowed down their souls, and
worshipped every form of animal existence; birds,
beasts, reptiles, and every thing, however obscene
and loathsome, which moveth upon the face of
the earth. Take the testimony of Herodotus:—

"Egypt, though bordering on Libya, does not abound in
wild beasts; but all that they have are accounted sacred, as
well those that are domesticated as those that are not. But
if I should give the reasons why they are consecrated, I must
descend in my history to religious matters, which I avoid
relating as much as I can; and such as I have touched upon
in the course of my narrative, I have mentioned from necessity.
They have a custom relating to animals of the following kind:
Superintendents, consisting both of men and women, are
appointed to feed every kind separately; and the son suc-
ceeds the father in this office. All the inhabitants of the
cities perform their vows to the superintendents in the following manner: Having made a vow to the god to whom the
animal belongs, they shave either the whole heads of their
children, or a half or a third part of the head, and then weigh
the hair in a scale against silver, and whatever the weight
may be, they give to the superintendent of the animals; and
she in return cuts up some fish, and gives it as food to the
animals; such is the usual mode of feeding them. Should
any one kill one of these beasts, if wilfully, death is the
punishment; if by accident, he pays such fine as the priests
choose to impose. But whoever kills an ibis or a hawk,
whether wilfully or by accident, must necessarily be put to
death. . . . .

"In whatever house a cat dies of a natural death, all the

family shave their eyebrows only; but if a dog die, they shave the whole body and the head. All cats that die are carried to certain sacred houses, where, being first embalmed, they are buried in the city of Bubastis. All persons bury their dead dogs in sacred vaults within their own city; and ichneumons are buried in the same manner as the dogs: but field-mice and hawks they carry to the city of Buto, the ibis to Hermopolis; the bears, which are few in number, and the wolves, which are not much larger than foxes, they bury wherever they are found lying."—*Herodotus,* ii. 65—67.

I think, if you look at them, the statues of the two peoples will expound their character, and explain their history. There are few Englishmen who have not seen the rich remains of Egyptian art and life which are contained in the Museum of our country, and who have not staid to gaze curiously on thoses trange symbols carved in stone by the Egyptian priests, which as yet half hide and half reveal the secrets of the primæval ages of history. Into the vexed question as to the duration of man's existence upon this earth, which, not from this ground alone, is being urged upon our attention, I have happily here no call to enter. Science treads boldly, not to say defiantly, on ground which is claimed in the sacred name of revelation; and has, not seldom, been compelled to recall her dicta and retrace her steps. Perhaps the reason of this defiant attitude is partly the jealousy with which narrow theologians have watched her explorations. A happier age is dawning; and whatever may be the final judgments of science on matters which fall fairly within her domain, theologians are thankful now to believe that it can but end in the establishment of a higher harmony between man's knowledge and the essential truth of the Word of God. One thing, at any rate, has been made clear by the study of Egyptian monuments, that the writer of the Pentateuch must have known Egyptian life thoroughly, and must have had a native right to discourse of Egyptian things. And the world is full of buried witnesses to the truth of God. Every stone of the Desert, could it speak, would testify that Israel passed that way.

The early history of Egypt is still buried in confusion, through which an orderly track is being slowly opened by the efforts of the ablest scholars of our time. From the time of Pharaoh Necho and his grandson Apries, or Pharaoh Hophra, who succeeded B.C. 595, who cross the track of the Scripture narrative, the course of Egyptian history is clear. In the reign of Hophra, Greeks first appear upon the scene, and the history of Egypt becomes inwoven with the general history of the civilized world. In 523 B.C. the native dynasties were overthrown by Cambyses the Persian, and the Pharaohs disappear from history.

There can be no doubt that the Egyptian
idolatry, being of a peculiarly degrading character, had plunged the people into the very
depths of anarchy and moral pollution, when the
Persian fire-flood swept the whole system away.
So swept the fire-flood of Jewish conquest through
Canaan, when the land was "weary of its inhabitants," and purged them out.   Some baptisms
must be of fire.   About 400 B.C. the Persians
relaxed their grasp, being fully occupied with
Greek affairs; and a native monarch, Amyrtæus
the Saite, occupied the throne after a long life of
struggle against the Persian rule.   He reigned
from 414 B.C. for six years in tolerable prosperity,
and was magnificently interred in a green breccia
sarcophagus which you may see now in the British
Museum.   In the year 350 B.C. the Persians re-
conquered the country; but at the disruption of
the empire of Alexander the Great, Ptolemy
Lagus, his ablest general, possessed himself of
the sceptre, and under his successors Alexandria
became the most wealthy and splendid city of the
East.   Under Augustus Cæsar it became a Roman
province, Alexandria being still one of the most
important cities of the empire, and for three centuries, at any rate, the most learned school of
the Christian Church.   In the 5th century, Alex-
andrian philosophy, Christianity, and society seem

to have fallen again into that state of utter demoralization, of hideous vice, which marked the close of the dynasty of the Pharaohs; and in 640 A.D. God again swept it by a fire-flood, and the fierce Mahometan conquerors trampled its pride and splendour in the dust. With them it remains to this day. But the cycle of time brings strange compensations, and Alexandria, as the key of the route to India, may again become one of the most important cities of the world.

I proposed to myself two objects in this present discourse. In the first place, to give you a little condensed information about the country and people, of which some of you might be glad; and, in the second place, and as the main subject, to inquire what it is in Egypt which makes it the symbol of that world, that state of nature, that "house of bondage," out of which in all ages God calls His sons.

That it is so employed in the Scripture, needs no proof. Why it is so used, it is worth while to consider. Babylon is not more identified in Scripture with malignant Antichrist, than is Egypt with the ensnaring world. Why Babylon represents to us Antichrist, while Egypt represents the world, it is not difficult to show. And here let me say, that, by the word "world" I am not seeking to indicate any places, occupations, or

portions of the great human family. I find too
much of the "world" in what passes for the
Church, to dare to draw a visible line of demarca-
tion. By the world here and throughout, I mean
that without us—each one of us—which corresponds with the flesh within us; that which
tempts the too willingly tempted soul.

The character of the Babylonish despotism, the
ceaseless attempts of the Assyrian monarchs on
the liberty of the Jewish Church, the injuries they
inflicted on Palestine, and the ruin they brought
on Jerusalem, fully explain the one symbol.
Egypt, on the other hand, always assumed a more
passive attitude, or at any rate was the seductress,
rarely the assailant and tyrant, of God's people.
It was expressly as a safeguard against seduction
that the people were warned against going down
into Egypt for war-horses, Deut. xvii. 16. Egypt
was not malignant, but rather corrupt and effemi-
nate. In a word, the quintessence of the world.
How it was so, and what the symbol has to teach
us who are called as sons out of Egypt, I proceed
to show.

God could have sent the patriarchs down into
Assyria as easily as into Egypt. There must
have been that in the temper and character of the
Egyptian people and land, which made it specially
capable of showing the world its "form and

pressure," and of furnishing in its relation with God's people a type, clear and impressive for all ages, of the method of God's deliverance of a soul.

I shall consider two points. The character of Egypt, her life, and her influence on her children; and the experience of the sons of God in relation thereto.

I. The character of Egypt and her influence on her children.

I observe—

1. That Egypt was distinguished as the abode of a peculiarly easy and luxurious life. "Take thy fill, eat the fat, and drink the sweet," was her seductive song. The means of subsistence were inconceivably abundant. The very soil teemed with life. Trees and the nobler forms of animal life were rare, but the lower forms and the coarser—melons, cucumbers, garlic, dates, fish, fowl, and the like abounded. How coarse and foul are even the great beasts of Egypt, the crocodile and hippopotamus, compared with the splendid beasts of prey which are the terror of other and more highly organized lands! Everything in Egypt has the mark of grossness on it. The higher faculties of man had little stimulus, the lower being surfeited with food. The luxury

of the Ptolemaic court was excessive.* In Egypt, as in the world, there was all that could lay the soul to sleep under its vine and fig-tree, and reduce it to the level of the brutes which the Egyptian worshipped as more wise and wonderful than man.

This easiness of the terms of life is fatal to the noblest elements in man. Look at Naples. No heroism can be extracted from the Lazzaroni. Give the fellow a bit of bread, a slice of melon, and a drink of sour wine, and he will lie all day long on the quays, basking in the sun and the glorious air; and what cares he if empires rise or totter to their fall? Egypt was the Naples of the old world; wealth, luxury, elaborate refinement, of a kind not inconsistent with grossness; but no moral earnestness, no manhood, no life. Nature wooed man to her lap in Egypt and won him, bathing him in luxurious pleasures—Egypt was the world.

Moreover, Egypt was cut off very much from all the political and intellectual activity in which Babylon was compelled to share. There was the stir and progress of life at Babylon. It was in the current, it must move on or sink. The highway of human progress passed through Babylon. Its situation related it inevitably to the leading

* See the elaborate description in the fifth book of the *Deipnosophists* of Athenæus.

peoples of the world. It would probably be just to date the commencement of the higher civilization of man from the fall of Nineveh, and the rise of Babylon to be the leading city of the East. Babylon lay in the track of commerce, in the path of progress; was brought into fruitful relations with neighbouring and even distant peoples, and was compelled to play a conspicuous part in the drama of the world's history. But Egypt, in her quiet nook, a cleft in the desert, enfolded by jealous wastes on every hand, was out of the line of march. She could " live to herself and die to herself," as was not possible for Babylon. She could play away her strength and her life in wanton pleasures at her will. Sense, the pleasures of the world, pamper the self in man till it kills and buries in its slime all the noble, unselfish, and distinctively manly powers; and thus Egypt nourished her children to wantonness, sloth, and emasculate manhood : feeding them, lulling them, caressing them, as the world, it may be, is caressing you; but robbing them, as the world is robbing you, of heaven and of God.

2. Egypt is the image of the wanton world herein. It was full of the wisdom of this world, the wisdom of the understanding, which prostitutes itself easily to the uses of a sensual and earthly life. Man is not a beast, nor is earth a

2

wild beasts' den. It is full of beautiful and glorious
creations of human intellect and force; but if the
name of God is not on them they bear the badge
of vile service, and lend themselves readily to
unmanly use. When the sacred fire was cold in
the temple of art in the sixteenth century, to
what uses did men like Romano lend most willingly their consummate powers? What fruit did
the complete intellectual culture of the eighteenth
century bear to the world? Egypt was in a sense
the wisest of ancient nations, and yet her wisdom
was worth least to mankind. She covered the
land with cities and temples, invented arts, discovered powers, attained to a strength and stature
whose grandeur has not yet been fully revealed.
Yet where are the temples of Karnak, of Denderah?
What are they? Jerusalem is still the magnet of
all hearts, Rome the shrine of all priestly power.
We still think, by the logic which Aristotle developed; and the constructive men of our time, the
harmonists of long sundered spheres, in philosophy are Platonists to the heart's core. But
Luxor, Memphis, Heliopolis — the floods have
left them stranded, buried in the sands of time.
The world looks at them with wonder, and
steals their treasures to adorn her capitals; but
the Obelisk of Luxor is not more alone and
strange in the focus of modern civilization than

is Egypt in modern history. She has given us
no heroes. Mighty conquerors seem to have
swept over vast regions, but none of them had
genius to consolidate the empires which they
won. Cyrus, Alexander, Cæsar, tread still with
imperial step in history. But Ramses, Sesostris,
Amenophis, who knows more than their names ?
Even such is the wisdom of this world, which
cometh to nought. "Where is the wise, where is
the scribe, where is the disputer of this world ?"
Dead as the memory of Egyptian conquerors.
That which lives must have some portion of
diviner life and higher wisdom ; that which is of
the earth earthy, as Egypt was, perishes as Egypt
has perished, and its very ruin is choked by
sand.

The seeds of great things were in Egypt in
rich abundance, but she could not nourish or
force them to maturity. Even so, in the world's
dust and slime the seeds of glorious things lie
buried, waiting for the quickening breath of the
Spirit of the Lord. The wisdom of Egypt was
fruitless, wonderful as it was ; it availed only to
make the priests luxurious tyrants, and the
people miserable, soulless slaves. It simply established and maintained a system which studiously
destroyed all elements of freedom and dignity in
man ; and has left the world, as its one legacy, a race

of the most abject slaves and drudges, the pity of travellers, the sport of domestic rulers, for two thousand years. There is something profoundly sad in the account of what their wisdom had brought them to, which is given to us by the Father of History, who saw it there four hundred and fifty years before Christ :—"At these convivial banquets, among the wealthy classes, when they have finished supper, a man carries round in a coffin the image of a dead body carved in wood, made as like as possible in colour and workmanship, and in size generally about one or two cubits in length ; and showing this to each of the company he says, 'Look upon this, and then drink and enjoy yourself, for when dead you will be like this.'"—*Herod*. ii. 78.

And is not this the world ? Is not the wisdom, which might have traced the path to heaven, busy clearing and paving the path to hell; making life more cheap, death more trifling, man more beastlike every day? Is not this the world's work in you? Does it nourish and expand the real life of your being, cultivate your highest nature, and hold your lowest under firm control : or is it thickening daily the crust that is growing round your spirits, whereby celestial messengers more seldom reach them, and auroral radiance, gleaming through the heavenly spaces, is more rarely seen? Does the world nourish the habit of self-communion, of heavenly contemplation, of prayer? Egypt did not this for her children; the world does it not for you—Egypt is the image of the world. Such was Egypt in herself and in her influence on her children. Now let us consider—

II. The experience of God's children there— its influence on a people conscious that they had a soul to be saved.

1. They went down to Egypt with the fairest prospects—certainty of sustenance, and promise of wealth, honour, and power. They were to settle in Goshen; better, richer land than the bare hills which would be their only home in Canaan, whose rich valleys would be mainly occupied by the native inhabitants—land in every way suited to yield pasture to their flocks. I am not criticizing too keenly their motive in their descent to Egypt—but they went *down* to Egypt in more senses than one—as we all of us mostly go *down* to a great worldly success. And though it was brought about by most striking providential agencies, and was ruled by God for his own great ends, I am not sure that we are bound to believe that the motives were pure and unworldly which drew them thither. Jacob wanted the higher

courage of Abraham, who sent Lot *down* into the rich valleys while he remained himself by the altar of his God. Some thought of the flesh-pots mingled with fraternal feeling; doubtless they went down to prosper, as men go down to win a fortune by their daily toils. And to how many of us is that fortune a Goshen; and if we can get hold of any Joseph who can settle us there, God keep us from idolatry! The memory of Hudson's statue is not yet cold. Still they found themselves in Egypt in a very simple and natural way, and in a very comfortable and prosperous world.

And why should we refuse the gifts of fortune? Why should we not make the best of the good things that God puts within our reach? Why should we not pass as many pleasant hours in this dull world as possible? Is not

"Dona præsentis cape lætus horæ, ac
Linque severa,"

the true philosophy of life? So the world woos us. We are born in it, God placed us here, God gave us these keen senses, these imperious appetites, and the means of their fullest indulgence; and why should we tighten the rein? See you no new reason why Egypt, when the patriarchs dwelt there, was a fit and full image of "the world?"

2. They had not lived there long, before, rich and fruitful as was the land, they began to find their life a bondage.

The cattle throve; they had fine possessions, and a monarch's favour. But they were men with living souls in them, as well as with cattle and stuff. They had heard the name of God; God knew *them* by name, and had inscribed them as heirs of a better country. They could not rest. Egypt was strange to them. They could not amalgamate with the inhabitants. The Egyptians came to feel it; alienation sprang up and bitterness. Egypt laid chains on them to keep them in her service, while they groaned and writhed, and sighed to be gone—to be free. And rich as the world's pastures may be, propitious as may be its kings, the soul of man grows uneasy in its abodes. There are moments of utter heart-sickness amidst plenty and luxury, such as a sick child of the mountains knows, tossing on a purple bed of state : " Oh, for one breath of the sunny breezes, one glance at the shadows sweeping over the brown moorlands; one breath, one vision, would give me new life." The very prosperity makes the soul conscious of its fetters. The man gets hide-bound with formalities, swathed in respectabilities, meshed in proprieties; he lives in a round of weary, frivolous, heartless occupation, which kills the very soul of pleasure, and makes life, whose every sensation was once so joyous, a clog and a pain.

3. The moment comes, in every experience, when the bondage becomes too grievous to be borne; when the spirit cries out and wrestles for deliverance, and the iron, blood-rusted, enters the very heart.

"And the Egyptians made the children of Israel to serve with rigour: and they made their lives bitter with hard bondage, in mortar, and in brick, and in all manner of service in the field: all their service, wherein they made them serve, was with rigour."—Exodus, i. 13, 14.

"And Pharaoh said, Behold, the people of the land now are many, and ye make them rest from their burdens. And Pharaoh commanded, the same day, the taskmasters of the people and their officers, saying, Ye shall no more give the people straw to make brick, as heretofore: let them go and gather straw for themselves. And the tale of the bricks, which they did make heretofore, ye shall lay upon them; ye shall not diminish aught thereof: for they be idle; therefore they cry, saying, Let us go and sacrifice to our God. Let there more work be laid upon the men, that they may labour therein; and let them not regard vain words. And the taskmasters of the people went

out, and their officers, and they spake to the
people, saying, thus saith Pharaoh, I will not
give you straw. Go ye, get you straw where ye
can find it: yet not aught of your work shall be
diminished. So the people were scattered abroad
throughout all the land of Egypt, to gather stubble
instead of straw. And the taskmasters hasted
them, saying, Fulfil your works, your daily tasks,
as when there was straw. And the officers of the
children of Israel, which Pharaoh's taskmasters
had set over them, were beaten, and demanded,
Wherefore have ye not fulfilled your task in
making brick both yesterday and to-day, as heretofore? Then the officers of the children of
Israel came and cried unto Pharaoh, saying,
Wherefore dealest thou thus with thy servants?
There is no straw given unto thy servants, and
they say to us, Make brick: and, behold, thy
servants are beaten; but the fault is in thine
own people. But he said, Ye are idle, ye are
idle: therefore ye say, Let us go and do sacrifice
to the Lord. Go therefore now and work; for
there shall no straw be given you, yet shall ye
deliver the tale of bricks."—Exodus, v. 5—18.

It is a chapter out of our own history. The
men became conscious of their higher vocation,
and wept and pleaded more earnestly; and their
tyrants yoked them more tightly, and loaded them

more heavily; till, like Job, they cursed God's
light and hated life, in bitterness of soul. And
the soul in its Egypt, the world, drinks deep of
this experience. The moment comes when it
wakes up and says, "I am a slave;" "I am a
beast;" "I will shake off this yoke;" "I will be
free." Then begins a battle-agony; a strife for
life and immortality—the end either a final,
eternal relapse into captivity, or an exodus into
the wilderness and to heaven.

Let the soul fight its own battles, and the most
heroic struggles shall not save it. Let it follow
the Captain of Salvation, and gird on the armour
of God, and death and hell shall not spoil it. It
shall sweep as "on eagles' wings" through the
toils and perils of the desert, and rest at last in
the "rest that remaineth for the people of God." I
believe that once, at any rate, God leads every man
to the edge of this desert: "There, where the
flame column lights the path through the darkness
is the way of a free man to liberty and heaven.
Behind you are the flesh-pots, the melons, the
fish, and the garlic, enough of them to surfeit
you. Now choose, and for ever."

Choose now, and choose for ever. You cannot
make the tale of bricks which the devil demands
from you. When have you had a moment's rest
in his service, a moment's hope? How often

have you cursed the bondage, and writhed under the yoke! How often have you hurled fierce anathemas at the lusts which enslave you, as you felt, with a darkness of heart to which the gathering gloom of death were as morning twilight, that the world was conquering, that your resistance was weaker daily, that the battle would soon be over, and your soul in the outer darkness for ever! Or perhaps you are satisfied with Egypt, its flesh-pots and flavours; you do your daily service like a task, wearily, if you may but play or wanton when it is done. You spur the jaded senses with fierce excitement: the casino, the gambling-house, the masquerade, if the burning brands do not drop too thickly, are the only pleasures that have the taste of pleasure to your surfeited heart. I know not what to say, or how to deal with you. Will you lie there and rot among your pleasures, as Egypt lay and rotted; and then be swept out into the outer darkness, where *" the worm dieth not, and the fire is not quenched for ever."*

But if there be one pang of pain, one cry of weariness, one aspiration for liberty and life, I preach to you an exodus. Choose, choose now, choose for ever—the flesh-pots of Egypt, the eternal darkness, or—EXODUS INTO THE WILDERNESS WITH GOD!

Sermon ii.

Out of Egypt have I called My Son.

Compare Exod. xii. 30-41, *with* Matt. ii. 15.

EGYPT is the " house of bondage," where God's
children are enslaved—the land of easy subsistence, of worldly wisdom, of carnal completeness :
yet of bondage to the spirit which has caught the
tones of a divine vocation, has heard a promise,
has executed a covenant with God. The bondage
becomes more bitter as the soul becomes more
conscious of aspiration and duty,—as it strives
for liberty and pants for life. The world exacts
its tasks, the devil demands his tale, with more
cruel despotism, as the voice of the Lord is heard
cleaving the darkness, and calling forth His sons.
At length the case becomes quite desperate. The
question is of life or death. "I can no longer gasp
in this dense atmosphere, steaming with the
smoke of the flesh-pots, and stinking with the
fetor of corruption,—I must go forth. In the
desert there is air, light, and freedom, and beyond there are worlds which are the spirit's

home." Then begin throes and struggles which
rend the very substance of the being, and tear
the fabric, of our world. The world and hell
muster all their power to crush us; heaven's
bright hosts throng thither to aid. Nature seems
to groan and shroud herself in gloom during that
mighty travail; all heaven, all hell, battling for
the possession of a soul. Then amidst porten-
tous gloom, shivering with terror and shrinking
with weakness, the soul passes out of its bondage,
through mountain gorges and walls of water,
pressed by foes and led by God, till it stands at
length a free soul under the lustrous canopy of
the desert heaven; and sees, with an awful joy,
breaking forth into triumphal hymns, a broad sea
flowing between it and the land of its bondage,
and its tyrants dead upon the shore. Such is the
picture of a soul's deliverance, which the scripture
history presents to us. I shall in this discourse
endeavour to present to you, as vividly as I can,
the leading features of this exodus of Israel, and
thence illustrate the exodus of the soul.

During the period of their abode in Egypt, the
seventy souls which went down with Jacob had
multiplied and become a nation—"six hundred
thousand that were men, besides children," as-
sembled in Succoth on the eve of the exodus.
The increase appears to be enormous. But, in

truth, it is but a fair allowance, considering all that was in their favour, the immense fertility of Egypt, the abundant nourishment, and the extent to which polygamy still prevailed. It is to be considered, too (as Mr. Drew has pointed out in his able and scholarly book on Scripture Lands, note, p. 30,*) that the total number of Hebrew immigrants must have been considerable, far exceeding the seventy of the house of Jacob "which came out of his loins."—Gen. xlvi. 26, 27. A family had come down into Egypt, a nation was ready to depart. The Israelites did not belong to Egypt, they never had a home there. There was something infused into their composure which made them of finer quality than the slaves of Egyptian plenty; they were a race of higher strain, and in bondage they could not rest. True, it had weakened them, demoralized them; much of their freedom was crippled, and their fineness marred. But no more could the Prodigal herd with the citizens of the swinish country, than could Israel, all bedimmed and degraded, herd with Pharaoh's slaves.

The character and conscious destiny of the race, buried from common eyes in the sensual life of the multitude, stood out, in one man's form

* *Scripture Lands*, by the Rev. G. S. Drew, M.A. Smith, Elder and Co.

and history, with preternatural clearness. There
are these "prærogative" men in all ages, in whom
the capabilities and tendencies of a race or community come out and express themselves. Men
who, by a life of toil and sacrifice, bring out the
latent possibilities of their brethren, and make
the people, after long discipline, what they are
themselves by the vocation of God. Moses,
nursed in the very lap, fed from the very bosom,
of Egypt, felt that the blood of his race had
some diviner tincture than that of the smooth,
soft, wanton, wondering Egyptians, among whom
he abode. He loved the desert more than the
city; the free range of open pastures better than
the fanes of temples, or the palaces of kings.
By a strange chain of circumstances God led him
forth into the desert, and trained him there, in
freedom and solitude, for the grandest work ever
committed to the hand of man. Moses is the
man of Israel. You must see Israel in his mirror,
if you would understand, as God understood,
what varied powers the people had in them. And
thus, if you would understand man, you must
"see Jesus," in whom what man shall be appears.

Moses, according to God's universal plan, was
thus disciplined; hardened and sharpened to be
God's instrument of deliverance. He came back
with a calm but unconquerable resolution to

redeem his race. Meantime, while God was educating the leader, the world was preparing the masses for deliverance ; was pressing them so hardly, smiting them so sharply, that in very desperation at last they were ready to achieve liberty or die. Then follows a series of most tremendous portents, by which the people were uprooted from Egypt, their very lusts and passions tamed and quelled ; while Egypt was set before them, not as a tyrant, who, if he smote and burdened them, at any rate fed and housed them, but as an embittered enemy, between whom and themselves there must henceforth be battle of life or death. After these dread miracles Egypt was to them no longer a house of bondage, but as a valley of death, as a gate of hell. The last judgment, the most awful, made eternal schism between them and Egypt. Egypt herself cast them forth in terror, and besought them to depart out of her coasts.— Exodus, xii. 29–33.

From out the shadow of that death-haunted night, themselves pallid with dread, they passed forth. The powers of the world to come were acting visibly on that theatre—the secret of the Lord was laid bare. They went forth, not naked and crouching, as captives, glad of life on the meanest conditions, but as men girt for their life-

work; "harnessed," they faced their future.
They reclaimed, at the world's hand, all the
treasures of which ages of bondage had robbed
them; they "asked," not "borrowed," but
asked with open face of the Egyptians jewels
of silver and jewels of gold and raiment, and
they bore them forth as men that had a right to
them, and would use them in the service of the
living God. The Egyptians gave their treasures
as to men favoured of heaven; and one day all
the world's wealth and splendour, now lavished
on its idolatries, shall pass into the hands of Christ,
and bear the inscription, "Holiness unto the
Lord."

Thus harnessed, with their wives and little
ones, with every fleece and every hoof, with
jewels of silver and jewels of gold—not at all
as men stealing away from their acknowledged
master, but as subjects seeking the service of
their rightful king—the children of Israel went up
with all their armies out of "the land of Egypt,
the house of bondage."

It is a matter of extreme difficulty to trace
their path. That they crossed the Red Sea into
the wilderness of Sinai is clear; but where they
crossed and by what route they reached it, is
fiercely debated among the best scholars, even
at the present day. The stations are Ramses,

Succoth, Etham, and Pihahiroth, the passage of
the Red Sea, and the encampment in the wilderness. But none of these stations can be fixed
with certainty, and no theory can be constructed
which is entirely free from difficulty. Moses, it
must be remembered, was familiar with the whole
region; a man, moreover, of large forethought
and resource, prepared for this great movement,
and therefore, we must suppose, prepared with
some general plan of their course. The difficulty
is how to bring the children of Israel into such a
station as that of Pihahiroth, without attributing
to Moses an utter want of skill and foresight as a
leader; or without, on the other hand, according
to the apprehension of some, even orthodox,
critics, drawing too largely on the supernatural,
which mostly appears to sustain and strengthen
the practical wisdom of the man who had been so
richly endowed for his work.

We shall not, probably, be wrong in placing
Ramses in the neighbourhood of modern Cairo*
—at any rate in that district of Egypt. From
that point a tolerably direct eastern course would
bring them to the head of the gulf which forms
the western arm of the Red Sea. Succoth was

* This, however, is by no means certain. Very able
scholars, following the LXX., identify Ramses with Heroopolis
—considerably to the north-west of the head of the gulf.

their first station. It could not have been far from Ramses. It means "tents," and was probably a mustering-place for those who were journeying eastward through the desert for the purposes of traffic or war. Their next station was Etham, "on the edge of the wilderness;" and here the difficulty begins. The Gulf of Suez manifestly stretched, in ancient times, far to the north-west of its present head. It is quite possible that the passage took place on some point which is now part of the isthmus, whose features are now all but obliterated by sand. Etham would seem, from the narrative, to be some place whence the desert might be reached by an easy route; whence, indeed, it was possible to pass up northwards, and follow the track, "by the way of the sea," to Palestine; or, bending to the south-east, seek the real desert by the wilderness of the Red Sea. There, at Etham, on the edge of the desert, a strange, and, humanly speaking, inexplicable message reached them. "And the Lord spake unto Moses, saying, Speak unto the children of Israel that they *turn* and encamp before Pihahiroth; between Migdol and the sea, over against Baalzephon, before it shall ye encamp by the sea."—Exodus, xiv. 1, 2.

This direction turned them back from their route round the head of the gulf, and brought

3—2

them down its *western* side, at some distance from the sea. They are expressly told to *turn*. There are two possible explanations. Either Moses led them too far southwards, and was in danger of finding himself on the coast of the gulf, at a point where there was no prospect of crossing, and was then told to turn *northwards*, that he might double its head, when he found himself cut off by the Egyptian forces, and was compelled to encamp in the gorge on the border of the sea; or, he was fairly *en route* for the desert, by a track which he knew well, when he was deliberately told to turn southwards, into a difficult and mountainous country, where he might find himself cooped up in a wild ravine, with the Egyptian host behind him, the deep sea in front of him, and the cliffs on either hand so precipitous and close up to the edge of the gulf, that there was no way of escape for him northward along the shore.*

I believe the latter to be the true explanation, and that this apparent entanglement was so ordered by God. Their strange course, in turning southwards from Etham to the mountainous country on the Egyptian coast of the Red Sea, filled the scouts who were observing their march with wonder. They no doubt bore the

---

* See an interesting and able report on this subject, by Captain Moresby, in Aiton's *Lands of the Messiah.*

tidings to Pharaoh, "they are entangled in the
land, the wilderness hath shut them in." These
tidings evidently directed and quickened his pursuit. It would seem that they reached a gorge
in the mountains of which the exit was securely
barred by the sea. God's direction was explicit.
No human arm, no human wisdom was to work
their deliverance. What follows, in the fourteenth
of Exodus, completes the wonderful story. "*Fear
ye not, stand still and see the salvation of God; the
Lord shall fight for you, and ye shall hold your
peace,*" was the inspiring word of Moses. And
this is the key of the whole narrative. That they
might stand still and see God's salvation, they
had been led into such straits. And thus, from
a narrow cleft of the mountain, barred behind by
all the forces of Egypt, and in front by an arm of
the sea, they were brought forth with an high
hand and a stretched-out arm, out of the land
of bondage. The broad free expanse of the wilderness at last spread round them, its brilliant sky
and burning stars above them; and a broad sea,
deep and still as the waters of Lethe, swept
between them and the scenes of their slavish
tasks, their swinish pleasures, their careless serfdom, to flow on for ever. "*As for the Egyptians
whom ye have seen to-day, ye shall see them again no
more for ever.*" Then while the solemn desert air

was hushed about them, and the morning sunlight bathed the scene of their triumphal exodus, and poured a flood of golden splendour around the camp of God's redeemed, rang forth the notes of the most magnificent jubilant hymn that human lips have ever uttered or heaven has ever heard : "And Miriam the prophetess, the sister of Aaron, took a timbrel in her hand; and all the women went out after her with timbrels and dances. And Miriam answered them, Sing ye to the Lord, for He hath triumphed gloriously, the horse and his rider hath He thrown into the sea."—Ex. xv. 20, 21.

Thus Israel completed the exodus. Thus God redeemed His sons. In the wilderness of Shur we leave them awhile, to consider what this wonderful exodus has to do with us—how Israel's history is the painted picture of our own.

I. We cannot treat this as an isolated fact in history. As I have already shown, Egypt is the type of the cunning, careless, wanton world out of which in all ages God is calling His sons. And the exodus remained a living fact in history. The infant Jesus went down into Egypt, as the infant Israel went down, not to repeat the exodus, but to illume afresh its fading lines. The descent of Jesus into Egypt is just a divine index of the significance of this history to man in all his

generations. His wilderness was Judea, his own
Jerusalem; like ours, the home of our nativity,
the theatre of our life-work, our nearest, dearest,
most beautiful and familiar things. I have likened
Egypt to the house of bondage in which each
one of us labours. I have now to show how out
of Egypt God is calling His sons. "His sons!
Yes," some of you will say, "let me but know
that I am one of the elect race, the chosen generation, the royal priesthood, and I come forth at
once! God forbid that I should waste here,
among bricks and flesh-pots, the force which will
put Canaan into my power! But how am I to
know? The cases are not parallel. Suppose I
leave my Egypt, and fall in the fruitless effort to
force my way uncalled to the promised land!
Show me my vocation; show me my name on
the muster-roll of God's elect host, and I am
ready at this moment to take up sword and shield
and go. In the case of Israel every man knew
himself called, every child of Abraham was in-
cluded in the vocation; to every child of Abraham
those awful miracles sealed the promises of God."
AND THEY SEAL THE SAME TO YOU.

I say at once, that the whole history of Israel
would be quite dark to me if I could not look
upon it as a picture of God's dealings, not with
an elect circle of men, but with mankind. I read

in the Gospel that "*God loveth the world*"—the world in its rebellion. I read that "*Christ died for all men.*" That as the hour of His agony drew near, He took the whole world to His heart of love, "*And I, if I be lifted up, will draw all men unto Me.*" I am told that the book is given to me to teach me this : that every line of it has a distinct relation to its great end—the proclamation of a Gospel to a whole human world. Its last cry of invitation is to "*Whosoever is athirst, whosoever will ;*" and with this the revelation is sealed. I take up my Bible, and a casual glance shows me that three-fourths of its bulk is occupied with the history of this people. I am driven to the supposition that the history of this people is a microcosm, in which I can see the history of all peoples—that Israel is, in little, all the world. A closer inspection of the Word sustains the supposition. There is absolutely no other key. Unless we take the kingdom of Heaven to mean the whole mass of those who have heard the proclamation of Christ's Kingship, and know themselves amenable to His laws, then the people of Israel is not, and cannot be made, typical of the kingdom of Heaven. Once lay it down as a principle that there are those in the world whom, by a distinct act of His Sovereignty, God calls out of the world, and leads forth to a pilgrimage which, despite many backslidings and short-comings, terminates inevitably in heaven, and you may shut up your bibles, you may shut up the book of experience, you may shut up the history of Israel specially—sovereignty is all that you have to do with; search for evidence of that, it will save you all further trouble; and if you find no evidence of that in yourself or in other men, at least you know your destiny, it will save you all further hope.

If I were compelled to say to you, my commission is to call certain of you, who have God's mark upon you, out of this congregation into the living fellowship of the Church; some of you being Israelites though unconscious, some of you being of the world, Egyptians in blood, habit, character, and inevitable destiny; the only point of uncertainty being as to who was of the one, and who was of the other side,—I declare to you solemnly, I would shut up this book, and shake off the dust of my feet as I leave this desk, as a testimony against the most solemn mockery which a man can enact before the face of God. That God has His own in all ages; that out of this company there are those who will join that sacred band, and some who will snuff the flesh-pots of Egypt, and laugh at liberty and divine joys, I cannot question; alas, it is made daily too clear!

That none can join that holy company except by the Father's grace and attractive power, seems as solemnly plain. What can "effectual" mean except that which is penetrated with the strength of God? But that God has already settled it— has put a mark on one and another, and decreed to this one an exodus, a desert pilgrimage, and a triumphant entrance into Canaan, whilst to the other the flesh-pots are left in indifference or scorn—is a conception of His relations and ways to man which does violence to the deepest convictions of the human spirit, and the clearest statements, the most earnest and heart-searching appeals of the word of God.

I believe solemnly that each one of you, to whom these words may come, is elect as Israel was that night; that to each one of you the summons comes as distinctly, as peremptorily from God, "*Arise ye, and depart, for this is not your rest.*" They were an elect race. Let us ask wherefore, and to what.

Wherefore? They were of the race of Abraham: that marked them; that constituted their distinctity. And you are of the race of the second Adam, who "seeing that the children were partakers of flesh and blood, Himself also took part of the same." That is your distinctity. You are of the same race, the same flesh and

blood as Jesus; and all who wear a human form
and understand a human voice, God calls forth
from Egypt: His voice is even now piercing,
flashing like electric fire through the gross
darkness which enwraps the land of bondage in
which they torment and strain His sons, "Come
forth to freedom, life, and heaven." If Israel
was of the race of Abraham after the flesh, never
forget—let it shame you in your abject serfdom,
your swinish pleasures—you are after the flesh of
the race of Christ. "Awake then, sleeper, and
arise from the dead, and Christ shall give thee
life."

And to what were they elect?

To what did God call them, deliver them,
bring them out with a high hand and a stretched
out arm? Was it to Canaan, to triumph, to
glorious rest? Yes, in His will He called them
to all this, but failing their will, how many of
them fell in the wilderness! He states, in the
most solemn terms, that it was His will to bring
them into Canaan; then, as their will went not
with His will, He swears as solemnly, that they
shall not enter into His rest. This opens up an
awful abyss of speculation. Who hath resisted
God's will? What finite being can resist Him
"who doeth according to His own will among
the armies of heaven, and among the inhabitants

of earth; none can stay His hand, or say unto Him, What doest thou?" You will find a grand distinction, in scripture and in life, between what God wills and what God decrees: when He says a thing shall be, it must be. When He says He wills it, if it is within the region of the moral activity of the creature, the will of the finite creature may counterwork the will of God. "*He wills all men to be saved.*" There were those of whom the Saviour testified weeping, "*But ye would not.*"

One feels that in this region it is easy to darken counsel with words without knowledge; there are deep mysteries on every hand. It is well if we can find some clue to guide us even a little way. I am far from imagining that I can dispose of the difficulty by a few weak words. Had Egypt no vocation as well as Israel? It is a dark mystery. But we can see that, in order to understand even a portion of God's ways, we must recognize humanity at large and through the ages, as well as the individual man, as having distinct existence before God. It is only on the scale of the universal, that much of His method can be understood. But how much remains dark after all our efforts! "O the depth of the riches both of the wisdom and knowledge of God! how unsearchable are His judgments, and His ways past finding out! For who hath known the mind

of the Lord? or who hath been His counsellor?
Or who hath first given to Him, and it shall be
recompensed to him again? For of Him, and
through Him, and to Him, are all things: to
whom be glory for ever. Amen." Let us be
deeply thankful that God has given us His great
love to *the world* in Christ, as the clue to guide
us through the maze of His counsels. We cannot
err if, understanding all that love includes, we
take it as our constant guide. One shudders,
sometimes, at the flippant fluency with which
some theologians, standing consciously on the
safe side of the line of effectual calling, expound
all that God is doing in judgment on the other.
Some say they "glory in a God of judgment."
I believe in the judgments of love, and hold the
judgments of love to be the most awful which can
be conceived; but I am thankful that I have
learnt to glory, as I pray that you, my brother,
may be able to glory, in a God who " IS LOVE."

I find, then, the most perfect parallelism
between your case and the case of Israel. You
are called to an exodus. You are called to get up
from your slavish lusts, your sensual pleasures,
and go forth. He calls you all forth from Egypt
as His sons—calls you forth to the desert, the
fiery pillar, the manna, the spiritual rock; and
while you aim at Canaan, His will, His heart are

on your side. Be loyal ; take His yoke upon you, and dare His service, and the pursuers of Egypt shall not reach you, the rangers of the desert shall not spoil you, the usurpers of Canaan shall not stay you from the mastery of the Promised Land.

I proceed, in the second place, to sketch,

II. The moral features of the exodus.

1. There was a life in Egypt which had become insupportable to a *man*. A beast might bear it, a slave with a slave's heart might bear it, but a man with a spark of a man's spirit within him would choose rather the alternative of death. I have already painted the picture. I have shown to you how the bondage became daily more galling and profitless, until the slaves cried out for death to set them free. It is the picture of the state of a soul around which the devil's toils are closing, which has given up the hope of living in freedom, and leaps to death for change, at any rate, if not oblivion.

Think you not that, every night while you are calmly slumbering, there are poor devil-driven wretches prowling about our streets and bridges, looking down into the dark water rushing and glancing beneath them, and singing to them a song which the devil suggests will be a lullaby to anguish and remorse ? Think you that in our

crowded streets, in broad daylight, you do not
brush by many a faithful servant of Satan, who
is agitating in his distracted heart the question,
Can hell itself be more burning than these flames
which consume me now ? Yea, amid all the hum
of the world's thronged thoroughfares, the drowsy
hymn of its sleek prosperities, there enters into
the ear of the Lord God who made it all, a ceaseless bitter cry against the strain of the world's
bondage, over the sweat and blood of the soul
wrung out and wasted in the dust. And there is
not one of you that has not felt the iron searing,
scorching into the very heart's core. There is
not one of you that has not wearied, and sickened,
and cried out, though vaguely and fitfully, for aid.
And God is looking down upon it all. His patience
touches its limits. Hear His word ; translate it
into your modern speech ; it is His word to you
this day :—" And the Lord said, I have surely
seen the affliction of my people which are in
Egypt, and have heard their cry by reason of
their taskmasters ; for I know their sorrows ; and
I am come down to deliver them out of the hand
of the Egyptians, and to bring them up out of
that land unto a good land and a large."—Exod.
iii. 7, 8.

2. They saw the stroke of heaven fall on all
that adorns, enriches, and nourishes a worldly life.

There was a pomp, a pride, a sensual glow in the life of teeming and magnificent Egypt, very ensnaring to man's wanton heart. The sweet water of the Nile—sweetest water in the world, sweeter than wine and honey to an Egyptian—the broad fields of corn, the teeming life everywhere, the beautiful cattle, the crowded population, the elastic air, the brilliant sun-light, the burning stars— these Egyptians worshipped it all. What is good, what is God, but these ? And the scathing curse of heaven fell upon it all. The Israelites saw the awful forms of the ministers of the Divine judgments moving amidst the pomp and splendour, and it withered, crackled, and became as fuel to the flame before their eyes. Never before or since has the world had such a lesson, on the meaning and worth of civilization without God. And when the sword of the destroyer swung through the heavy air, and smote every first-born in the land, they understood, in the very core of their trembling consciences, that the world's wealth and splendour without God may be Hell. And God hath revealed it unto you. You have had your idols; they have been ground to powder, and you have tasted their bitter dust. Nothing that a soul can be tempted to trust to in contempt of God has been spared. Your business has failed, your cattle have fallen, your children—a tender mercy it may be to them

—lie in the graveyard, and in bitterness of soul you have been made to feel that the universe itself, and all it doth inherit, were an apple of Sodom, unless it came to you from the hand of the Lord, and were consecrated by His benediction to your use.   It is the dread hour of a soul's vocation, when these plagues fall on its idols; God is calling it out of Egypt. Egypt is full, not of flesh-pots, but of wailing and death. To stay is not only to grovel in bondage, it is to grope in outer darkness; it is to mate with the devils in hell.   For if God has shown to you the vanity of your idols, the loathsomeness of your lusts, and you still cling to them, it is the devil you worship, it is hell you cling to : the cloak, which we name "the world," is stripped from off them, and these are the realities behind.

3. There is a Divine leader—a man commissioned and inspired by God.

Of all classes, slaves are the most dependent on leaders; and, when led, most terrible to their tyrants. When the Roman slaves found leaders, they became the most formidable enemies of the State. But how shall these poor Israelites be free? Unused to independent action, unskilled in arms, unbraced for war, who shall organize and head them; who shall uplift their banner, strike the first stroke, and by his strength and

4

courage inspire them with the hope of victory?
In the very crisis of their history, when the inso-
lence of their tyrants and the misery of their lot
had culminated, a divine leader stood in the midst
of them, and declared that the Lord God Almighty,
the Master of the Egyptians, the Master of the
universe, was on their side.

There are times when man is specially conscious
of his spiritual dependence, when his heart is
open to Divine monitions, when from the depth
of his spirit he prays, "Except thy presence go
with me, carry me not up hence." Man can
blink the aspect of the heavenly presences in his
daily tasks and pleasures; but when the deeper
fountains are stirred, when the stagnant pool
of his serfdom is swept by the storms of life,
when his idols perish, his landmarks fail—how
piteous, how abject often, his cry to the God
whom he has forgotten or scorned, for aid! Then
how gentle, how generous, how loving, how hope-
inspiring the response! A man steps forth, clad
in all the meekness and patience of sorrowful
humanity, yet inspired with all the strength and
wisdom of the eternal Word of God, and clasping
us with the love of a brother, the strength of a
captain, bears us forth into open battle with our
foes. Moses stood forth, and all the heavenly
hosts stood with him. The people, yearning to

know if God was with them in their perilous enterprise, heard his voice and dared the exodus. The force that upholds the heavens and crushes hell, expressed itself in that voice and gesture. He stood there—the divine man—pledge to them of an everlasting victory.

"And now, seeing ye are compassed about with so great a cloud of witnesses, lay aside every weight and the sin which doth so easily beset you, and run with patience the race which is set before you, looking unto Jesus, the author and finisher of your faith; who, for the joy that was set before Him, endured the cross, despising the shame, and is set down at the right hand of the throne of God." "Consider the Apostle and High Priest of your profession, Christ Jesus," who in the house and the work in which Moses wrought as a servant, represents God as the Son. No mere man can take the headship of humanity. For us it has been assumed by "Emmanuel," "God with us." Hell is strong; but He who hath the keys of death and hell is stronger; and He is with you, young pilgrim, and will bury the universe in ruins before one hair of your head shall, unpermitted, fall. Well may you cry, tormented by inward traitors and pressed by conquering foes, "O miserable man that I am, who shall deliver me from the body of this death?"

4—2

Look up! a glorious Captain of the Lord's host is here; His title is, "Mighty to save." Those foes that press you, He has already grappled with and conquered; their blood empurples His triumphal raiment; He waves his consecrated banner—the Cross, by which He won the victory —and passes onward, onward, to complete the triumph and to gather the spoils of the war. Lift your hand and swear to follow Him; grasp His banner and pass on, cross-bearing in His tracks, and you shall fight a good fight on the arena of life's battles; and, dying with a freeman's shout of triumph on your lips, pass up to share the glory of your Captain, and reign with Him on His recovered throne.

4. We discern a condition of utter dependence on the strength and faithfulness of God.

They were delivered by a Divine Work. Shut up there in Pihahiroth, arm of flesh could not help them; the right hand of God was their only aid. "Fear ye not, stand still, and see the salvation of God," is the word which is passed through their host. If God comes forth, there will be triumphant deliverance; if God fail, there will be slavery and death. I do not enter on any theological argument to sustain the plain sense of the words of St. Paul, "Wherefore we conclude that a man is justified by faith without the works of the law." But I say to every one who is beginning to stir in his bondage and pine for freedom, pray God that the hour may come when, it may be in anguish of heart over the wreck of all your worldly hopes, you are brought to cry, "What things were gain to me, those I have counted loss for Christ; yea doubtless and I count all things but loss for the excellency of the knowledge of Christ Jesus my Lord: for whom I have suffered the loss of all things, and do count them but dung that I may win Christ, and be found in Him, not having on mine own righteousness, which is of the law; but that which is through the faith of Christ, the righteousness which is of God by faith."

The time will come when it will be revealed to you that, unless your salvation rests on a Divine Work, it rests on a basis of sand: that unless your righteousness is God's righteousness, it can never bear the blaze of celestial sunlight; that unless your life is the Divine life, the heavenly air will wear and waste it to a wreck. A God-Man must your leader be, and a Divine deliverance must He work. Shut up between Migdol and the sea, you will one day look back with dread on pursuing Egypt, forward to the moaning sea with despair; and unless your soul, emptied of self-trust, yet most trustful—cleared of worldly hopes, yet most hopeful—can stand still and see the salvation of Christ, "of Christ Jesus and Him crucified," that valley will be the grave of your soul. But there, in the agony of despair, is the Divine deliverance; for, "when there was no eye to pity, His eye pitied; when there was no arm to save, His right hand and His holy arm wrought salvation." Stand still! not here in Egypt, among the flesh-pots; but there, on Calvary, amid the deepening gloom, by what seems to be the grave of a world's hope, and see the salvation of God.

5. The last feature of the exodus which I dwell upon is the free, broad desert; the world, the universe before them; a broad, deep sea flowing between them and the land of bondage; and their tyrants dead upon the shore.

If you have ever come forth out of some deadly agony—from watching the death-struggle and the victory of life in one most dear—battling with winds and storms on a reef in the wild ocean —or some commercial crisis through which you dreaded that the fabric of your fortunes, which you had been years in building, would melt like a wave from under your feet—you may share the joy of those redeemed ones when they stood free in the wilderness, watched the broad sunlight gleaming on the track by which they were

to journey to their land of promise, and their
tyrants dead upon the shore. A broad sea swept
between them and Egypt for ever. The gate by
which they had passed to liberty was locked, by
God's own terrible hand, against the pursuit of
even the most daring foes. "Here, then, is freedom. The air is bright, the scene is grand and
inspiring; here we can live as men, and be free."
Do not be misled by the word desert. As I shall
prove to you in my next discourse, there is very
much that is sublime, very much that is soft and
beautiful, in that wilderness. Life there was harder
than in Egpyt, but nobler; though not harder—
not so hard—as that of our Scandinavian forefathers; the grandest race that has ever quickened
the flow of the life-blood of our world! To see
the stormy armies that were closing round them,
tossed as the sport of the stormier sea; to know
that Egypt had met with such an overthrow as
would guard them for ages from any assault; to
see that all before them was their own, that by
that shore the past chapter of their captivity was
sealed up for ever, and that they commenced a
new life-course from that hour; these were the
springs of the joy which inspired that magnificent
hymn, which rang over the waters their last farewell to the land of their toils and tears; and
this joy of the Lord was to be their strength

through the wilderness, and bear them, as on eagles' wings, to their own beautiful and glorious land.

And so, when the burden of your guilt and wretchedness rolls off before the Cross on Calvary, when the deep sea of the Divine forgiving love sweeps over the past and obliterates its shame, when you lift with the arm of a freeman the consecrated banner, and cry, "Christ is my Leader, the free wilderness is before me, and Heaven!" such joy shall thrill in your heart as shall burst forth in music, which may mingle with the harpings of the seraphim before the throne of God and the Lamb.

Oh, the glorious sense of liberty, of wealth, of life, which gushes up in the heart of the man who has made the exodus, and sees his tyrant taskmasters dead behind him on the shore! The devil? He is a beaten foeman; Christ shattered his throne and seized his spoils when he cried out, "It is finished," "and ascended up on high, leading captivity captive." The world? The plagues of God have stripped it of its beauty, the painted and jewelled wanton is made bare, and we loathe what once was our lust. Sorrows, toils, struggles? We hail them. A free man exults in the manly exercise that is wasting to a slave. We glory in tribulations, we delight

in toil, we leap to conflict. Discipline is our life.
And Death? See we not Him who grappled
with the grisly Terror, and tore the iron crown
from his brow? With a song, then, through
Christ, we affront him; we pass with a victor's
step before the prison-house where he rules in
chains. "O death, where is thy sting? O grave,
where is thy victory? The sting of death is sin,
the strength of sin is the law. But thanks be to
God who giveth us the victory through our Lord
Jesus Christ."

Sermon iii.

The Way of the Wilderness.

" But God led the people about, through the way of the wilderness of the Red Sea."—Exod. xiii. 18.

THESE words expound to us a whole philosophy of life.   The Way of the Wilderness has become a household word in Christendom, and this decision of Jehovah is the proclamation of the law of man's earthly life.   It repeats, substantially on the same grounds, and for the same reasons, the first sentence on the man who had made himself a slave by sin.   My text is a new and illustrated comment on the words, " And unto Adam he said, Because thou hast hearkened to the voice of thy wife, and hast eaten of the tree of which I commanded thee saying, Thou shalt not eat of it : cursed is the ground for thy sake ; in sorrow shalt thou eat of it all the days of thy life : thorns also and thistles shall it bring forth to thee ; and thou shalt eat the herb of the field ; in the sweat of thy face shalt thou eat bread, till thou return unto the ground ; for out of it wast thou taken ; for dust thou art, and unto dust

shalt thou return." Gen. iii. 17–19. Read also
Exodus xiii. 17—22. These passages should be
read together, for together they explain the toils,
struggles, sufferings, and desert wanderings of
this our life.

Palestine is the England of the East.* It is
the only natural home in those regions of a free,
independent, industrious, and noble people.
Cyrus expressed a deep truth, which is one of the
chief keys to human history, when he said sadly,
after the settlement of his hardy Persians in the
rich Mesopotamian plains, "The soil which
nourishes such fruits and flowers will not nourish
warriors." This relation between the people and
their home had more to do than any careless
student of history would suppose, with the
strength and liberty, the prosperity and glory of
the most remarkable race which has ever played
its part on the great theatre of the world.

Palestine presents a most striking contrast to
the physical character of both Egypt and Mesopotamia. Their rich soft luxuriant plains, their
tame and monotonous outlines, threw up in more
striking relief the brilliant variety of the hills and
the valleys, the brooks and the rivers, the meadows and the terraced mountain slopes of Canaan.

* A decided likeness, especially to the northern regions of
England, has been discerned by many observant travellers.

The vast plain of Mesopotamia offered no variety, the ranges of mountains were too distant to enter as living features into the composition of the landscape. It was the dreariest of all monotones —a rich one. In Egypt the monotony was of a different but as complete a character. The land of Egypt was a narrow strip of the richest and greenest land conceivable, following the course of the river for more than five hundred miles, the river neither gaining nor losing much in breadth or swiftness; for it receives no tributaries from the point, on the borders of Nubia, where it issues forth from its first Cataract, to the broad Delta through which it discharges its waters into the bosom of the Mediterranean. This narrow belt of soil, the average breadth of which is hardly more than seven miles, is flanked on either side by a range of most bare and desolate limestone mountains, whose plateaus are arid wastes, whose cataracts and avalanches are streams of sand. For some hundreds of miles these level ranges enclose the river; above Thebes, the sandstone crosses them, and about the quarries of Silsilis lends, at any rate, the variety of brilliant colour to the monotony of the narrow mountain gorge, in the hollow of which green Egypt lies. The range of the sandstone is but small; it soon yields place to the granite of Nubia, which, wild

and grand as the long level limestone table mountains are tame and expressionless, forms the
southern boundary of the most prolific region of
the earth.   But the granite region is beyond the
boundary of Egypt proper, and its children play
but slight part in her history.

Thus, in every direction around Palestine, in
the contiguous habitable countries, there is a
somewhat dreary monotony in the landscape,
and a luxuriant, almost wanton, productiveness
in the land; two conditions as unfit for the unfolding of the higher and more godlike part of
humanity as can well be conceived.   Palestine,
on the other hand, presented a winning variety,
both of form and expression: every hill, every
valley, every village, had its distinct feature of
character and beauty whereby it was known and
loved.   The land received its people as a bride,
and they entered it with a lover's eagerness.
Read the Song of Solomon, if you would see
how every nook and corner of the country was
laden, to the eye of a Jew, with an expression of
human beauty.   You might search long the
records of Mesopotamia or Egypt for such a witness of the character and charm of their land.
Moreover, it was a country of mountain passes
and narrow defiles.   Each range of mountain was
a battlement, each pass might be made a Ther-

mopylæ by a free and determined people, as Maccabæus proved. It was a home worth defending, and probably more easy to be defended by a small but courageous people than any other portion of that region of the world. The vast monotony, the soft wanton air, the cloudless skies, the luxuriant herbage of Egypt, formed a background, which served as a relief to Palestine in the memory of the people. For slaves, Egypt might be the meet and sufficient habitation; but out of Egypt, into such a home as Canaan, God must call His sons. But by what road? *"And God led them not through the way of the land of the Philistines, although that was near; but God led the people about through the way of the wilderness of the Red Sea."* From Etham, on the edge of the wilderness, there were two roads to Canaan. The one in a north-easterly direction, across the great northern limestone plateau of the desert, to the southernmost city of Palestine; the way by which Jacob "went down," and by which his funeral procession "went up" to lay him in the grave of his fathers. From Ramses to Gaza is a journey of about ten days. The way is easy, rapid, and safe; but it was not the route selected by Moses, under the guidance of the Lord. The other route I will endeavour in a few words to describe.

From the head of the Red Sea it takes a south-easterly course towards the lofty range of mountains which occupy the triangle, bounded on two sides by the Gulfs of Suez and Akaba; and on the third or northern side, by an irregular sandy plain, which divides the great mountain region from the vast monotonous limestone tract which forms the desert between Palestine and Egypt, and which has its slope steadily towards the Mediterranean Sea.

The mountains which occupy the angle of the peninsula approach in their highest peaks 10,000 feet above the sea level; and it is through the ravines about their northern slopes, and the broken, sandy tract which sweeps almost in a semi-circle from Suez to Edom, between the sandstone and granite on the one hand, and the limestone region of El Tih on the other, that the way of the wilderness lies from Egypt to Palestine—entering it by the south-east, on the shores of the Dead Sea. I will endeavour to condense the accounts of the most intelligent students of the physical geography of this region whose works I have met with, and give you, as far as I can, a general notion of it in a few words.

The central mountain chain of Syria, the Lebanon, falls off to the south into "the rolling limestone hills" of Judea, and, continuing its

course towards Africa, forms a vast desert plateau
of an average elevation of two thousand feet:
this is the desert between Palestine and Egypt,
to which I have referred. This table-land, very
dreary and monotonous in expression, occupies
the whole country, from near the Mediterranean
on the north, to the broad sandy valley on the
south, which separates the long horizontal line
of limestone mountains supporting the desert
plateau from the angle of the peninsula occupied
by the range of Sinai. By the great desert
valley, which sweeps round by a grand circuit
between the limestone on the left and the bolder
sandstone and granite formations on the right,
from the head of the Gulf of Suez to Akaba, the
children of Israel journeyed with their armies.
The left, or northern, side of this "Debbet-er-
Ramleh" has little character or variety—it is the
old limestone rampart of the Nile valley prolonged
into the desert, with mainly the same features;
but on the southern side the traveller finds a
scene of strange grandeur, of awful sublimity,
not perhaps to be paralleled by any other mountain region in the world. In many very important points, its features are unique. It is a
mountain range of a twofold character. The
chain which immediately fronts the traveller, as
he takes his departure from the Egyptian edge of

the wilderness, is of rich red sandstone, singularly varied and magnificent in colour, which, running down from the desert east of Jordan by Edom, traverses the peninsula of Sinai, and, crossing the Gulf of Suez, reappears in Upper Egypt, in about latitude 26° N., where it forms the quarry of many of the most magnificent cities and temples in the land. This narrow belt of sandstone mountain, all aglow, if not ablaze, with colour, excites the enthusiasm of every observant traveller. From the way in which it is described to us by men whose eye is evidently to be trusted, we are led to believe that nothing more splendid, in point of colour, is to be met with even in the most favoured regions of the world. But this is no more than the outwork of the granite range of Sinai, which tosses its black and jagged peaks into the clear air beyond. The rock of Sinai is granite and porphyry. We meet with it again in Nubia, throttling the Nile in its narrow gorge at Syene, where it forms the quarry out of which sphinx and obelisk had been carved in successive ages, in monotonous repetition, which is Egyptian to the heart's core.

In the Sinaitic peninsula this granite system is remarkable for its stern sublimity, its awful stillness, its singular resonance, and for the few lovely valleys which nestle in its deep recesses, clothed

5

with the richest verdure, and adorned, if not with stately, with shadowing palms. Along the base of this wild region the pilgrim of the desert passes, having the low limestone plateau on his left, and on his right the bolder sandstone, crowned by the sublime peaks of Serbâl and Sinai, with frequent and exquisite glimpses of the blue Gulfs of Suez and Akaba on either hand. It is the way of the wilderness from Suez to Palestine; and I imagine, after some study of what travellers of various lands have said about it, one of the most striking and impressive routes in the world.

I do not wish to anticipate the description of the desert scenes which will illustrate the successive stations, whose moral meanings and lessons we have to trace. I simply wish to present to you a glimpse of its broad features, that we may enter more fully into the reason for which it was selected as the way of the children of God. I have said something on the general geological character of the region—that is, its skeleton; now let me give you some general notion of its aspect—that is, the way in which its bones are clothed with flesh. It will be needful, as the lawyers say, to dismiss from your minds the notions which naturally associate themselves with the word desert. We generally understand by

the word, broad, desolate, arid tracts of sand.
If you read the Pentateuch, you will find the
allusions to sand singularly few. The people
suffered little or nothing from the sands of the
desert. The fact is,—and as Dr. Stanley well
observes, it affords a valuable negative testimony
to the truth of the narrative,—that sand is the
exception in the desert of Sinai. Such sand-
wastes as are found in the deserts of Lybia, are
here unknown. The word most commonly employed to describe this region means literally "the
pasture." "The pastures of the wilderness" are
celebrated in the Psalms. The term describes the
broad open waste which affords pasture sufficient
for a nomad tribe wandering with their flocks.
Everywhere along the track which I have described, you meet with a thin and scanty vegetation ; while, here and there, are scenes of splendid beauty and luxuriance ,where a great people
might encamp and live in plenty through successive years.

These scenes of beauty, these oases of acacia,
tamarisk, and palm, are rare. Travellers reckon
but three, of any importance, between Suez and
Edom ; but there is ample evidence that in the
desert of Sinai, as in the inner recesses of Switzer-
land,* nature has been growing more savage and

* I was much struck by the observation of a Grindelwald

5—2

barren for ages; that as man's courage and strength have compelled her to yield her habitable parts to his dominion, she has made her wastes more barren and desolate. I cannot stay to dwell at length on the proofs; but there is ample evidence that the desert, when Israel crossed it, though presenting the same general features which meet the eye of the modern traveller, was more rich in wood, water, and verdure than now. Within the memory of man, vast palm groves have disappeared. Of the acacia (Shittim-wood), of which there was sufficient in the region of Sinai to make the whole framework of the tabernacle, hardly a trace remains. About Rephidim, Amalek—a strong people manifestly—strove with Moses and his nation, where now a few Bedouins can hardly find pastures for their flocks. It was a waste then as now, incapable of cultivation; but more richly clad with verdure, and offering more numerous stations where, in the lap of plenty and beauty, a great multitude might rest.

Murmuring against the barrenness of the waste is not the chronic disease of the pilgrim-nation, it is rather an acute symptom at rare intervals;

pastor, whose hospitality I once enjoyed, that nature in that region is becoming more savage every year. The old road across the great plateau of the Oberland from Grindelwald to the Vallais, is quite lost.

and this testifies to the general sufficiency of the
desert supplies, and tolerableness of the desert
life. I regard this as a point of very large importance, because it presents a striking analogy
between that desert and the way of man's pilgrimage until the present day. God leads none
of us by the rapid and easy path to knowledge,
fortune, or happiness. We all of us travel by a
path which has long stretches of barren and weary
march, and here and there only soft resting-places,
flashing like emeralds on the diadem of the desert,
where we may wait and sleep and play awhile,
before we gird up our loins and pursue our toilsome way. There is a Debbet-er-Ramleh of
grammar, arithmetic and logic, between the young
school-boy and his Canaan of knowledge. I suppose you are not altogether in love with your
daily tasks, whose monotony becomes wearisome;
but they must be done before you can ungird and
lie down in some oasis of social communion, and
live for the moment a life whose sensation is bliss.
I say the oases are few, but, brethren, they are
sure. No true pilgrim can miss them. Not more
surely did Israel find sufficient though scanty
pasture through the whole desert way, with oases
of beauty and plenty at due intervals, than does
man find his bread sure under the hardest circumstances, with appointed seasons of joy and even

rapture; mounting up, in the holiest and most pilgrim-like, to the "joys unspeakable and full of glory." The short way might bring us to rest and glory sooner, but the rest would relax, and the glory blind us. We travel by a longer, harder path; that muscle may be disciplined by toil, courage assured by conquest, and self-government studied in many a season of shame and pain. Then the crown will fit us, rest will be calm and noble activity, and glory we shall wear like kings.

Such is the broad general reason of the way of the wilderness to Canaan. When we come to examine it more in detail, we shall find everywhere suggestions which explain and justify God's method in the ordering of our lives. The text gives an indication, but not an explanation. There was a clear reason why they should not go by the way of the sea, which the dullest could comprehend. The Philistines were there, a powerful confederate people. The conquest of Canaan would be too great an enterprise for a disorganized company of escaped slaves. God is the author of order in the Church and everywhere. His miraculous hand but makes the order of His ways more sure. The disciplined only can win and hold a kingdom. To be disciplined they went forth—to grow into a nation, to be trained to war, to be nursed to a noble manhood, and then they would be able to fulfil the great counsel of God. Among the special reasons of their guidance by that path, the following may be noted :—

I. They had been sated with the magnificence of man's works; God led them forth into the wilderness to show them His works in their native grandeur, and to refresh their exhausted hearts and spirits by the vision of the splendour of His world.

The desert is, geographically, the mediator between Egypt and Canaan, and in its physical features it partakes strangely the character of both. In the wilderness they learnt to mark and cherish the physical features of their habitation—a great step in the development of beings who had been used to the rich but wearying monotony of the Delta of the Nile. They saw both the sublime and the beautiful in nature, and they acquired a touch both of strength and softness which was the first rudiment of the education of their souls. In Egypt they had seen the marvels of *man's* handiwork. The pyramids were already built, and clear from base to summit ; and there the sphinx stood sentinel—a long avenue of the most vast and impressive sculptures in the world. They saw those scenes in all their splendour, whose faded glories men now make long pilgrimages to behold. And then God led them forth where they might see His temples, His pyramids and obelisks of granite and porphyry, His pomp of colour, and all the mystery and splendour of His construction of the world. There can be little question that the great Egyptian monuments borrowed their sublime forms from the types of nature. The pyramids and obelisks of the granite range of Nubia suggested the monuments of Memphis and On. An obelisk stands there still, amid the ruins of On, which shot its delicate shaft into the brilliant air that morning when Joseph wedded the daughter of Potipherah, and penetrated the mysteries of the temple of the Sun. Egypt copied God's works on a scale of matchless grandeur, and then fell down to worship them; and God led his people forth to see the Divine originals, and worship in their solemn presences not the creature, but its Lord.

The glorious range of Horeb, blazing with more brilliant colours than ever Egypt knew: the black, jagged mountain peaks—one of them virgin still—rent and tossed in the most massive, impressive confusion; the palm-groves nestling in their deep recesses, and the torrents, though rarely, rushing down their channelled flanks, tuned the spirit of the people to a higher key-note than had been struck in Egypt, and commenced, in purifying awe and stimulating wonder, the education of their souls.

An extended knowledge of nature has always attended—I do not say caused—all the great eras of the outburst of the human intellect and spirit. It were a curious question to consider what the conquest of the East did for the Augustan age of the Empire ; what the Crusades, regarded as mere discoveries of a larger world, did for the awakening European life of the 13th century, and what the discovery of a new and wondrously beautiful hemisphere did for the imagination and practical force of the men of Elizabeth's day. And so God led His people forth into the desert to see His rock-built palaces and temples ; to hear the even fall amid the breathless silence of the wilderness, to watch the sunlight burning on the sublime peaks of Serbâl or Sinai, and then touching with a softer, tenderer lustre each point and slope, till it flashed gaily in the dewdrops which gemmed the desert verdure at their feet ; and there they learnt how solemn is life, how wonderful is nature, how awful and glorious is God. Egypt had killed this sense, which had been quick in the breast of their patriarch sires ; God regenerated it under the peaks of Sinai, and consecrated it to Himself.

And God has this vision for us. Twenty years ago, we were tempted to complain that science was stripping the mantle of wonder off creation; and in that marvellous book of wisdom, *Sartor Resartus*, our Cato complains, "It has come about that now, to many a royal society, the creation of a world is little more mysterious than the cooking of a dumpling; concerning which last, indeed, there have been minds to whom the question, *how the apples were got in*, suggested difficulties." But the process is like scaling the outer crust of the gem or shell. Science has unfolded beneath, new marvels, new glories, before which the boldest and most self-sufficient are compelled to bow. God has filled the world with forms, hues, tones, which are an everlasting wonder, if we will go forth to enjoy them; and which will tend, if we live with them much and lovingly, to keep pure and simple our easily bewildered and sophisticated hearts. Nature is a book which would confound the world's wisdom if earnestly read. How small our passions amid the strife of elements; how petty our fancies and follies under the solemn canopy of the stars! God leads us as He led them, where we can see all this and be rebuked and silenced; and blush with

shame at our beggarly idolatries, when we know
the name of Him who built and adorned the world.

II. God led them forth by the way of the
wilderness, that He might reveal not nature only
but Himself.

God sought to lead no tumultuous, uncultured
rabble to Canaan, but a people knowing themselves and knowing Him. A rabble they were
when they came out of Egypt, with all the follies
and vices of a rabble; when they entered Canaan
they were an organized nation of disciplined, self-
controlled, resistless men. He led them into the
wilderness as He leads us, that He might meet with
them, speak with them, reveal Himself to them, and
teach them to know themselves in knowing Him.

"Who is the Lord?" was their cry when
Moses came to them. The life in the wilderness was the answer. Ra—Ptah—Kneph—these
are no gods, mighty as are their images and
splendid as are their fanes. The Lord, on that
awful night when He led them forth from Egypt,
destroyed their reverence for Egypt's gods for
ever.* When He planted their feet on the free
soil of the desert, He began to make known to
them His power, character, and name. His
word brought the deluge of waters over the flower

* Even in their lapse into idolatry, Aaron "proclaimed a
feast unto the Lord."

of the Egyptian forces; His visible splendour marked out their mysterious way; His hand spread the manna under the dewy veil on the bosom of the waste, and drew from "the flinty rock" the living stream, to supply, purely and freshly, their daily needs. His voice thundered on Sinai, and declared a law to them; His finger traced, on the tables of stone, the fundamental basis of a moral society; He expounded the sanctions of right and the meaning of truth; He made them know, as no nation before or since has known, that all the force of world and devil cannot stay the man who is in the Lord's highway of duty; that curses cannot wither nor enchantments entangle him; that the very stars in their courses fight for him, and confound his foes.

To give room and time for this revelation, the Lord led them round by Sinai, as He leads us round the wilderness of the world. He takes us "round" by ways of toil and want, that we may learn to know Him as the master of our tasks, and the husband of our need. He brings us to sorrow and bitter complaining, that He may work for us—while every sense is strained to watch it—a deliverance greater than our dreams. He leads us, conscience-stung, to the mountain of testimony, that we may learn the awful form of duty, the sacred limits of life; and

sends us forth, as He sent Israel, men full-armed
for the moral conflict—wise, strong, resolute,
unconquerable, because knowing ourselves, our
way, our work, and HIM.

III. God led them into the wilderness, that He
might there cultivate their manly qualities, and
fit them to hold the possessions they might win.

Discretion comes by experience, experience by
endurance of pains and toils. He led them, by
this way, "to prove them, and see what was in
their heart." He needed not to know; He forecast their character. But He wished them "to
know themselves, and to know that He knew
them, that He might place their relations with
Himself on a firm basis of wisdom and truth.
When they passed out of Egypt, they were the
weakest and most impatient of peoples; when
they passed into Canaan, they were the strongest
and most enduring. A comparison of Numbers xiv. and Joshua i. will make this abundantly
plain. This development was the work of the
wilderness; they had to be educated there to
win and to hold the Promised Land. How nobly
does Paul develop this thought, in Galatians iv.
1–9.! This is the key to the history—"The
child under tutors and governors, until the time
appointed of the Father;" we shall have to use
it again and again to unlock the meaning of the

wilderness life. To spare a child the toils and
pains of education, is the most grievous wrong
that a father can inflict on him. Thus did not
God spare His sons! From the day when they
sang their triumphal hymn upon the desert
shore, to the day when they "passed over
Jordan," their life was one continued discipline : each station, each experience, had a distinct office in relation to the formation of their
character; was sent to add to them a virtue which
would be an instrument of conquest or government, and a spring of strength, not in time only,
but eternity. Not simply to keep them out of
the way of the Philistines, but to drill them till
they could master their enemies; to nurse them
till they could bring forth a Samson, a David,
who could compel the Philistines to own their
supremacy, He led them by Sinai, and trained
them, by self-conquest, to conquer the strongest
foes. They came at last on Canaan, not as a
scattered band of marauders, but with the shock
of a thunderbolt : you feel that the battle is won
the first moment that they set their feet on the
land. And those men in the desert, hard as was
their way and fare, were making history. Bunsen
says,—"History was born that night, when Moses
led forth his people from Goshen." The narrative of their toils and struggles is the oldest and

most precious of historic records, and their way-book has become the heirloom of the pilgrim world. " Behold, we count them happy which endure."

And you who are out in the wilderness, faithless and heartless, like a sailor on a dark sea unlit by stars, learn from Israel the grand reason of your pilgrim vocation, and the end to which it will be guided if you follow the highway of God. God finds you a slave: He would make you a son. You are not the lawful slave of wanton Egypt ; you have the King's mark upon you,—the King of kings is waiting to redeem His own. Come forth, then, come forth to freedom ! breathe the free air, scan the broad horizon—it is your land of wandering ; see the soft blue hills swelling in the distance, the gleaming of rivers, the shadow of woodlands—it is your land of rest.

One word, in conclusion. The desert was the vestibule of Canaan ; life—not the Egypt, but the wilderness of life—is the vestibule of heaven. The scenery of the desert was the transition from the paralysing monotony of Egypt to the stimulating variety of Palestine. Learning how to live in the desert, they were learning how to live in a more beautiful and wealthy land. Not a day of their discipline could be spared. There was not an act of their wilderness life which was not a preparation for their home. Let

it consecrate life and the world to your apprehension, and make all the deed and patience
of the present sacred, to know that it bears a
great future in its breast. There is not a line
of form, a tinge of colour, a tone of sound which
you reverently study here, which is not giving
you the key to the forms, the hues, the harmonies
of celestial worlds. All that is grand and beautiful on earth is an apocalypse, a glimpse through
the veil, of the pomp and beauty of eternity.
These earthly things, from the blade of grass that
crisps beneath your footsteps, to the Alp, that
hides its maiden peak in the white bosom of the
skies, are but images; their ideal forms are the
realities of God's kingdom on high. The stripes
of chastisement, the sobbings of the new-born
spirit, the tears, the wailings, have their counter-
parts there, in crowns, in joys, in songs. Live
boldly, then, and freely, like the king's heirs in
the wilderness; make all the beauty and blessing
of this broad world your own : and the day cometh
when you shall pass with solemn joy, with familiar boldness, into a wider universe, bathed in the
lustre of a more glorious sun. "Come, ye blessed
of my Father," ye who have sustained the toils
and learnt the lessons of the wilderness, "inherit
the kingdom prepared for you from before the
foundation of the world."

Sermon iv.

Marah: the Well of Bitterness.

" So Moses brought Israel from the Red Sea, and they went out into the wilderness of Shur; and they went three days in the wilderness, and found no water. And when they came to Marah, they could not drink of the waters of Marah, for they were bitter: therefore the name of it was called Marah. And the people murmured against Moses, saying, What shall we drink?"— Exod. xv. 22–24.

God led His sons by the way of the wilderness, because it was capable of being the theatre of a nobler, purer, freer life than they could have lived in Egypt; than they could have lived, till disciplined, in Canaan. There was room for a man to breathe there, and work, and prepare himself by the development of all his nobler faculties to take a high part in all the great battles of the Lord. The word, as I have said, employed to describe the region means "the pastures," suggesting anything but thoughts of desolation and death. Waste it is in one sense, but everywhere clothed with a thin vegetation, brightening, as often occurs in limestone regions, wherever a spring gushes up from its not utterly arid bosom,

6

into some of the fairest, richest, sunniest pastures
which deck the mantle of our world.   The mountain passes—for there are such between Suez and
Edom—with all their rich variety of scenery, are
peculiarly bold and splendid; most elevating to
the spirit of a nomad people, who had been nursed
in the lap of luxuriant wanton Egypt, to the
dulness and carelessness of slaves.   The points of
beauty and interest are rare, but most rich when
reached.   I know not that it is otherwise in life.
It is a full repayment for the toil of days of weary
march over burning plains, to rest beneath the
palm groves of Feiran, to wander amid the glens of
Mount Serbâl, or from the peak of Sinai to sweep
the horizon of one of the most glorious prospects
in the world.   God loves not monotony and barrenness. These are not characteristic of the homes
of his elect races: and let us be sure that the
land of the pilgrimage of his first-born had scenes
of interest and features of fitness not easily to be
matched upon this earth.   Mark you, it was no
Eden.   Of that their first day's journey into the
wilderness gave unmistakeable witness. And earth
is no Eden; but seamed and scarred though it be
with the lava-floods of evil, it is liker still to
heaven than to hell.   And this wilderness was the
vestibule of Canaan; its free broad horizon, its
hills and mountain peaks, its rare but exquisite

valleys, its springs and winter torrents, were in contrast with Egypt, in concord with Canaan. These were the first buddings of the beauties of Palestine; their first vision of the land of rich freedom and variety in which God meant them to spend their glorious days. It was no scene of prison discipline, but of manly education; no home of mean furniture and narrow resources, but rather of stimulating varieties and brave excitements; the meet training-ground of the race who were to guard the palladium of the law and the liberty of man, amid those enervating Eastern climates where despots lorded it easily over herds of slaves. The wilderness offered a fair field for a freeman's education; each moment, he would have impressed upon him that his maintenance was in his own hand, and under God's. The individualizing process, which is the necessary preparation for a high communion, would go on there with singular rapidity. Each man would be educated to take thought for himself and his dependants; while the common lot of so great a company, their common sufferings, dangers, and deliverances, would nurse their nationality and develop their common, *pari passu* with their individual life. Nowhere on earth probably, could a bondman be trained so readily to be a freeman and the member of a nation, as in that wilderness.

It was, moreover, as I have said, the vestibule of Canaan, more like beautiful and fruitful Palestine, with all its wasteness, than was Egypt with all its fertility; much as this fair earth with its soft beauties and shining splendours, its meadows and mountains, its morning brilliance and tender evening shadows, is the vestibule of heaven. The earth was cursed for Adam's sake; but, like the wilderness, it had left in it vestiges neither faint nor few of Eden. The rains break up the images of stars and snow-peaks in the clear bosom of a mountain lakelet; but watch well the broken mirror, and you will find strangely beautiful and even perfect vestiges of the image which has been destroyed. And thus, too, the pomp and the splendour of our home, the flush of dawn and the sunset glow, the clear stars and the gleaming flowers, the broad snow-fields in their pure whiteness, and the virgin peaks which shoot up from their bosom to lose themselves in the veils of heaven, are images, broken images, but strangely beautiful and true, of the glories of that heaven of heavens which our sunlight doth not quicken, and where we shall see the heavenly models after which all that this world holds was made. This great world of ours has dreary monotonies—broad blank plains, steppes, and deserts, which are the wandering grounds of our common life; here and

there, like the desert of Sinai, it has oases of
sparkling freshness and beauty, which light up
the dulness of our daily marches, and bear witness
of other worlds.

Forth then into such a wilderness, through
stormy walls of waters, the Children of Israel
passed with their armies. "Egypt, farewell for
ever! Come toil, come struggle, come want, we
are pledged to a freeman's march through the
wilderness, to seek our ancient freeman's home."
This was the spirit of the exodus, the spirit which
inspired Miriam's hymn. And now we picture
them to ourselves as they stand ranged in ranks
on the shore of deliverance, filling the broken
plain which lies between the range of limestone
mountains, supporting the great central plateau
of the desert, and the sea. Doubtless there was
something in the freedom and breadth of the
desert landscape which exhilarated and inspired
them; something, too, in its monotony and vast-
ness which impressed them with a sense of the
solemnity of the life on which they were entering,
and its dependence upon God. Through the first
day's march the novelty of the scene, the freshness of their experience, sustained and cheered
them. The deep blue waters of the gulf, crested
with foam, would lie to the right hand of the
host; and ever and anon we can fancy a bright

band of youths and maidens darting forth on to
the sands where lay the wreck of the army of
their foes, and making the very air palpitate with
the chorus, " Sing unto the Lord, for He hath
triumphed gloriously, the horse and his rider hath
He cast into the sea." Moses and the leaders
would hold on their careful way. The great mass
of the host would doubtless follow patiently in
their tracks; but on either hand, we can imagine,
the more adventurous would spread out upon the
shore or in the desert, exploring the wonders of
the new world into which they had been led forth
so mightily by the right hand of God.

Some impression of the character of their first
days' experience may be gathered from the words
of a recent traveller by the same route :—

" Towards noon we left the shade of the old
palm, and launched out upon the scorching waste.
From a slight rise of sandhills, a burning region
spread out before us ; an irregular plain of sand
and gravel, extending from the foot of the mountains Er-Rahab, which support the great inland
central plateau of the desert, down to the shores
of the sea ; its surface is indented slightly by
occasional wadies or valleys, here merely irregular
depressions in the level, caused by the passage of
the winter floods from the mountains to the sea,
and dotted by scanty tufts of coarse grass and

withered gritty-looking shrubs, which the camels in passing generally caught at with avidity, but sometimes refused. After the continuance of rains, however, these valleys freshen up and afford pasturage to the flocks of the neighbouring small tribe of Terâbîn Arabs, whose encampment lies beneath a singular and conspicuous peak on the left, called Tâset Sudr, or the Cup of Sudr, from a fountain there. The shipless sea appears on our right, and the dark mountains of Attaka beyond, with the opening of Wady Tawarik. In one of these wadies we encamped at sunset.

" Oct. 5.—Off before sunrise, commencing the labours of a most toilsome day. Plain, mountain and wady in a blaze of white heat, ' lie like a load on the weary eye,' and seem as if they had just passed, all palpitating, through a fiery crucible. Truly this beginning of their desert course must have appalled the Israelites. We picture them toiling over the burning expanse—here, too, we learn that they were destitute of water : a fearful privation ! In the afternoon we leave this wearisome plain, and ascend the first range of the white limestone hills, and get peeps of the mountain region beyond. Winding among these hills, at sunset we reached the fountain Howârah, and encamped, at a short distance beyond.".— *Forty Days in the Desert*, pp. 30, 31.

In considering the moral meaning of all this, I remark,—

I. That the first day's journey, in spite of the splendid scenery of the coasts of the gulf, is probably the most wearisome and monotonous of the whole way. Sand-storms, white limestone plains, the dust caked into a hard surface intensely hot and dazzling, no water, no trees—it is as if the desert put on its dreariest dress to greet its pilgrims, and gave to them at once a full taste of the toils and wants which they must endure in traversing its wastes. From Marah there is hardly a single day's journey which does not cross the track of some green oasis, some well or thin filmy stream which clothes itself with verdure, and makes itself known from far by its tamarisk or palm. But from the shore on which they sang their hymn of triumph over their despoiled and beaten foes, they went three days' journey into the wilderness, and found no water. Whether they had filled their skins at the wells now called Ayoun Mousa—or, as is probable, since they are not mentioned in the narrative, had depended on the supplies which they brought with them out of Egypt, this terrible three days' journey through a land of drought, under a blazing sun, must have filled them with dread forebodings and bitter regrets. Travellers who *know* the stations of the wilderness, and when and where they shall come upon water, describe the journey through those dusty wastes as most disheartening. But this people had come out into a strange land : what knew they of the springs of Elim and the oasis of Paran ? They knew only that they were in the wilderness : was this to be its character ? As they pressed on in the track of their leader, dust-covered, parched, staggering in the blazing heat, their very hearts melted within them. Who can live in such a desert ? God, in very vengeance on our sins and slavishness, hath brought us out into this wilderness to die !

The first day's journey would probably pass cheerfully enough. The novelty, the remembrance of their miraculous deliverance, the sense of free-dom, and the sight of the deep blue waves rolling between them and the land of bondage, would fill them with confidence and hope. But, as they pressed on during the second day, and found the desert grow more waste and parched ; as they lost sight of the mountains and the sea behind them, and swept the near horizon in front—treeless, life-less, and unutterably desolate and repulsive, their hearts would sink, and they would exchange ex-pressions of distrust of Moses and doubt of God. The second night they encamped out under the lustrous star-lit tent of their desert home ; and

they felt, probably, that the next day would decide
their destiny—that the next night would find them
at home in the desert, naturalized to its life, or
dead.   The morning broke, and still the treeless
waste stretched out before them, silent, bare, and
blank as death.   But one feature of the scene as
they advanced, we may well imagine, cheered them
to endurance.   The far horizon in front was
bounded, not by a line of level sand, but by sharp
mountain summits, tossing their peaks into the
sky in wild disorder, and suggesting irresistibly
the thought of torrents, glens, the shadow of the
great rocks, and groves of palms.   But for that
vision of mountains with its rich suggestions, we
may well question whether they could have endured.   At length a dark line on the bound of the
horizon took shape as they approached it, and
palm-trees and a belt of verdure promised water to
the thirsty host.   Not more eagerly does the ship-
wrecked seaman, floating on a crazy raft at the
mercy of the waves, strain his sight to catch the
first white speck in the distance which may be-
token an approaching sail ; not more earnestly
does a mother watch the pallid face of an infant
in a death-crisis of fever, for the first calm breath
which may tell that life has gained the mastery
over death, than does the desert pilgrim watch for
the dark spot on the line of his horizon which

tells him that water is within reach. An oasis, with its springs, was in sight. New courage animates the host. Each eye flashes—each limb is re-strung. "God has not failed us: He has but tried our courage, and now He will richly supply our need." Loud hallelujahs would ring through the resonant air; and, perhaps, a strain of their triumphal hymn would break forth again, and over the awful silence of the desert the solemn exulting chorus would float:—"Sing unto the Lord, for He hath triumphed gloriously, the horse and his rider He hath cast into the sea."

And now about those three dreary days in the wilderness without water: Such a host must journey slowly. They would easily consume three days in traversing a distance which a modern traveller, well mounted and guided, could travel in two days, or even, by a great effort, in one. The distance from Suez to Marah is not formidable, but it was enough to try the patience and courage of a host, so burdened, most severely; and to lead them to look at the desert not as a home, not even as a land of pilgrimage, but as a grave. Mark you, it *was* a wilderness, a waste country; no home for such a people, but a training-ground. Amalek might be content with its scanty pastures and live, dead to the world, dead to history, in the valleys of Paran. But Israel was to move on to Canaan,

to occupy the Eden of the East, to mingle in the
congress of mankind, and to make not *a* history
only, but History.   And God made them see that
it was no home for them ; their first impression of
it never left them.   " That great and terrible
wilderness wherein was no water," expressed
the memory of those first days' journeys.   God
showed to them its sternest countenance, that
they might not grow wanton and lust after its
beauty ; and only when the desert character had
thoroughly impressed itself on every heart, did he
lead them into the groves of Elim, the vast
luxuriant valleys of Paran, and unfold to them
the riches and splendours of the land.

And is it otherwise in life ?   Is not the same
character impressed for us on earth and life, when
we enter on its sterner era, when we leave the
home of our childhood, the Egypt of our careless
half-developed youth, and go out into the wilderness, to wander freely there under the law of duty
and before the face of God.   Does it not seem to
all of us strange and dreary ?   Who ever found
the first aspects of duty pleasant ?   Is it holiday
pastime, the first grappling with the realities of
life ?   Who has not been choked and parched by
the hot dust of the great desert ! though it be full
of looms, and mill-wheels, and manifold activity,
it is a desert at first to us before we get accus-

tomed to its atmosphere and at home in its life. The first march into any unexplored region of duty or thought, is like that three days' march into a weary land. Well does the schoolboy know it as he plods into the wilderness of study, and faints under the first experience of its dryness and dust. Let him but hold on awhile, and he will find springs and palm-trees, where he may rest and play; but it wants large faith and a goad of sharp necessity to get him through the weariness of those first days. God does not conceal from any one of us the hard and stern conditions of our discipline. The very first step out, under His guidance, brings us in front of the real perils and privations of the way. We are, none of us, coaxed on by soft slopes of sunny pasture, and meadows enamelled with flowers, till we find ourselves entangled in the desert and the way shut against our return. It is all honest and open, if stern, this method of Providence. Over the very threshhold of our pilgrimage is written, as on those glaring plains, " this is a land of wandering, not of rest." " Through much tribulation we must inherit the kingdom." " If any man will come after me, let him deny himself, and take up his cross and follow me."

We are saved from repeating the errors and follies of Egypt, or are at least warned against

them, by the pain of our first march out into the
free world. It bears witness to us of our present
condition; heirs as we are of the first sentence,
whose brand still blights the earth. That first
sentence on God's sinful child received prompt
execution : "So he drove out the man." That
very night, as the shadows fell over the waste
where no human footsteps had ever trodden,
Adam knew that God was in earnest, and that
he was to be a pilgrim to the end of his days.
More dread to him than the Desert of Sin to
Israel, was that broad Mesopotamian wilderness.
The shadow of his guilt fell around him blacker
than the night, and shrouded all things. The
memory of bright Eden, lost to him for ever,
filled him with anguish, and darkened all the
brightness of the world. And the young heir of
salvation, the son of the second Adam, must in
the flesh, on earth, master the same experience,
drink the same cup of bitterness, and be taught
all the lessons of pilgrimage the first moment
that he enters on his career. The echoes of the
hymn of deliverance have hardly died down in the
distance when some practical conflict, toil, or
sacrifice reveals to him the essential character of
the life which he undertakes. In the place of perpetual songs, some dry, dull plain of duty has to
be trodden ; and in place of all-sustaining Divine

strength, his first experience is of his own weakness and weariness, even in a heavenward way. Oh brethren! it is in the history of all pilgrims of duty, that three days' thirsty march into the wilderness. The first stage is the true trial. It is along the first day's march that the bones of the fallen whiten the sand.

But on the third day, as I have described to you, an oasis appeared in the distance, and the eager host struggled up to the springs to repay themselves for their thirsty toil. "*And when they came to Marah they could not drink of the waters of Marah, for they were bitter; therefore the name of it was called Marah. And the people murmured against Moses, saying, What shall we drink?*"

There is nothing very striking or beautiful about the well of Marah—nothing to redeem its bitterness, of which quality the word has become a symbol wherever the Pentateuch is read. We do not find any hint of dying women and children pressing up to the well to drink. They were probably by no means in utter extremities. Their supplies, fairly husbanded, would have spared them the agonies of a caravan dying of thirst. Still they were near enough to extremity to press up to the spring with eager haste, and to feel the full bitterness of the disappointment, when they found that the water was nauseous and worthless.

It was the certainty of supply, when they saw the dusky verdure on the far horizon, which aggravated their sufferings, when they came up to it and found it naught. For three days they had borne up bravely—there were no wells in sight; they braced themselves to endure. But when a well appeared they were ready for indulgence, the strain was taken off; all unbraced, they gave themselves up to pleasure and rest. And then the disappointment mastered them : "*And the people murmured against Moses, saying, What shall we drink?*"

It is a trite saying, that disappointment is the hardest of all things to bear. Hardest, because it finds the soul unbraced to meet it—relaxed, at ease, and tuned to indulgence and joy. A man can make up his mind to anything, and take it calmly. He can live under the hardest conditions, and bear them cheerily. There is nothing so elastic and self-accommodating in the universe as man. The conditions under which human beings have lived and flourished are most startling to us in these easy days. Man delights to proclaim himself king of circumstance, and can maintain his royalty, though in want and exile. Tell him what he *must* do and bear, and he will do and bear it, and much more beside. He strikes his average of expectation, and thinks himself happy with but a little beyond. " Consider that thou

deservest to be hanged, and it will be a happiness
only to be shot," says Carlyle, somewhere, in a
sardonic mood. But disappointment embitters
and maddens. It may be the smallest fraction of
good, a little morsel of delight which a wealthier
or happier would spurn; no matter if it be but the
killing of the prisoner's spider, or Mungo Park's bit
of moss discovered; whatever we are not braced
to meet, saddens or gladdens us far beyond vastly
larger and more momentous things which we have
wrought up into the average of life. Who has not
muttered "Marah" over some well in the desert
which he strained himself to reach and found to
be bitterness? Have you found no salt waters
where you thought to find sweetness and joy?
Love, beauty, the world's bright throngs, marriage,
home, the things which once wooed you and promised to slake the thirst of your soul for happiness, are they all Elims, sweet springs, and
palms? Oh, what fierce murmurings of "Marah"
have I heard from hearts wrung with anguish,
from souls withered and blasted by a too fond
confidence in anything or any being but God!
Believe it, no man, with a man's heart in him,
gets far on his wilderness way without some bitter
soul-searching disappointment; happy he who is
brave enough to push on another stage of the
journey, and rest in Elim, "where there are

twelve springs, living springs, of water, and three-
score and ten palms."

But we must not leave Marah yet. No spring
so bitter that God cannot heal it ; no want and
misery so utter that a cry to Him will not bring
effectual aid. *"And Moses cried unto the Lord;
and the Lord showed him a tree, which when he had
cast into the waters, the waters were made sweet:
there He made for them a statute and an ordinance,
and there He proved them, and said, if thou wilt
diligently hearken to the voice of the Lord thy God,
and wilt do that which is right in His sight, and wilt
give ear to His commandments, and keep all His
statutes, I will put none of these diseases upon thee,
which I have brought upon the Egyptians: for
I am the Lord that healeth thee."*   Ex. xv. 25, 26.

This miracle completes the lessons of Marah,
and offers many pregnant suggestions.

Marah was no accident. It is according to the
law by which we all live, and under which we are
all trained. God led them thither. He spread
those dazzling sands for their first paths ; He
made their first well a bitter one ; and He was
near to watch their suffering, to make it minister
to their health as pilgrims, and to bring them,
wiser and stronger, on their way.

A question has been raised as to the precise
nature of the miracle. Did God create the trees

at that time for the purpose, and really *give* them
as well as *show* them to Moses? Or had He
caused a tree to grow in the desert, which had
power to sweeten the brackish waters, and thus
help all travellers at their need? The strict
letter of the narrative favours the latter view;
and travellers have sought out, in all ages, some
desert tree, or shrub, in which this healing
quality might be found. Many have been discovered possessing it, in some measure; some
the Arabs use constantly for this purpose; and
Dr. Johnston, in his *Chemistry of Common Things*,
explains at length how the bark of a certain tree
has power to precipitate the mineral particles
which embitter the waters, and to make them
sweet and clear. It is a beautiful provision of
Nature in lands where she deals hardly with her
children. The desert is full of such compensations. As, when one sense is lost, the loss is
strangely supplied by the new activity of the
rest: so when the ordinary supplies fail the pilgrim of the wilderness, there are ready strange,
unknown helpers, like ministering angels, to meet
his need.* And never, through your whole
wandering, shall you find a well of bitterness

* These mutual compensations of the senses are very
singular, and are worthy of the closest study. It would
seem as though each sense extended itself through the body;

which God, if you cry to Him in faith and hope,
shall not turn to sweetness; never shall you
miss some bright celestial messenger to show
you a talisman which shall turn your mourning
into dancing, your despondency into exulting
joy. Still, Marah was no resting-place : God
compelled it to yield them a moment's solace
and refreshment, that they might press on to
the bright valley which He had carpeted and
decked for them, where they might rest awhile
and brace themselves for more earnest toils.

" *So God showed him a tree, which when he had
cast into the waters, the waters were made sweet.*"
That the tree was there in the desert at all, was
the grand miracle. That Moses should be led
to recognize and use its ministry, was but a
subordinate wonder: a declaration, not a suspension, of the order of God's world.

I make two notes on it.

1. That in God's benignant arrangement for
the good of His creatures, the bane and the anti-
dote, the infection and the cure, the pain and
the solace, lie close together. No man has to
wander far for healing, no man has to cry out
long for food. It is notorious that the most

so that the soul with all its organs is in presence in every
part, though it has its special presence-chamber, where it
transacts in detail the business of its life.

common sources of pain and injury, and their cures, are found in close proximity. Old women's simples have a deeper method than science dreams. In the spiritual world, most surely the word which saves is "nigh us, even in our mouths, and in our hearts." If the world is near and the devil, Christ and all good angels are nearer. Cry, cry aloud! cry promptly and earnestly to a present Saviour; and, as the light parts and scatters the mists of the morning, the Lord the Saviour, with all His powers, breaks through the gloom, and is at your side. This bitter well may be your first heart-searching hour of anguish. "The Lord hath forsaken me, and my God hath forgotten me," is the cry of your desolate heart. "This first hope has cheated me, all others are mockers. Go to! the earth is bankrupt, and life is a snare." "Stand still, my brother, and see the salvation of God." There is a tree which God hath cast into the fountain of the world's bitterness; by killing the sin which poisons it, He hath made it sweet and clear. "Look unto Jesus, the author and finisher of thy faith, who for the joy which was set before Him, endured the cross, despising the shame," and drink again, the water shall refresh thee; then hasten on, thy home is in the land whose waters can never fail. "*There*

*is a stream there of water of life, clear as crystal,
proceeding out of the throne of God and of the
Lamb. And there thou shalt hunger no more,
neither thirst any more; the sun shall not light on
thee nor any heat, for the Lamb which is in the
midst of the throne shall feed thee, and shall lead
thee unto living fountains of waters; and God shall
wipe away all tears from thine eyes."*

2. It strikes me that we have, in this miracle,
most important suggestions as to the philosophy
of all miracles.

I believe that the object of all miracles is to
maintain, and not to violate—to reveal, and not
to confound—the order of God's world. All true
miracles are revealings of the living God in
nature; blazing letters, to show to the blinded
and sensual what His hand is daily doing for
the beautifying and glorifying of the earth and
life. The Lord has planted virtues of healing
in drugs and balms; and the hand of Jesus,
touching that palsied limb, reveals to us the
fountain from which daily these blessed healings
flow. The Lord is showing thee thus who healed
that fever, who soothed that racking pain; "who
forgiveth all thine iniquities, who healeth all thy
diseases, who redeemeth thy life from destruction, and crowneth thee with His loving-kindness
and tender-mercies."

And what does the calming of the stormy waters which St. Matthew describes to us expound? The Lord hath shut up the storms in the deep ravines that open on that blue Galilean sea, and the Lord's hand ever loosens their bands when the land is thirsty, that they may sweep cool showers over the panting plains. And the voice of Jesus, shedding sweet peace as from an angel's wing over the storm-vexed waters, reveals the Being whose word maintains, calm and constant through the ages, this commerce and circulation of the elements—this ceaseless benediction of the world. *"This is the Lord's doing, and it is marvellous in our eyes."*

The wonders reveal the wonder, the standing wonder of creation. They strike again the key-note of its order, and tune again the concords of these lower spheres. But let us understand that God's miracles will remain but marvels, aimless and voiceless, such as brutes tremble at in a storm, until we learn that the thrilling of the life along the nerve tissues of the body, as it bathes its breast in the morning freshness or the balmy sweetness of the spring; the melody of birds, the dewy brilliance of flowers, and all the grace and splendour of the universe, are "shown unto us by the Lord."

Sermon v.

The Springs and the Palm-Trees of Elim.

*" And they came to Elim, where were twelve wells of water,
and threescore and ten palm-trees: and they encamped there by
the waters."*—Exodus, xv. 27.

THE first stage out of Egypt into the desert of
Sinai is, as I have said, the most wearisome of the
whole route. Three days' journey into the wilderness and no water! and their first well Marah
—bitterness! God help them, if this was to be
the common texture of their experience. There
was no lack of graves in Egypt ; all the toil and
pain of the exodus might have been spared. And
this history is profoundly true to life and to man's
experience. Who has not been rudely awakened
from his day-dreams of joyous liberty? Who, in
his young career, has not knelt to drink of many
a fountain which he found to be bitterness, and
straightway flung himself passionately on the
sand, cursing fate, life, and even God ?

I suppose that to all the young pilgrims of God
the first days of joy and bliss appear like a paradise regained. Sin pardoned ; the chain of the

captor broken; the land of bondage fading in
the distance; the tyrants dead upon the shore.
The glow of victory, the sense of liberty, the vision
of glory, conspire to make the first day's journey
a rapturous triumphal progress, a realization of
our dream of heaven. We need the three days'
journey, and the springs of bitterness, to disen-
chant us; to reveal the wilderness around and
before us, and bring us to the condition of sober-
minded Christian warriors, entering on a battle-
field, the prize of which, after long stern conflict,
will be victory in death. The humbling experience
of our first station remains through life a whole-
some memory: we find Marah again whenever
we are tempted to forget the wilderness, and rest
as though our heaven were won. It is strange,
passing strange, to the carnal understanding, that
the first station of God's elect host should be a
well of bitterness; but to those who consider it
steadily the strangeness will become familiar, and
they will recognize the most friendly form of the
fatherly discipline of God. And ever, that we
fail not utterly, close by Marah we shall find,
when we have learnt its humbling lessons, an
Elim with its springs and palms.

Few stations in the desert are so difficult to
identify as Elim, in spite of the marked features
which it presented when Israel encamped under

its shade. There are not a few halting-places
which might answer the description, between the
well of Howara and the desert of Sinai; but as
we learn that the people subsequently encamped
by the Red Sea, in the Wilderness of Sin, in
Dophkah, in Alush, before they reached Rephidim
—(compare the narrative in Exodus with the
table of their stations in Numbers xxxiii.)—it
seems manifest that Elim must be in the near
neighbourhood of Marah, and before, entering
the mountain region, they would lose sight of the
Red Sea finally. Looking at the matter from
this point of view, it seems safe to conclude that
Elim must have been the Wâdy Ghurundel, of
which the following description will convey a
tolerably clear idea :—

"This proved a very interesting but fatiguing day. I left
the encampment at an early hour, and reached the edge of
Wady Ghurundel—a considerable valley, filled with wild tamarisk and other bushes—in about two hours. The principal
spring wells out at the foot of a sandstone rock, forming a
small pool of clear water, bordered by sedges, and looked
highly refreshing after Ayûn Musa and Howara. There was
even, delightful sight! a little grass, and birds were hopping
about, enjoying the rare luxury. The water, trickling off,
pursues its way some distance down the valley, forming a reedy
marsh, interspersed with thickets of bushes and dwarf palm-trees,
and a considerable quantity of tamarisk, with other shrubs; and
as there are also considerable masses of similar vegetation above
this point, there are, probably, several other springs which

nourish it. Altogether it was a reviving sight in the thirsty desert; and I saw no spot which could so well correspond with the wells and palm-trees of Elim, through the entire route to Wady Feiran. Filling our water-skins, we proceeded down the valley, encountering here and there a few straggling Arabs of the Terabin, with their flocks, and passing more water and vegetation. In rather above an hour, the blue sea peeped in through the western opening of the Wady, on the left of which, like a portal, rises a noble mass of slaty stone, deeply hollowed out, and throwing a broad cool shadow into the sandy valley, truly ' the shadow of a great rock in a weary land.' "—*Forty Days in the Desert*, p. 33, 34.

Such was the scene in which they rested, but without doubt fairer and brighter far than it appears to the modern traveller. They seem to have remained some days, at any rate, in this encampment and its neighbourhood, for it was not until " the fifteenth day of the second month after their departing from the land of Egypt" that they came into the Wilderness of Sin. And here I must interpose a remark, which will need to be borne in mind as we follow the course of the people on their path to Canaan. We must by no means suppose that when " the people" is spoken of, the whole mass of 2,000,000—men, women, and children—is necessarily meant. Such a body could not travel in one band. Moses and the leaders with a considerable company would travel by one path; great companies, pursuing the same

main track, would travel by others.   Ghurundel,
with its springs and palm-trees, would be the
head-quarters of Moses and the chieftains; but
there are springs in the valleys all round, and
the people would doubtless distribute themselves
under their leaders, and find water and shelter as
they could around the central camp, which is
recorded by name in the Sacred Text.   This consideration, together with the fact that the desert
was manifestly more fruitful in those days than at
present, will help us to understand how so vast
a host could find food and shelter there.   You will
not fail to note that the miraculous interpositions
are, on the whole, but rare.   Until they encamped
in the Wilderness of Sin they seem to have found
supply, partly from the natural productions of the
country, and partly from the stores which they
brought with them from Egypt.   As they plunged
into the wilder regions of the desert, the hand of
God was disclosed to them, miraculously supplying
their need ; and they learnt that *" man doth not
live by bread alone, but by every word that proceedeth
out of the mouth of God doth man live."*

Let me beg you to consider—

I. That Elim rises before us as the representative of the green oases, the spots of sunny verdure,
the scenes of heavenly beauty, wherewith God

hath enriched, though sparingly, our wilderness world.

"And they encamped there by the waters." How cool and fresh the words fall upon the ear! So fell the gurgling of the springs on the ear of the thirsty host, as they flung themselves on the grass under the thick shadow of the palm-trees, and drank a draught which for the moment was a draught of bliss. The hot, blank silence of the desert had been around them—not a sound in the air, not a moving thing upon the sand. It is the very drearihood of silence—that desert stillness, the desolation of death. Suddenly the freshest, brightest, most living music of nature gushes out into the silence, water babbles and glances, grass springs, tamarisks and palm-trees spread; and a very paradise nestles in the bosom of the waste. We must tread that weary silent path if we would know the full breadth of the music of those fountains, and share the joy of those parched and exhausted pilgrims, who encamped there by the waters, and cast themselves under the shadow of the palms. And Elim stands not alone, the one oasis of the desert; scenes yet brighter and fresher, broader tracts of fertility, we shall meet with as we attend their march. There is no desert upon earth which has not its Elims. Even the vast wastes of Central

Africa are known to engirdle tracts of beautiful
and densely peopled table-land. It is the broad
character of earth. Were it all Marah, life would
not be tolerable, even for sinners and slaves. Its
Elims make it a marching-ground to freemen
and saints. Marah is the mark of the curse.
God has burnt His sentence deep into the bosom
of a sin-stricken world. But He seeks to set the
heart of the sinner, not towards the wastes of
desolation in despair, but towards Himself and
His heaven in hope; and He has brightened the
desert of life with many a scene of beauty and
splendour which are a prophecy of the better
world. We cannot walk far on earth without
stumbling upon the springs of bitterness; but he
who is led of God shall not want the groves and
fountains of Elim to cheer and strengthen him in
his way. I think it very deeply important to
bring out the mixed character of Israel's desert
experience, believing as I do that it furnishes the
key to our experience of life.

This world is not all bad; its marches are not
all bare. *" Cursed is the ground for thy sake "*
—and because for thy sake, it is not cursed
utterly. It is not all black, bare, lifeless, as
the crust of a cold lava flood; a prison-house for
reprobates, instead of a training school for sons.
Sin broke up its Eden for ever; brushed the

bloom from its beauty, the freshness and brightness from its smile.   There is a sad tone about
the world's countenance.   On the whole, it is a
careworn and death-stricken world; and it looks
like it.   The shadows lie more thickly than the
sunbeams; the winter reigns more mightily than
the spring.   The deepest undertone of poetry and
art is a lamentation; earth is dressed to be the
theatre of a tragedy of life.   The optimists are
ever mastered, in the end, by the severities of
reality; and Epicurus, in the long-run, sets the
fashion of suicide.   It is tragic, is life; all
peoples have felt it; and earth is fashioned and
draped to be the theatre of man.   I do not
indulge here in platitudes about the falling leaves
of autumn, and the deepening shadows of night,
because I believe that any particular phenomenon
of nature may be tuned by man to his mood if
he will.   But I think that I have on my side
man's firmest convictions and earth's clearest
expressions when I say, that in the half-lights
of man's life here the shadow predominates, and
that the minor ·rules the music of the world.
They were not the most foolish and shallow-
hearted of people who believed that night was
more potent and prolific than day.   (Tacitus,
Germania, sec. XI.)   But while I see this broad
character on life and man, and read in it the

fulfilment of God's sentence on His sinful child—
I say *His*, for He distinctly refused to cast off
and disown him; He rather sought, by the promise of a Redeemer, in that very hour to link him
at once in gratitude and hope more firmly to
Himself.—I see further, that God has not given
earth up, any more than man, to be the devil's
portion; and keeps alive, in the heart of its wildernesses, scenes of verdant freshness, of radiant
beauty, which link it in close kindred with heaven.
I believe of this earth of ours that there are scenes
where heavenly visitants might fondly linger,
which need but the transfiguring celestial sunlight to be beautiful and glorious as the heavenly
land. I have seen, from mountain summits, the
mists part for the moment, and through the rift—
apparently in the heavens, the landscape beneath
and around being all veiled from sight—I have
seen the hills and meadows, the cities and rivers
of a fair island, floating in the midst of a sea of
intensest blue, touched here and there by silvery
crests of foam. I have seen the vision glow in
the lustre of such sunlight, as seemed to realize
the images of the Apocalypse; and then, as I
watched it swimming in this sea of golden glory,
the mists have gathered again on the vision, and
left me only the memory of a glimpse of a celestial
land.

Such *Christian* saw from the summit of the Delectable Mountains, such Moses from Pisgah's crest; such John, when he saw heaven opened in the Apocalypse; such we may see, some day, when the mists and veils of life are parted for ever, and the whole breadth of the heavenly Canaan appears. Mere fancy! some of you say. I think not. Our world is as our being; and if in us there are here, in the midst of the dust and sweat of the conflict, fore-shinings, rare but clear, of the glories in store, let us be well assured that it is not otherwise with our world. But the outer sphere attends the inner, and is but its index and expositor. And inwardly to those who seek them, in the very stress and strain of the battle, there come moments when they mix with angels and taste the sweetness of the fellowship of heaven. I often think of Jacob at Mahanaim, where the angels of God met him; and I am well assured that, were we purer and simpler-hearted, *we* might more often meet them. It is not that they are cold and reticent, for what is their joy, their work for Christ? "are they not all ministering spirits sent forth to minister to them who shall be heirs of salvation?" And these Elims of the soul, these seasons of deep repose and joy, these hours of unspeakably dear and tender communion with the Saviour, when He brings

us into His banqueting-house, and His banner
over us is love, when we drink of the river of
the water of life, and eat of the fruit of the tree
which, self-willed, in Adam we lost, but which,
humble and believing, in Christ we regain, are
like these oases, of heavenly texture. They are
sent by Christ to teach us tenderly that the
ground is cursed, not to torment, but to task and
train us; and that even here we may find, if we
will it, much both within and without us which is
most like heaven.

This, then, is the first teaching of Elim—its
perennial sermon. Those fountains gurgle, those
palm-trees wave through all the ages, to refresh
the wilderness of the world.

II. The nearness of Elim to Marah opens up
to us a deep truth in the spiritual history of man.

Had they pushed on instead of murmuring at
Marah, they would have found all they sought,
and more than they hoped for, at Elim. Ah!
the time we waste in repining and rebelling—
scheming to mend God's counsels! How many
Elims would it find for us, if employed in courage
and faith! But that is not the main point here.
It was quite natural that the people, after three
days' weary march, should rest at Marah; and
the Lord, in mercy, heard their cry, and sweetened the bitter waters, as we have seen. But the

next stage, from Marah to Elim, was a short one
—a brief day's march—some six miles, no more;
" and they encamped there by the waters." How
near is the sweetness to the bitterness in every
trial! it is but a short step to Elim, where we
may encamp and rest. The brightest spots of
earth are amidst its most savage wildernesses,
and the richest joys of the Christian spring ever
out of his sharpest pains. Think you that Paul
had not found a Marah, and an Elim not far from
it, when he wrote this chapter of his history? " I
knew a man in Christ about fourteen years ago,
(whether in the body, I cannot tell ; or whether out
of the body, I cannot tell : God knoweth ;) such
an one caught up to the third heaven. And I
knew such a man, (whether in the body or out
of the body, I cannot tell : God knoweth ;) how
that he was caught up into paradise, and heard
unspeakable words, which it is not lawful for a
man to utter. Of such an one will I glory : yet
of myself I will not glory, but in mine infirmities.
For though I would desire to glory, I shall not be
a fool; for I will say the truth : but now I for-
bear, lest any man should think of me above that
which he seeth me to be, or that he heareth of
me. And lest I should be exalted above measure
through the abundance of the revelations, there
was given to me a thorn in the flesh, the mes-

8—2

senger of Satan to buffet me, lest I should be
exalted above measure. For this thing I besought
the Lord thrice, that it might depart from me.
And He said unto me, My grace is sufficient
for thee : for My strength is made perfect in
weakness. Most gladly therefore will I rather
glory in my infirmities, that the power of Christ
may rest upon me. Therefore I take pleasure in
infirmities, in reproaches, in necessities, in perse-
cutions, in distresses for Christ's sake : for when
I am weak, then am I strong."—2 Cor. xii. 2—10.

These abundant revelations were like a well in
the wilderness ; but how soon did he find its
sweetness bitterness, until he was led down from
his high places to the spring of Christ's sufficiency, and the shadow of His love ! This again
is no accident, this nearness of Marah to Elim.
The humbling pains of disappointment tune the
soul for the joys which the next station of the
journey affords. It is when we have learnt the
lessons of the wilderness, have girt our souls to
its toils and privations, and are resolved to press
on, cost what it may, in our heavenly path, that
springs of unexpected sweetness gush up at our
very feet, and we find shade and rest, which give
foretaste of heaven. The fresh young pilgrim,
full of natural force and fire, content to trust
to the common supplies of the desert, scant

as they may be, if he may but press through
to a home beyond, will find springs of bitterness enough.   His first well will fail him;
his natural courage and strength will die down
in murmurs; and, unless he can look humbly
to a Father's eye and hand, and cry unto Him
who is able to deliver, he will lie down and
die at his first station, and leave his bones to
whiten the sand.   Many such dread records has
the desert.   Pilgrims, who started high in heart
and high in hope as you, but who never got
beyond Marah; they looked to an arm of flesh—
a man's courage and endurance—and, when it
failed them, their carcases fell in the wilderness.
Those only who march in faith, under the heavenly Leader, reach the next station, and encamp
there by the waters of God's strong grace and
quickening love.   And through our whole career
the same truth meets us.   Emptied of self, we
are filled with the joy of God; when we are
weakest, then are we strongest in Christ; dying,
we live.   "We are troubled on every side, yet not
distressed; perplexed, but not in despair; persecuted, but not forsaken; cast down, but not
destroyed: always bearing about in the body the
dying of the Lord Jesus, that the life also of
Jesus might be made manifest in our body."

Let a man, in the bitterness of his disappoint-

ment, when some spring of this world to which
he had trusted has failed him, have faith to say—
" O send out Thy light and Thy truth : let them
lead me; let them bring me unto Thy holy hill,
and to Thy tabernacles.   Then will I go unto the
altar of God, unto God, my exceeding joy: yea,
upon the harp will I praise Thee, O God my God.
Why art thou cast down, O my soul ? and why
art thou disquieted within me ? Hope in God :
for I shall yet praise Him, who is the health
of my countenance, and my God"—(Psalm
xliii. 3–5)—and you shall soon see him en-
camping under the palm-trees, and making the
very air resonant with the song—" Bless the Lord,
O my soul : and all that is within me, bless His
holy name.   Bless the Lord, O my soul, and forget not all His benefits : who forgiveth all thine
iniquities; who healeth all thy diseases ; who redeemeth thy life from destruction ; who crowneth
thee with loving-kindness and tender-mercies."—
Psalm ciii. 1—4.

  " Let not your heart be troubled."   " Verily,
verily, I say unto you, that ye shall weep and
lament, but the world shall rejoice : and ye shall
be sorrowful, but your sorrow shall be turned into
joy.   A woman when she is in travail hath sorrow, because her hour is come : but as soon as
she is delivered of the child, she remembereth no

more the anguish, for joy that a man is born into the world. And ye now, therefore, have sorrow : but I will see you again, and your heart shall rejoice, and your joy no man taketh from you."
—John, xvi. 20—22.

Marah and Elim are together everywhere. Life is born out of the womb of death.

It is to me very significant, that Moses made the people enter into a kind of fresh covenant at Marah. He rebuked their murmurs, proved and confirmed their faith, rekindled their hope, and straightway they found themselves in Elim. My brother! weeping by some salt fountain, groaning under the burdens or writhing under the stings of life, get thou up and renew thy covenant; cry unto God thy maker, who giveth songs in the night: and hearken! there is the gurgling of water in the distance, the song of birds, the breath of flowers, the shade and fruit of palms,— go down to Elim and rest. "The Lord is my shepherd; I shall not want. He maketh me to lie down in green pastures : He leadeth me beside the still waters. He restoreth my soul: He leadeth me in the paths of righteousness for His name's sake. Yea, though I walk through the valley of the shadow of death, I will fear no evil, for Thou art with me; Thy rod and thy staff they comfort me. Thou preparest a table before me in the

presence of mine enemies : Thou anointest my
head with oil ; my cup runneth over. Surely
goodness and mercy shall follow me all the days
of my life : and I will dwell in the house of the
Lord for ever."—Ps. xxiii. "And when they
came to Marah, they could not drink of the
waters of Marah, for they were bitter : therefore
the name of it was called Marah. And the people
murmured against Moses, saying, What shall we
drink? And he cried unto the Lord ; and the
Lord shewed him a tree, which when he had cast
into the waters the waters were made sweet :
there he made for them a statute and an ordinance, and there he proved them, and said, If
thou wilt diligently hearken to the voice of the
Lord thy God, and wilt do that which is right in
His sight, and wilt give ear to His commandments,
and keep all His statutes, I will put none of these
diseases upon thee, which I have brought upon
the Egyptians : for I am the Lord that healeth
thee. And they came to Elim, where were twelve
wells of waters, and three-score and ten palm
trees : and they encamped there by the waters."—
Exodus, xv. 23—27.

III. Let us endeavour to discern the principle
of this alternate sweetness and bitterness of
life.

"*They came to Marah, and they could not drink*

of the waters, for they were bitter." How is this?
Why are the promises of nature so delusive; why
are the brightest things so treacherous? does God
make things to deceive; does heaven stamp falsely
the coin it issues? are these false shows—these
trees that fruit not, these springs that refresh not
—God's work or the devil's? are they the signs
that God has left the world to the evil one, and
these the fruits of his baneful sway? The fairest
spots of His earth are seamed with lava floods.
The gardens of the world, Naples, Sicily, Lisbon,
are arched over caldrons of seething fire. How
shall we explain this? "God is good and doeth
good;" the Scripture saith it, and we gladly
believe it; our hearts clasp the truth, and refuse
to let it go; but how shall we understand this?
God refuses to be judged by these things: they
are His work, and in His world; but they are not
final; they exist not for themselves, nor because
He loves them. They but attend the human as
satellites: nature is as man is; if you would
understand the sweetness and bitterness of Nature,
you must study not her, but man and God. To
study nature otherwise, separate from man, a
creature complete in itself, and as far as it reaches
the complete expression of the mind of God, is to
fall at last into hopeless confusion. These lights
and shadows of nature, this glow and gloom, are

caught from a higher sphere. Nature is but the
reverse of the medal whose obverse is man. The
ultimate reason of the bitterness of Marah, is the
sin in the heart of Israel and all pilgrims; the
ultimate reason of the sweetness and freshness of
Elim, is the mercy that is in the heart of God. I
am not saying that God put either the well or the
palm-trees there with a special view to that particular journey, and the private sins of Israel's
heart. But just as their particular sin was a stream
from the fountain of all sin, so that particular
Marah was a rill from the fountain of bitterness
with which sin has poisoned the waters of the
world. Nature has become hard, stern, and frugal
of her stores, because we have become selfish and
wrongful. It is we who make the bitterness; the
malign elements in nature are all our work. Eden
had none of them: an evil spirit has marred the
good constitution of the world. How manifest it
is that an evil heart is at the bottom of all the
bitterness and harshness of nature, let our daily
experience teach us. There is not a day in which
we are not fouling some bright stream of goodness, or turning some sweet fountain into bitterness by sin. Our own spirits cannot alter the
essential qualities of things, but they can alter
their character to and effect on us. We cannot
make gloom daylight, or harshness sweetness, but

we can smile at the harshness, and make the night bright with song.

There is a fearful power in the human spirit to make God's brightest blessings bitter curses. Who was it who wanted to die, because God had found a deliverance for a great city in which were half a million of doomed men? And there is, too, a royal power in the human spirit to transmute curses into blessings, and to be happier by Marah than another shall be in Elim, who has the bitter waters of selfishness at his heart. There is no suffering so terrible that man cannot smile at it, no blessing so pure that man cannot make it a source of misery and shame. At the door of your own spirit lie all the pangs and wretchedness you have known. You have cursed fate and fortune, and protested that you were the most wronged and persecuted of men. But the mischief lies not in God's constitution of the world, nor in His government of it, but in your hearts. You have found, in trifles, that Marah became Elim in an instant, when you swept envy, malice, and selfishness, for the moment, clean out of your breast. Look into your own spirits when you are moaning with anguish or shrieking with fury, and see what hell-born passions are raging there; what corrosive poison of hate or lust is searching with malignant fangs for the very vitals

of your soul. You, persecuted, tormented, the
victim of Fate! Why you would moan and curse
if you were standing, with all bright spirits round
you, in the bowers of Paradise, or before the
Eternal Throne! Sweep the heart clean of lust
and passion; slay not sins, but sin; sacrifice, not
selfishness, but self; and there is no Marah between you and Canaan, unless you raise self from
its tomb again, and set it up in your heart beside
the Lord.

It is fearful to hear men blaspheme the goodness of Providence and the order of God's world,
when their hearts are not resting on them, but
wrestling against them with suicidal energy, inflict-
ing, with their own hands, the wounds that drain
the very life-blood of their souls. Many a pure
spring you have thus filled with bitterness. Business, home, the marriage bond, the parental tie,
some rich success, some new acquisition, study, or
friend, some fresh apocalypse of the beauty and
glory of the world,—you have blighted and blackened all of it by lust, selfishness, passion, or
hate; and now, by your bitter well, which your
own lustful and envious heart has poisoned, you
are crying out in anger and frenzy against God.
How beautiful is earth, how blessed is life, to the
man who rests his heart on the bosom of his
Saviour! The bitterest water he drinks with a

blessing, and it becomes sweeter than honey in his mouth. How earnestly do I wish that I could make you understand, that the springs of the sorrow of life are in you; of the sweetness, the Elim, in God! Elim, as we have seen, was close to Marah. Jesus, "when he had overcome the sharpness of death, opened the kingdom of heaven to all believers." That last drop of bitterness He drank, and then passed up to His throne. Songs of celestial gladness hailed His entrance. "Thy throne, O God, is for ever and ever; a sceptre of righteousness is the sceptre of Thy kingdom. Thou hast loved righteousness and hated iniquity, and therefore God, even thy God, hath anointed Thee with the oil of gladness above Thy fellows." It is true everywhere, through the whole scale of life. The Divine Master and Captain, the humblest pilgrim, "shall drink of the brook by the way, and therefore shall he lift up the head."

The spring of our Elim is Faith. We may lie down beside the still waters, and bless the shepherd who has led us into the green pastures; and straightway, growing wanton, change our Elim into a waste. The Elim of the soul is the presence of the Saviour—the word of His mouth, and the touch of His hand. Lose that and your springs sink, choked by sand; your pastures wither and become burnt and bare; your sun goes down at noon, and a thick Egyptian darkness draws its pall over the soul. Earth has no Elim where you are secure against the devil's seductions. One Eden he has destroyed, and its very place,

> " Like an image in a mountain lake
> Which rains disturb,"

is lost. And sin will destroy every Eden, unless Christ is your rock in the desert, and your cool shadow in a weary land. What baffled energies and wasted days we have spent in working out, by the strength of our own arm, some conquest, or wrestling against some great evil in the world! At last, weary and desolate, we have cried out to Him to whom we should have sought at first, and a heavenly peace has spread through the stormy regions of passion,—a soft rest has bathed our strained energies, a new quick life has thrilled through every vein and fibre, and, " *believing*," we have entered into rest.

I said that earth had scenes whose beauty is of heavenly texture—whence, as from some Pisgah summit, we might look into the heavenly land. I now say that we may make life of heavenly texture, and live on earth as already at home with God. Who realizes this, is another question; but there is no barrier, physical or metaphysical, to hinder it. Let us live in holy and loving intercourse with Jesus, and the flowers shall spring out beneath our footsteps, and the music of running waters shall attend us through the whole journey to the close. There are some whose clear, pure, childlike hearts seem to have won this privilege. Earth is to them an Elim : to their clear sight there is, in common things, a radiance, a glory, which we scarce discern in miracles. Each daily mercy is touched as a gift from the warm hand of Christ, and wakens musical thanksgivings; and each common trouble loses all its bitterness, being sweetened inexpressibly by the assurance of the Saviour's love. I have known men—I have one now in my mind's eye—whose citizenship of both worlds seems already perfect; who here, through purity, see a beauty and enjoy a bliss which we must be purged by death to make our own. Blessed pilgrims! they rebuke our faintness and stir our courage. The end is no dream; they see and touch it; let us be strong and valiant, we too shall grasp it at last. "Thou wilt show me the path of life; in Thy presence there is fulness of joy, at Thy right hand there are pleasures for evermore." "As for me, I shall behold Thy face in righteousness. I shall be satisfied when I awake with thy likeness."

It may be that I am speaking to some whom God has led forth into bitterness as of death. It seems as though He had mingled His strongest cup for

you. "Deep calleth unto deep at the noise of
Thy water-spouts; all Thy waves and billows are
gone over me," is the cry of your spirit. And
now He is making a "statute and an ordinance"
to prove you. Again and again He has led you
out to the edge of the wilderness, and you have
trembled and recoiled as you looked abroad over
its free wastes. And then He has laid the yoke
upon you more heavily. You have groaned and
fainted under the tyrannous cruelty of sin. And
now, in the last extremity, you go forth again, and
you halt by the first springs : Marah! it is all
bitterness, everywhere! I may as well go back
and die! "*Turn thee, turn thee, why wilt thou
die ?*" To go back is to die among the flesh-pots,
and rot there like the brutes. Turn thee! gather
all thy courage; call the all-conquering Spirit of
God to aid thee. Lift thine hand now, in a perpetual covenant. Give an everlasting yea to the
vocation of God, and lo! there wave the palms,
there gush the fountains of Elim; encamp there
by the waters, and meditate on a pilgrim's life
and "the rest that remaineth" beyond.

Thus we may transmute through life, if we will,
Marah into Elim by faith. Shall I be departing
from the true monitions of my subject, if I speak
for a moment of the bitterness of death ? You may
conquer every trial, but the last trial still awaits

you. You may sweeten every fountain of bitterness, but who shall sweeten the bitterness of death? Death is the second and completer Exodus—the passage of the pilgrim soul to a world of which the wilderness had bright foreshinings; whose gates through the whole pilgrimage gleam starlike in the blue distance, whose brightening glories measure our growing nearness to our home. But the river of death runs cold and drear between the pilgrim and those homes of the blessed. We may take a brave heart up to its brink, but there is a pang of sharp anguish to be mastered as its waves swell up around the breast and choke us; as with long gasps the spirit struggles to breathe still the air of a world it loves the better as it is to pass forth from it for ever. To die! It is the bitterness of life!—the last and sharpest struggle with the tyrannous king. Blessed be Christ, that as the moon which lights our pilgrimage sets in the wilderness, and casts a last pale gleam on the wastes where we have fought and suffered, the sunlight of the higher world flings the glow of its dawning splendour over an Elim, brighter, softer, more blessed, than even our most daring dreams. And there the victorious sufferers, " having conquered the sharpness of death," are resting, encamped by the waters; they share the triumphs of courage and patience, and wait till we join them,

9

to seek with us the Jerusalem of the skies. "And there the sun shall no more go down, nor the moon withdraw itself, for the Lord God shall be their everlasting light, and the days of their mourning shall be ended for ever."

Sermon vi.

The Bread of the Wilderness.

" He fed thee with manna (which thou knewest not, neither did thy fathers know) ; that he might make thee know that man doth not live by bread only, but by every word that proceedeth out of the mouth of the Lord doth man live."—Deut. viii. 3.

THE people broke up from their encampment by the waters in Elim, and resumed their wilderness march.   The next stages of their pilgrimage would lead them through some of the most strangely magnificent mountain scenery in the world.   They had first to traverse the successive wâdys of the sandstone region, whose intensely brilliant colour surpasses anything which is to be met with, at any rate within the ordinary tracks of civilized man ; and then the wilder and grander granite world spread its grim peaks and passes before them ; conducting them, by approaches which cast the sphinx avenues of Egypt into the shade, into the inner court of that sublime temple, where they were to hear the voice and behold the glory of Jehovah, and pass through the great crisis of their history.

9—2

The higher mountains of the peninsula of Sinai gather themselves into three chief clusters, whose loftiest peaks are known as Mount Serbâl, Mount St. Catherine, and Um-Shômer—the most distant and the loftiest, whose peak, until recently at any rate, no human foot has scaled. The broad character of this region is sterile sublimity. The silence, the desolation, the grand form and colour of the mountains, produce an impression on the mind of every imaginative traveller, which remains sacred, wholly apart from all the other experiences of life.

The sublimity of the grandest Alpine peak is tempered by a veil of grace; the exquisite softness and roundness of the snow outline, the murmurs of cascades which fill the air with music, and the bright starry flowers which gem the earth at your very feet, lend a touch of grace and even gentleness to the most awful mountain forms. But in front of Sinai no brook, no tree, no flower, no bird, gives animation to the scene: it is blank desolation; grandeur—but as of a Titan petrified in death. Into this region they were steadily advancing. The horizon in front of them was already cut by lines of rich variety and beauty. It was an education to look upon them, and to learn that by that path God would have them pursue their way. Elim has many sisters, in the neighbouring valleys. There is some exquisite scenery in the passes between Elim and Rephidim, with visions here and there of the blue waters of the gulf, one peep of which Dr. Stanley thus describes :—

"Another glorious day. We passed a third claimant to the title of Elim, the Wâdy Tayibeh, palms, and tamarisks, venerable as before; then down one of those river-beds, between vast cliffs, white on the one side, and on the other, of a black calcined colour, between which burst upon us once more the deep blue waters of the Red Sea, bright with their white foam. Beautiful was that brilliant contrast; and more beautiful and delightful still, to go down upon the beach and see the waves breaking on that shell-strewn, weed-strewn shore, and promontory after promontory breaking into those waters right and left: most delightful of all the certainty—I believe I may here say the certainty (thanks to that inestimable verse in Numbers xxxiii.),—that here the Israelites, coming down through that very valley, burst upon that very view—the view of their old enemy and old friend,—that mysterious sea, and one more glimpse of Egypt, dim in the distance in the shadowy hills beyond it. Above the blue sea rose the white marbly terraces, then blackened by the passage of the vast multitude. High above those terraces ranged the brown cliffs of the Desert, streaked here and there with the purple bands which now first began to display themselves. And as the bright blue sea formed the base of the view, so it was lost above in a sky of the deepest blue I have ever observed in the East."— STANLEY: *Sinai and Palestine*, p. 69.

This was their last vision of Egypt. Their sea was thenceforth to be the Mediterranean, the highway of the Tyrian commerce, the focus of all the activity of the ancient world. We turn with them somewhat sadly from their last view of their old home, though it had been a bitter one. Memory clings even to scenes of pain and sorrow. It is not without sadness that we bid any haunt, however mournful, farewell. But the call, "Speak unto the children of Israel that they go forward," rings again through the host, and they pass on across the burning plain of Murkâ, and by the gorgeous valleys which lead into Rephidim, the entrance to the great oasis of Paran—now the Wâdy Feirân—beyond whose palm-groves the solemn peaks of Serbâl rise. The sites of Dophkah and Alush (Num. xxxiii. 13) are quite lost, but Rephidim can be identified with tolerable certainty. It means "the resting-place," and must have been in the near neighbourhood of the great resting-place of the Desert, the paradise of the Bedouins. The plain of Murkâ, the wilderness of Sin, was the scene of their first murmuring for food; but it will be more convenient to trace their course to Rephidim, and consider together the whole question of their miraculous supplies, and their first battle with and victory over their foes.

The oasis of Paran—the Wâdy Feirân—is the widest and the richest of those splendid luxuriant valleys, which here and there, at rare intervals, relieve the monotony of the Desert route. It lies at the foot of Mount Serbâl, of which Dr. Stanley testifies, "it is one of the finest forms I have ever seen." The combination of the wild granite peaks of the mountain, its black shadows, its sterile silences, with the sparkling beauty of the broad oasis which nestled in its breast, presents a spectacle which I suppose can be seen only in those sublime deserts, through which God led His sons. This oasis was, in the days of Moses, the home of a people strong enough to dispute with Israel the passes of the mountains; and, down to the sixth century, was the seat of a settlement which was a bishopric of the Christian Church.

We identify Rephidim the more readily with Wâdy Feirân, because nature seems herself to have marked it out as the inevitable resting-place of the people on such a march. The fact that Dophkah and Alush were between Elim and Rephidim, compels us to look for the latter far on in the direction of Sinai. Again, it is evident that the people called Amalek (possibly a generic name for the rovers of the Desert) were established there. There had been no time since the exodus for an Idumæan people to have taken the alarm, and sent an expedition southwards to close the first passes of the Desert against the heirs of

Palestine. This resistance was evidently offered
by a people on the spot, fighting for their altars
and homes; and as Paran was the only region of
the Desert where such a people could find an
abode, the identification of Rephidim with the
Wâdy Fierân becomes almost a matter of necessity. The chief difficulty arises from the want of
water; Feirân being abundantly supplied. But
it is noted by travellers that the entrance of the
valley, which drains southwards into the Red
Sea, is twelve miles from the springs which feed
its verdure; and there, doubtless, Amalek met
Israel in arms to defend the entrance to their fair
oasis, which Israel forced, and enjoyed during a
long halt the beauty and fatness of the land.
There may be seen still, in all probability, the
very "hill"—the word in the original is specific,
not "mountain" but "hill"—on which Moses
wrestled in prayer for the victory of his people in
their first battle with the foes of the Desert; and
there, amid the glens and peaks of Serbâl, he
meditated and matured his plans, and prepared
himself for the next great act in the drama of his
life—the greatest act in the drama of the world's
life, before the advent of the Lord.

Some slight description of the aspect which
this oasis now presents to the traveller, will serve
to justify the views which I have presented as to

the rich variety, the splendid beauty, and, occasionally, the rare luxuriance of this way of the wilderness by which the people were led forth by the Lord :—

" But a sudden change awaited us ; about noon, at a turn of the road, the scene that burst upon us was more like the dream of a poet, than any reality in this arid wilderness. The cliffs on either hand still towered, bare and perpendicular, to an immense height; but instead of a gravelly valley, collecting and condensing the fiery rays of the sun, arose, as by enchantment, tufted groves of palm and fruit trees, producing on my mind a more vivid impression of romantic luxuriance than had been left by anything I had yet beheld in the East. . . . . Here, in the heart of that terrible wilderness of rock and sand, of the stunted bush and nauseous scanty pool, I pitched my tent beneath a tall group of palms, which bent shelteringly over it ; the spring coming down the valley, and rippling among green sedges, formed a small transparent basin at the foot of a fragment of limestone rock, fallen from the mountain wall above ; a beautiful natural altar, as it were, decorated with the light pensile foliage of overhanging turfeh-trees. The camels, relieved of their burdens, after drinking their fill, were scattered about the bowery thickets, cropping the thick blossom with avidity and unusual relish ; whilst the Arabs spread among the shady trees, revelling in the choicest beauty of their Desert home, the proverbial "paradise of the Bedouins." The palms beneath which I encamped were not the solitary ornament of a small oasis ; but the outskirts of a dense grove, extending for miles far up the narrow valley. On stepping out of my tent, I was at once in the midst of an almost tropical wilderness. In the palm-groves of Egypt the stems are trimmed and straight, and placed generally at regular intervals ; but here this most graceful of trees is half untended, its boughs spring direct from the earth, and form tufts and avenues, and dense overarching thickets of the most luxuriant growth, through which the sunlight falls tremblingly upon the shaded turf. Among them some few, shooting upright, lift high above the rest their lovely coronal of rustling fans and glowing bunches of dates; but the greater part assume that fantastic variety of form which only untended nature can originate; some, wildly throwing forth their branches, droop to the ground like heavy plumes, laden with a graceful burden of fan-like boughs which almost kiss the turf; others, crossing and intertwined, form mazy alleys of exquisite verdure; the clear stream bubbles freshly on the edge of these arcades, and the deep solitude is vocal with the song of birds; the wind, sweeping down the rocks, plays over the rustling foliage with the gentlest murmur; and, shut in by two lofty walls of rock from the dreary Desert without, the traveller, lulled in a dreamy and delicious repose, heightened by his past weariness, forgets awhile its perils and privations, and the long distance he has yet to accomplish across its drouthy sands."—*Forty Days in the Desert*, pp. 51, 52.

Having thus sketched the scene, and traced the history, let us study its moral meanings, and draw forth some portion of the rich instruction which it affords.

I. They broke up from their encampment in Elim in an enervated and murmuring mood.

"*And they took their journey from Elim, and all the congregation of the children of Israel came into the wilderness of Sin, which is between Elim and Sinai, on the fifteenth day of the second month after*

*their departure out of the land of Egypt.   And the
whole congregation of the children of Israel murmured against Moses and Aaron in the wilderness :
and the children of Israel said unto them, Would to
God we had died by the hand of the Lord in the land
of Egypt, when we sat by the flesh-pots, and when we
did eat bread to the full; for ye have brought us forth
into this wilderness, to kill this whole assembly with
hunger."*—Exod. xvi. 1-3.

They had eaten of the fat of the wilderness and
become wanton, and they began to lust even for
the fat of Egypt, the slave's portion ; the lot of
the freeman already seemed too spare and hard.—
Wisely, indeed, was the wilderness appointed for
our wanderings.   Wisely was Adam sent forth
into the land in which *"in the sweat of his brow he
must eat bread."*   Bread won more cheaply may
fatten the body, but it sends "leanness into the
soul."   I never heard that money won by gam-
bling or thieving brought a blessing with it to
its possessor.   Did you ever hear of speculation
enriching either mind or heart ?   At the time of
the great railway mania, any lad who could squint
along a level could earn large sums by surveying,
while the fever lasted, especially in the early days
of November.   One, who knew the whole thing
thoroughly, told me that he had never met one of
them who had been blessed by his gains.   Money

which comes cheaply goes cheaply, and leaves no
benediction.   God's inscription on His coin is
LABOUR.   It is of another mintage, when that impression cannot be traced.   Men dream away life
at Naples, Palermo, or Constantinople.   It is the
men who have to battle with the Northern seas,
and wring a harvest from the Northern climate,
who support the great characters in the drama of
history.

God does not multiply our Elims, for He cannot trust us there.   He gems the earth with them,
to teach us that it is not all blasted, that we are
not a cursed race in a cursed world.   He sets
them before our eyes as witnesses that there are
worlds where there is no bitterness in the fountains, and where man shall find more than a
Paradise regained.   But He suffers us not to
linger there; and when He leads us forth, He
knows that we shall be but murmuring pilgrims,
till privation and toil have braced our moral
muscles again, and restored the poise of the
pilgrim soul.   How many of us have come out
of our Elim strengthened?   From out some cold
salt-bath of calamity we have come forth again
and again renewed.   But Elim! who can bear its
sweetness and softness! who does not grow wanton
by its gurgling waters and rustling palms?

They are the very finest and purest natures

which are tuned to a higher key in Elim; most of us get let down to the level of the key-note of this wanton world. To enjoy the season of rest and refreshment with a high-souled resolution to hold on the way, as soon as the rest has renewed us, how hard! how rare! God's richest mercies we steep in bitterness; His most beautiful gifts and seasons we abuse to His loss. Rare are these palm-groves on earth. The marvel is, that they are not rarer; but that God's wisdom is merciful, it would be an utter waste. But it is a bitter thing that rest and plenty make men wanton, and that our Father is driven to the severer methods in dealing with our sensual souls. Rest in Elim, but dare not to ungird. Drink; but like Gideon's men, "lap" as in haste. Sleeping, let your loins be girt, your lamps burning, your staves ready to your hand—prompt at the first signal to renew the wilderness way. Grow wanton there, and you make, as I have said more at large, the whole world a wilderness; and your next station will find you crying for the flesh-pots of Egypt—the fodder of slaves.

II. The first stage of their journey brought them out into a vast sandy plain, where there was real danger, to the eye of sense, of their dying of hunger.

Elim had re-heartened them after Marah. But

the wilderness of Sin renewed their pains and terrors, and "the whole congregation of the children of Israel murmured against Moses and Aaron."

Their cry after the flesh-pots was the fruit of Elim. They had renewed there the blunted edge of their lust. The old appetites resumed their sway, as they sat by the waters and ate of their flocks; when they went forth their murmurs broke out with new fierceness, as of lust rekindled, and in spirit, at any rate, they gave themselves again to be slaves. Beware of rekindling the flame of a dying lust or appetite. Starve it—it is the only policy. Let it taste again, let it but look again, it flushes up into full fever glow, and you are once more enslaved. The thirst for blood may lie latent in a tiger while blood is denied; let him but lap a drop of it, and the passion is all aflame.

Still the danger, to the eye of sense, was a real one. Their flocks and herds had been nourished in the pastures of Elim, and had revived after their three days' burning march; but what hope was there of saving them in the end? A new course was before them; still no pasture, no water! and when the flocks and herds were dead what should nourish them in the waste? The danger to men who had no vision of the Invisible, was pressing and real. *Their* dread of it was faithless and shameful. God was the God of the waste and of the flesh-pots; the plenty of Egypt and the dearth of the Desert were alike from His hand. He had broken for them every morsel they had eaten in Egypt; His hand, curbing the stormy waters from their path, had led them forth into the wilderness; and what were its wastes that they should frustrate His purposes, or refuse to nourish His beloved?

Then follows the history of two of the most stupendous miracles recorded in the Word of God.

"*Then said the Lord unto Moses, Behold, I will rain bread from heaven for you; and the people shall go out and gather by a certain rate every day, that I may prove them, whether they will walk in my law, or no. And it shall come to pass, that on the sixth day they shall prepare that which they bring in; and it shall be twice as much as they gather daily.*"
"*And when the dew that lay was gone up, behold, upon the face of the wilderness there lay a small round thing, as small as the hoar frost on the ground. And when the children of Israel saw it, they said one to another, It is manna: for they wist not what it was. And Moses said unto them, This is the bread which the Lord hath given you to eat. This is the thing which the Lord hath commanded, Gather of it*

every man according to his eating, an omer for every man, according to the number of your persons ; take ye every man for them which are in his tents. And the children of Israel did so, and gathered, some more, some less." . . . *" And the people thirsted there for water ; and the people murmured against Moses, and said, Wherefore is this that thou hast brought us up out of Egypt, to kill us and our children and our cattle with thirst ? And Moses cried unto the Lord, saying, What shall I do unto this people ? they be almost ready to stone me. And the Lord said unto Moses, Go on before the people, and take with thee of the elders of Israel ; and thy rod, wherewith thou smotest the river, take in thine hand, and go. Behold, I will stand before thee there upon the rock in Horeb ; and thou shalt smite the rock, and there shall come water out of it, that the people may drink. And Moses did so in the sight of the elders of Israel. And he called the name of the place Massah, and Meribah, because of the chiding of the children of Israel, and because they tempted the Lord, saying, Is the Lord among us or not ?"* Exod. xvi. 4, 5, 14–17 ; xvii. 3-7.

Such is the startling statement of God's book ; such the strong belief of the Jewish people through all their generations, confirmed by the words of the Lord Jesus. And I firmly believe it simply as it is here set down. God was beginning the education of an infant race ; He was teaching again the lessons which in the darkness consequent on the Fall had been forgotten or obscured. And this was among the first : " MAN SHALL NOT LIVE BY BREAD ALONE, BUT BY EVERY WORD THAT COMETH OUT OF THE MOUTH OF GOD."

The reality of this miracle has been attacked in all ages. Travellers have brought back wonderful accounts of the honey dew which falls in the Desert, and nourishes the exhausted traveller; also of the tree manna, which exudes in large quantities from the tamarisk-tree, and covers the whole ground; both which answer, in some very qualified degree, to the description in the text. There seems to be no doubt about the natural productions of the Desert, though it is difficult to get at the whole truth about them. It seems to me that the Arabs are clever cicerone, and tell the traveller what it pleases him most to hear. The Rationalists come back with explicit Arab testimony in one direction, and the Orthodox with as clear statements in the opposite one. Doubtless they are prompt to answer leading questions, and lie liberally, we fear, when well paid. But we may freely accept the account of travellers on the subject of the natural manna. I should be as little inclined to doubt that many natural rills are found springing out of the rocks of the Desert. God does not contradict Himself,

10

or dishonour nature, by his miracles. I should anticipate that this miracle, like all miracles, would be a revelation; an unfolding of the inner springs of the mechanism of nature there; an exaltation and perfecting of some handiwork of nature for His people's good. It seems most likely to me that there should be some natural substance there, to be the bread of the desert to the few wanderers; and that God, as with the loaves and fishes, and the wine at Cana, multiplied and purified it exceedingly, and made it a perennial store for the supply of His children's need. The gift of the manna was unquestionably a miracle; the quality, the constancy, the Sabbath supply, and its cessation, as reported in Joshua v. 12, all mark it out as a miraculous supply of what was truly a marvellous need—for the miracle of miracles was the presence of that people there— and it does not trouble me, it rather instructs me and deepens my sense of the wonder of the works of God, when I hear that manna is still in small quantities to be found in the Desert, and that streams start freshly out of rocks in a very remarkable and unexpected way. God's care of His people is not a constant suspension of the laws which govern and bless His creatures, but a more full and rich application of them, that they may bestow the whole blessing which their hands

contain.   The order of things is good; God's
miracles even cannot mend it; they but disclose
it, and apply its blessing directly to the child
whom He instructs and tends.*

Israel had to learn that it was quite as wonderful that they should have been fed in Egypt, as
that they should eat bread in the Desert; that
the one as well as the other was the distinct and
wonderful handiwork of God.   Many streams
they had passed gushing out of the rocks as they
had journeyed, and had drunk, unmindful of the
hand which held the cup to their lips.   It needed
that they should be perishing, and be visibly supplied by the hand of God, before they understood
the great wonder, their daily sustenance, and
learnt that daily "by the word that cometh out
of the mouth of God doth man live."   That
bread and that water were in a sense living—fresh
angels' food.   They must have had a special
sweetness in them, compared with the waters of
the cisterns which we hew—puddles fouled and
muddied by the hoofs of our vagrant desires and
lusts.   But this bread even, the angels' food,

* See, on the whole subject of the miraculous, the masterly
Discourse on Revelation, published many years ago by
A. J. Scott, A.M.; which seems to me to be the quarry from
which many views on miracles, now fully current, have been
hewn.

10—2

nourishes not a spirit: "The Father giveth us
the true bread from heaven." "The bread of
God is He which cometh down from heaven and
giveth life unto the world."

And think you, brother pilgrim! that in any
waste to which you are led forth by God's angel,
His bread and water can fail you? Think you
that if you go up out of Egypt, shake off the
fetters of any bondage that weakens and de-
grades you, He will leave you to starve in the
desert? Man of business! struggling to live
honestly and bravely, flinging off the bonds of
the habits which reign in the Goshen of commercial wealth and splendour, think you that your
bread and water are other than sure? Let this
history of Israel teach you: it was written for
your learning. Go forth, and the dews shall feed
you, the rock shall give you drink; but not one
hair of your head or of those who depend on you,
be you but brave and faithful, shall be harmed.

Oh! how fearful are we when we get out of
our Egypt into new scenes, where the familiar
supplies and associations fail. So long as we had
it in our own hand, our own garden, our own
cooking-pot, none so confident as we! But
abroad in the desert, among rocks and sands!
Can waters spring from the flinty rock, and bread
grow out of the dry ground? Yea, all this is

possible—easy to Him as your leek and melon beds in Egypt ; but one thing is impossible, impossible for ever, for the supplies of God to fail a trusting believing soul. Men lay up for their children " where moth and rust corrupt, and thieves break through to steal," and think they have done well, and made all sure ; while the riches of faculty and character, which can never perish, and the blessing of God, which can never grow old, seems to us but an uncertain heritage for our beloved. And so we, blind as we are to the real presence of God everywhen and everywhere, have to be brought low, and made to cry out of misery ; and then He shows to us, in our want and sorrow, what He had shown to us in our joy and plenty, but we would not see it, that every thing is by " the word that cometh out of the mouth of God."

Neither did they learn the lesson from these miracles perfectly. They had to be brought down again, and again, and again, and the lesson had to be reiterated, with indignant judgments, Beware ! "*how is it that ye do not understand ?*" Deep teaching of spiritual truth is there in these miracles, wonderful unfoldings of the mysteries of man's spiritual life. The outer life is the key to the inner ; as the body lives by bread, so the soul must live by Christ or perish. As they ate of that manna and drank of that brook, they were called to commune in love and confidence with their God, and be nourished unto life.

Alas! how few won the double blessing. They drank of that well and thirsted again, they ate of that bread and died. The world's food cannot nourish spirits, the world's pleasures cannot satisfy the infinite longings of a human heart. "Take thy fill, eat the fat and drink the sweet;" and then, if that be all, the fever of insatiate longing, the fire of ravening lust, through eternity. How calm and deep, amid the stirrings and rushings of the thirsty host to fill their water-cups at the rill which was flashing and gurgling through the sand—meet type of the wrestling, panting multitude who are thronging all the pleasure springs of the world—do the words of Jesus fall upon the ear: "*Whosoever drinketh of this water shall thirst again; but whosoever drinketh of the water that I shall give him shall never thirst, but the water that I shall give him shall be in him a well of water, springing up into everlasting life.*"

III. Rephidim was the scene of their first battle and their first victory.

In the first great act of the drama of deliverance, their duty had been simply to "Stand still and see the salvation of God." The hour was now come when they must "quit them like men

and fight." Not otherwise is it in the Christian
life. To rest on Christ, to "stand still and see
His salvation," is the true deliverance of a spirit:
this is redemption. But we must fight hard, as
if the victory depended on ourselves—not for
redemption, but as redeemed, if we would reap
all its glorious fruits.

The first foes of Israel were their kinsmen.
"And a man's foes shall be they of his own
house." Notably so in the first ages, and in
heathen lands; but even here, how hard it is to
take up an independent standing-ground among
one's kinsmen and familiars, and to be a saint
among one's friends! But come whence they
may, foes soon beset the young pilgrim: before
he has gone far, a long day's battle will test his
courage and strain his strength. Lusts and passions, which he thought he had slain for ever,
stand forth alive, and renew the conflict. The
Egyptians slain, new enemies throng round us.
Our pilgrimage must be a war-march, with battle-
music and banners: "JEHOVAH NISSI," "the
Lord my banner," we cry, and renew the fight.
How prone is the young soldier of Christ to think
that his first victory is a final one! But the outward tyranny beaten, the external enemy slain,
he finds, as Israel found, that the true battle of
life commences; that things and beings dear to

him as his own soul range themselves to oppose
his progress, or lurk as traitors within the citadel
of his own heart, ready to render it meanly to the
foe.   "If thy right hand offend thee, cut it off
and cast it from thee," is the charge which is laid
upon him.   "Thou therefore endure hardness,
as a good soldier of Jesus Christ," is the inspiring
cry of his Chief.   But the battle goes hard, the
foemen are many and strong, the heart faints,
the strength fails, the banner droops, and Amalek
raises the shout of victory.   "Who is sufficient
for these things?"   Who can bear the strain
and stress of this war?   Lift up your eyes and
behold the great Intercessor!   Behold the uplifted arms of Jesus, pleading your cause before
the Eternal Throne.   Pray! wrestle in prayer!
fight with heart uplifted!   The hand brave,
strong, prompt as Joshua's; the heart humble,
dependent, prayerful, as Moses', and hell has not
strength to master you :

> "By all hell's hosts withstood,
>   We all hell's hosts o'erthrow,
> And conquering them by Jesus' blood,
>   We still to conquest go."

Let your heart lose its hold on Jesus, your banner sinks, the enemy closes round it, the battle is
lost!   Nay, look once more.   Grasp once more
the consecrated standard, cross-bearing, renew the

fight; and that banner shall float victorious on all the storms that rage through the field of conflict; your steps shall be heard at length at heaven's gate as the steps of a conqueror, and shouts of triumph shall ring through the arches of the heavenly temple, as you bend before the Captain of salvation to receive your crown.

Sermon vii.

Sinai. The Revelation of the Divine Name.

" I am the Lord thy God."—Exod. xx. 2.

If we are right in the identification of Rephidim with the Wâdy Feirân, the great Oasis of the Desert, we shall have the less difficulty in determining the site of the Mountain of the Law. This giving of the law to the Jewish people, is the most solemn and pregnant event before the Christian era; it has but one parallel—the advent of Him who giveth the law to the whole human world. The sentence is profoundly true, that that day was the birthday of history. The whole significance of the exodus was developed before Sinai; and History, as well as Israel, was baptized there in the name of the Lord God " of all the earth." In the heart of that terrible and magnificent wilderness, He wrote His name above the tabernacle of man's history. Like the name of the architect of the Pharos, it has been overlaid by that of the kings, conquerors, and divine heroes of this world; but the clay crumbles away through the wear of the ages, and the name of the Lord God of Israel stands out grandly before us as at first.

The general term, Sinai, is applied to the centre group of the great mountain system of red and grey granite, which occupies the southern portion of the angle enclosed by the two arms of the Red Sea. The western group is known by the name of Serbâl, the eastern is Um-Shômer, the highest peak of the region; and the central group, loftier than Serbâl, lower than Um-Shômer, is Sinai. It consists of a cluster of summits, of which the highest, Djebel Katherin, commands a most magnificent panoramic view of the whole peninsula, and the two Gulfs, Suez and Akaba, intensely blue. The second and lower peak, Djebel Mousa, is the traditional scene of the giving of the law. Towards the north those two ridges blend in an elevated rocky plateau, which stretches some miles in a northerly direction, and flinging up some of the wildest and sharpest peaks in those regions (Râs Saseâfeh), descend suddenly in a sheer precipice on a perfectly level plain, enclosed by mountains on every hand, except to the east; there it bends round the spurs of the mountains, and joins the Wâdy-es-Sheykh, the great highway of that part of the Desert. Every traveller describes this scene as peculiarly grand,

and even sublime. The plain, the Wâdy-er-Râheh, is about a mile and a half in length, perfectly level, surrounded by steep cliffs on every hand; and in front of the traveller, as he descends the rough mountain pass, Nakb Hôwy, which is the nearest though most difficult route from the Wâdy Feirân to the Convent of Sinai, there is this range of magnificent precipices, Râs Saseâfeh, descending sheer into the level of the plain, and forming one of the most impressive panoramas which can be contemplated by the eye of man. As the traveller looks down on this level plain ·from the wild pass, Nakb Hôwy (the Pass of the Wind), it seems to be locked on every side by mountains; only on advancing it is seen to bend to the left round a bold promontory of rock, and to mingle with the great highway of the Desert; which, avoiding the Nakb Hôwy, sweeps round the outside of the mountain chain, from the entrance of the Wâdy Feirân to Sinai and Akaba.

The desolation in this land-locked sea of sand is utter; the silence profound. It is the inner sanctuary of Nature's great mountain temple. "If I were to make a model of the end of the world," writes one, "I would make it from the Convent of Mount Sinai." The forms of the granite cliffs which enclose the plain are singularly bold and strong. They have, at the same

time, a certain grand uniformity, like the avenue
—the dromos—of sublime sculptured forms which
led on to the shrine of the Egyptian temples.
God carved and piled the approaches to this great
mountain sanctuary, where His sublimity was to
be revealed.

I dwell on these particular features because
I believe in their significance. I believe that
God has established a special relation between
races of men and the forms of nature in the
country they inhabit; and that, further, there
is both mental and moral discipline to an
awakened, attentive spirit in the haunts of
nature which it frequents, and in the midst of
which the inner life brings forth its fruits. The
jaded head and heart, in our day, fly for solace
and refreshment to the glorious mountain regions,
where, amid the solemnities of glaciers and snow
peaks, our fretful spirits may gather strength and
calm. The valley of Chamounix, the Grindelwald, the Bay of Naples, the orange groves of
Sorrento, have been temples of worship and revelation to many an over-weary heart and spirit.
God is not more there than here, but our spirits
catch there more quickly the key-note of communion; they put off their veils, and pass more
simply, more wholly, from before the face of
nature to the face of God. Mere fancy! one tells

me, to whom Fleet Street is the oasis of the desert of life. To *you*, doubtless, it is mere fancy. But tell me, why did God lead forth this people into the heart of sublime mountain scenery, through its most difficult passes, to the very core of its grandest expression, when He would reveal to them His law and Himself? It was not the nearest way, it was not the easiest way, it was not the pleasantest way; but it was the right way, because beauty, splendour, sublimity, were there. The people, probably, would not journey by the narrow and difficult "Pass of the Wind," which I have described as leading from the Wâdy Feirân to the head of this small plain Er Râheh. The host, with the impedimenta, would follow the vast crescent-shaped Wâdy-Es-Sheykh, which bends round the outside of the mountains, and join Moses and the leaders in this narrow plain, on which they would look down from the summit of the pass, and see the level sand stretching like a sea up to the very foot of the Mount of God. They looked upon a scene which was destined to be ever memorable in the history of earth and eternity. Let me present to you the description, of a recent and most observant traveller :—

"We started at five, A.M. The camels went round by Wâdy Es-Sheykh; we took the direct route by Wâdy Solab,

which, passing by several deserted Bedouin villages of the
Arab serfs of the convent, with their lonely burial-grounds,
brought us to the foot of the Nakb Hôwy, the 'Pass of the
Wind,' a stair of rock, like that by which we had mounted to
the cluster of Serbâl, and by which we were to mount again
into the second and highest stage of the great mountain labyrinth. . . . We reached the head of the pass ; and, far in
the bosom of the mountains before us, I saw the well-known
shapes of the cliffs which form the front of Sinai. At each
successive advance these cliffs disengaged themselves from the
intervening and surrounding hills, and at last they stood out—
alone against the sky. On each side the infinite complications
of twisted and jagged mountains fell away from it. On each
side the sky encompassed it round, as though it were alone
in the wilderness. And to this giant mass we approached
through a wide valley, a long continued plain, which, enclosed
as it was between two precipitous mountain ranges of black
and yellow granite, and having always at its end this pro-
digious mountain block, I could compare to nothing else than
the immense avenue—' the dromos,' as it is technically called
—through which the approach was made to the great Egyptian
temples. One extraordinary sensation was the foreknowledge
at each successive opening of the view of every object that
would next appear ; as cliff and plain, and the deep gorges on
each side, and, lastly, the convent with its gardens burst
before me ; it was the unfolding of the sight of sights, of
which I had heard and read for years, till each part of it
seemed as familiar as if I had seen it again and again. Was
it the same or not ? The colours, and the scale of the scene,
were not precisely what I should have gathered from descriptions ; the colours less remarkable, the scale less grand. But
the whole impression of that long approach was even more
wonderful than I had expected. Whatever may have been the
scene of the events in Exodus, I cannot imagine that any

human being could pass up that plain and not feel that he was
entering a place above all others suited for the most august of
the sights of earth.   We encamped outside the convent, at the
point where the great Wâdy Es-Sheykh falls into the Wâdy
Er-Râheh, immediately under the corner of the cliff."—*Sinai
and Palestine*, pp. 73, 74.

Here, then, in this plain, and not in any of
the narrow gullies and broken ravines of the
mountain, doubtless the Israelites encamped;
and the pile of jagged cliffs rising sheer out of
the plain, and not the more distant summits,
would be the scene of the giving of the Law.   In
this site alone are to be found fulfilled all the
conditions which the narrative requires:—" A
mount which might be touched,"—which seems
to exclude the distant summits; a plain at the
foot of the mount, whence a complete view might
be gained by a great host; a situation in which
Moses might be able to hear the sound of song
in the camp, but not be able to see, as in some
of the lateral ravines by which he would have
to descend the precipitous cliff; room for the
idolatrous festival, and a brook coming down
from the mount, where the ashes might be
scattered, and the people compelled to drink.
There, too, bounds could easily be set about
the mount, lest the people should break through;
and, in a word, all the important conditions are

fulfilled. Dr. Robinson and Dr. Stanley join in
affirming that the general aspect of this site is
a most convincing argument; and that nothing
but the most conclusive evidence could induce
any one, who has carefully surveyed the localities,
to give up the belief that the Wâdy-er-Râheh
and the cliffs of Sasâfeh which overhang it, were
the scene of the giving of the law. The view
of the plain from the summit completes this
impression.

"The first thing to be done was, therefore, to gain the
summit of the other end of the range called the Râs Sasâfeh
(Willow Head), overlooking the Er-Râheh from above. The
whole party descended, and after winding through the various
basins and cliffs which make up the range, we reached the
rocky point overlooking the approach we had come the preceding day. The effect on us, as on every one who has seen
and described it, was instantaneous. It was like the seat on
the top of Serbâl, but with the difference, that here was the
deep, wide, yellow plain sweeping down to the very base of the
cliffs; exactly answering to the plain on which the people
'removed and stood afar off.' . . . There is yet a
higher mass of granite immediately above this point, which
should be ascended, for the greater completeness of view
which it affords. The plain below is then seen extending not
only between the ranges of Tlaha and Furei'â, but also into
the lateral valleys, which, on the north-east, unite it with the
wide Wâdy of the Sheykh. This is important, as showing how
far the encampment may have been spread below, still within
sight of the same summit. Behind extends the granite mass
of the range of Gebel Mousa, cloven into deep gullies and

11

basins, and ending in the traditional peak, crowned by the memorials of its double sanctity."—*Sinai and Palestine,* pp. 75, 76.

Now let us try to analyze and realize the moral meaning of the scene.

The first grand, all-comprehensive fact which we meet with is, that they were led up into the wilderness that they might enter into covenant with God.

"*And Moses went up unto God, and the Lord called unto him out of the mountain, saying, Thus shalt thou say to the house of Jacob, and tell the children of Israel ; Ye have seen what I did unto the Egyptians, and how I bare you on eagles' wings, and brought you unto myself. Now therefore, if ye will obey my voice indeed, and keep my covenant, then ye shall be a peculiar treasure unto me above all people : for all the earth is mine : and ye shall be unto me a kingdom of priests, and an holy nation. These are the words which thou shalt speak unto the children of Israel. And Moses came and called for the elders of the people, and laid before their faces all these words which the Lord commanded him. And all the people answered together, and said, All that the Lord hath spoken we will do. And Moses returned the words of the people unto the Lord.*"— Exod. xix. 3–8.

This is the prologue of the scene which follows,

which gives to it all its significance; a people entering into covenant with the "High and holy One who inhabits eternity;" "Who doeth according to His own will among the armies of heaven, whose hand none of the inhabitants of the earth can stay, or say unto Him what doest Thou?" "Who is above all things, and was before all things," "for whose pleasure all things are and were created."

I. God in covenant with man, is the condition of the existence and development of man's spiritual life.

Man is either a sinner under sentence, which it may please the Judge at any moment to execute; or he is a sinner spared on the distinct understanding that God is seeking his life and not his death. In the first case, no spiritual life is possible; if death, the death of the soul as the penalty of sin, is certain sooner or later, then morals have no meaning for man. The sooner it is over the better: "Let us eat and drink, for to-morrow we die." But this is not the condition in which a merciful God has left us. Adam did not so understand it when he went out from Eden. The occurrences of his life, and the particulars of his intercourse with God, are hidden from us; but thus much we gather from what is recorded of his history, that Adam cherished till

11—2

death a pious and thankful confidence in God, built on the first promise ; which confidence implies, of necessity, that he felt that his sin might be forgiven, that his wounds might be healed. However dark the wilderness might be compared with Eden, its twilight was the dawning which would not darken into night, but flash up into rosy day. Noah did not understand it so. He cherished the hope of his sire, that the cursed earth and the afflicted soul might look up with hope to God. Abraham did not understand it so. No malefactor, respited for a moment but surely doomed, did he walk with God in Palestine, but a man in covenant with his Maker—a man whom God had called His friend.

Now this sense, that man is not only reprieved for a time, but is a being concerning whom God has an object and a hope, a being with life before him and not death, unless he wills to die, under-lies all human moral activity and progress. And this is, in other terms, a covenant of God. It may not be expressed in what remains of the history of Adam ; it is expressed in the history of Noah and Abraham, and we are made to see that this was the rock on which they edified their lives ; and it is every man's rock who would have a foundation stronger than the quicksands of fancy and listless expectation ; who is not content just to take his chance with the creature which perishes and shall perish, but seeks to connect his life with God, who endures and shall endure. In some shape or other, some covenant of God must underlie the life and progress of the world.

You may say the sentences, which are here set down as the words of God's own lips, cannot be the words of Him whom "the heaven, even the heaven of heavens, cannot contain"—so serene, so lofty, so infinitely removed from our comprehension and thought. The idea of God speaking to men, making a covenant with men, enacting a code of express regulations, descending even to the minutest details of life, must be a dream of man's, not a thought of the mind of God. You may say that the very idea of a covenant with fallen sinners, the kind of expression of Himself which a covenant implies, is dishonouring to the ideas which we are bound to cherish concerning the absolute, infinite, and immutable God; who has established the system of the universe with that excellent wisdom, that He has left no room for any accident or contingency which might call for such a transaction as that which this passage records. But, in addition to the fact, that the most deep and serious history in the world declares that the world's chief heroes and saints *did* live by faith in a covenanting God—*did* accept

and seal a covenant with Him, and made their
lives noble and glorious by the resolution and
struggle to keep it,—you will find, if you consider
it closely, that without some distinct, exact expression of God's mind and will on the subject of man
and his future, the Fall must have buried man in
the darkness of death for ever. Remember the
sentence is *in* man, in every man, by nature.
Adam hid himself, every man hides himself,
when sin forces itself on his conscience; and he
knows that the doom is, and must be, death. The
despair of the sinner, but for God's mercy, would
crush him, would crush all of us, into the nether
deeps. And what know we of God's mercy? We
may spin fine words and fine thoughts about it
out of the stuff of our own imagination; but no
imagination of man has ever proved strong enough
to be the foundation of his higher life. We
may have learnt to think and talk of it familiarly
as a thing unquestionable; but for ages our forefathers have been living consciously in a covenant,
and all our ideas of God have been formed by it.
But ask that agonized father, plunging the bare
knife into the throat of his daughter, or flinging
his tender infant into that seething cauldron of
fire, what man, ignorant of the covenant, knows
of the mercy and forgiveness of God. Man lives
on the covenant; he builds his life on the

promises; it is the condition of his living at all in the sense in which a man may live. The notion of this wells up even in the midst of the pagan desert, and makes some green oases. It is the office of revelation to bring out the terms of that covenant (which, like all the higher bonds of relation between spiritual beings, becomes less explicit in terms as its spirit is better understood), that man may know and live by it, and attain to the strength and dignity of a being who is in solemn covenant with God.

God led that people out that He might make them understand the full terms of that covenant which He sought to establish with them, and call out their intelligence and spiritual activity in response. There their moral life began: there every man's moral life begins. No man lives—he only exists—till he has set his hand to the record of his divine relations and duties, and said in a covenant which he would rather shed his heart's best blood than abandon, "I will serve the Lord."

II. The second broad fact of the narrative is that God was seeking the covenant, not man.

Man was not finding God, God was finding man, and bringing him near unto Himself. And this is the profoundest fact in the history of the great universe. Redemption, spiritual life, the

glory and bliss of heaven, all spring out of it.
God seeking man, laying hold on man when
rebellious and forgetful; pledge of all longsuffering patience and tender love. The people
were bondsmen, slaves, "dead in trespasses and
sins," sitting by the flesh-pots, and forgetting
utterly in their rank flavour the bread of heaven,
when God's hand touched them, rekindled the
dying memories, and re-illumined the faded records
of their race. His hand led them out, having
nerved them for the path of peril by the prodigies
He wrought for their deliverance; and He guided
them by ways they knew not, feeding them daily
from His own hand in heaven, until He set them
in front of those beetling cliffs in that vast silence,
and expounded to them the terms of a fuller covenant with Himself. It is God who acts, man who
accepts; God who gives, man who receives; and
thus the hope of man has its strong resting-place,
not on the strivings of his own weak will, not on
the searchings of his own too easily bewildered
and blinded intellect, but on the eternal purpose
and love of God.

God cannot dispense with man's heart, will,
and intellect; He led that people there that He
might engage them in His service. Refuse Him
that service, and the covenant is worthless to you,
nay, is a witness against you to condemnation;

yield them to Him, and rest in the assurance that
your salvation depends not on your own weak
work, but on the strong arm of God. I find in
this idea, so powerfully developed in the narrative
of the exodus, a strong prophetic preaching of the
Gospel, which St. Paul more fully expounds:—
"For by grace are ye saved through faith; and
that not of yourselves: it is the gift of God: not
of works, lest any man should boast. For we are
his workmanship, created in Christ Jesus unto
good works, which God hath before ordained that
we should walk in them."—Ephes. ii. 8-10. We
talk of a covenant of works. The Jews understood it so; but there was a Gospel—a Gospel of
the grace of God in the heart of it. "I call
heaven and earth to record this day against you,
that I have set before you life and death, blessing
and cursing: therefore choose life, that both thou
and thy seed may live: that thou mayest love the
Lord thy God, and that thou mayest obey his
voice, and that thou mayest cleave unto him: for
he is thy life, and the length of thy days: that
thou mayest dwell in the land which the Lord
sware unto thy fathers, to Abraham, to Isaac, and
to Jacob, to give them."—Deut. xxx. 19, 20.

Man seeking to propitiate God, to lay down the
terms of a covenant under which he will consent
to live, to offer that which may make him accept-

able in His sight, in whose hand " is the soul of
every living creature, and the breath of all mankind," passeth down inevitably into the darkness;
man believing in and loving a God seeking *him*,
goeth up into the eternal day.

III. You will find two grand features in that
which was transacted there on the Mount of God:
God revealing Himself—God declaring His law.
This was God's covenant; the people had but to
say in heart and with voice "Amen." I shall
consider the first, in what remains of this discourse; the second, the philosophy of the dispensation of law, will need fuller consideration by
itself.

God declares His name.

The first lines of the Covenant were traced
when God declared Himself to Moses, "*And
Moses said unto God, Behold, when I come unto
the children of Israel, and shall say unto them,
The God of your fathers hath sent me unto you;
and they shall say to me, What is His name? what
shall I say unto them? And God said unto Moses,
I AM THAT I AM: and He said, Thus shalt
thou say unto the children of Israel, I AM hath sent
me unto you. And God said moreover unto Moses,
Thus shalt thou say unto the children of Israel, The
Lord God of your fathers, the God of Abraham,
the God of Isaac, and the God of Jacob, hath sent*

me unto you : this is my name for ever, and this is my memorial unto all generations."—Exodus iii., 13–15.

An awful question for a people to have to ask, What is the name of God ? To us, familiar as we are with the Divine name, the question is hardly comprehensible. Nothing is so difficult for a Christian in this nineteenth century to realize, as the experience of a man looking round with awe and wonder on this vast universe, and asking himself, without a clue to the answer, what meaneth this mystery of life? To the infants of humanity, each dawn and each spring was a fresh and prolific wonder. The Vedas contain passionate questions, whether the sun will rise again from the lap of ocean; whether the night, as it falls, is to be the grave of the world ? We see behind the curtain; we see the scope and capacity of the mechanism of creation ; and wonder—informed, instinct with knowledge,—gives place to faith, whereby, in a measure we are little conscious of, day by day we live. But, in the early ages, wonder was kept watching; every seed, every river, every reptile, every child, was enveloped in mystery : who could expound the whence and the whither of this manifold teeming life of the world? Every-where, in the springing corn, in the globe of fire, which by some unknown unfathomable power daily traversed the sky, was an element of mystery which eluded man's keenest searchings. Should he call this "God?" Should he bow down and worship the unsearchable, in every form of nature, in every movement and manifestation of life? Egypt had no better answer to the question. She worshipped birds, and beasts, and loathsome reptiles; and knew neither the name of man, nor the name of God. A calm, blank look of baffled wonder is her most divine expression; her Sphynx, too, is but half a man. To know God is the glory of a man; that is manhood, and that alone.

There is nothing to lift a man out of the whirl and suction of the great world engine, to stay him from swinging round helplessly with it in its circles as a mere atom of creation, but the knowledge of the name of God. This raises a man at once into the higher hemisphere of being. There is an eternal distinction between him and the creation which claims him, and will have him, unless he set up this protest, "I know and am known of God." And God declared His name—the Maker of the world, the Author and the Ruler of this manifold, mazy labyrinth of life. He laid His hand on every element in Egypt, and showed that it served Him. Bread and water, the staff of life, in the desert He had visibly consecrated with His hand. And now He set them before His grandest handiwork, and from the summit of the mount of God He proclaimed His name. The Lord, who had shown Himself king of every element and creature that Egypt worshipped, was there before them, in a cloud of splendour on which their eyes could not prevail to look. To some a nearer vision was vouchsafed. "Then went up Moses, and Aaron, Nadab, and Abihu, and seventy of the elders of Israel; and they saw the God of Israel; and there was under His feet as it were a paved work of a sapphire stone, and as it were the body of heaven in his clearness."—Exodus xxiv., 9–10. But all heard Him; all bowed down and worshipped Him; all heard from His own lips the solution of the baffling mystery. "I am the Lord your God." What an emancipation! Life was no longer a riddle, earth was no longer a maze. Egypt worshipped all things. Israel knew the Lord whom all things worshipped; they could look with a man's free and mastering glance on all beings and all things around them in the world.

The name of God is the key to the cipher of creation. Without the key, it baffles the finest intellect; given the key, it is open to the under-

standing of a child. Those hoary peaks, glowing
with sunset splendour, that pallid moonlight,
which threw a softening veil over their rough-
ness, and left the shadows deeper in the hollows,
were the creatures, the servitors of the Lord of
Hosts. They felt that a new and grander distinction grew up between themselves and wanton,
slavish Egypt. She confounded, they could dis-
tinguish, reverence, and magnify, the name of God.
It is the true secret of life for every one of us.
Nature, circumstance, the currents of life, master
us, till we know the Divine Name. We know
ourselves in knowing Him, and find in ourselves
the broken features of His likeness. We become
conscious of a life which it is foul shame, wrong,
and wretchedness to bury in the perdition of the
creature. Nature may still present to us many
insoluble problems. We may feel that there is
still an awful mystery in life—in the mixture of
good and evil in us, and in the world. But we
have the key. We can face the Sphynx, we can
hold up the head in front of the mass, force, and
witchery of nature, for we know the name of the
Lord. The first step towards the establishment
of the covenant was the revelation of the Divine
name.

2. It was a merciful name which the Lord
made known : " I am the Lord thy God, which

have brought thee out of the land of Egypt,
out of the house of bondage. I am the God of
thy fathers." How tender, how blessed the
assurance ! There was something awful in the
revelation of the Divine name, though it emanci-
pated them from all meaner dread. Like the
rill of bright gushing water amid those sterile
giant rocks; like a clump of fair, sweet flowers
amid a waste of desolate grandeur, else crush-
ing to sense and soul, was this soft word, " THE
GOD OF THY FATHERS," from such lips. To
know God, is the first step out to spiritual
freedom and manhood. To know that He is my
God, the God of my fathers, the God of my
pilgrimage, the God of my redemption,—that He
yearns over me, clings to me, and with a strong
right hand will save me,—lifts me up from the
freedom of a man to the joy and fellowship of a
son. God's revelation of Himself to Israel is full
of such touches of tenderness. What a principle
of unity, what a cement of national life is here !
" The God of our fathers " hath appeared to us ;
we are a chosen and peculiar people, we have a
name which God, the God of our fathers, has
bestowed and consecrated ; we can only lose it by
apostacy ; we cannot be despoiled of it by death."

Most blessed to Israel, most blessed to us, is
the revelation of the merciful name. What are

the toils and perils of the wilderness, what the
pangs of thirst and hunger, what the hate and
violence of foes? The Lord our God bears
us as on eagles' wings through the privations,
and dangers, and sufferings of the Desert, and
sets us unharmed, unstained in the Promised
Land. Consider then, faint-hearted one, " that
as a nurse cherisheth her child, so the Lord thy
God cherisheth thee."

3. The Lord's name is holy. " The Lord thy
God is a holy Lord."

A sensual-hearted man will fashion gods like
unto himself. A wise and earnest-hearted man
will "give thanks at the remembrance of God's
holiness." There is something affecting in the
struggle of man's heart, in all ages, to hold fast
the belief in the holiness of God. The lust of
man was too strong for his convictions, and his
gods grew to be as sensual as himself. But he
soon began to loathe and scorn them. Rome, in
the age of Christ, made merry with her gods.*
To persuade man that God winks at sin, and is
ready to go partners in pleasure, is to make man

* It is a very interesting question how far the atheism of
such a deep thinker as Lucretius was an earnest protest against
such gods as Rome told him of; a search after a more universal
law of creation than Jupiter could explain to him, and so far
his poem was constructive work.

blaspheme his Creator, and hate his very life.
To tell man that God hates sin, is to open up a
spring of hope and life to him, if he has heard
the merciful name of God; May I but know Him,
he cries, my soul may be saved. The covenant
declares such a God—" glorious in holiness," " a
hater of sin." Many and terrible were the witnesses to this in their national history; but the
loss of the sense of it would have been national
death. It is the great test of character. Can
you rejoice in the holiness of the Lord? Would
you have a God like unto yourself, or a God such
as the Scripture reveals to you, like whom you
may hope to become? To believe in the perfect
holiness is essential to all who seek to be sanctified—to be made pure in heart that they may
see God. How blessed the revelation that this
God of awful holiness, " who cannot so much as
look upon sin," has in mercy entered our world,
to put away sin by the sacrifice of Himself.
That He has made acquaintance with all the
experiences of our nature, has been " tempted in
all points like as we are," that He might succour
our need. Those who can give thanks at the
remembrance of His holiness are those who have
seen Jesus, the great high-priest, before the
throne. The law implies and necessitates the
Gospel. Moses is the sure forerunner of Christ.

12

Sermon viii.

Sinai. The Golden Calf—the Essential Nature of Idolatry.

"*Up, make us gods, which shall go before us.*"—Exod. xxxii. 1.

THE most patent fact of man's history as a spiritual being is idolatry. It is man's dull form of the recognition of the spiritual powers. It is man's Amen to the sentence of the perplexed and baffled intellect, "Canst thou by searching find out God? Canst thou find out the Almighty to perfection? It is as high as heaven; what canst thou do? deeper than hell; what canst thou know?" The 32nd chapter of Exodus is its complete natural history. In one day that people lived through the experience of the idolatrous world, from the first cry of the yearning want which begets the lust after an idol, to the last drop of bitterness in which, when it is ground to powder, we have to drink its dust. Israel lived a typical life. The history of this people is in little all history; and idolatry, the world's religion, receives its richest illustration from this record of Israel's life. It is manifestly a very deep question, and related very profoundly to man's spiritual nature in its present condition before God. It appears, not in paganism only, a· substitute for God among an ignorant and godless people, it appears in Judaism, it appears even in the Christian ages in the bosom of the Christian Church; it is *the* great temptation, *the* easily besetting sin of all time. That surely must have a deeper root than mere ignorance of God, which sets up its images in the full blaze of the sunlight of the noon of the Christian ages, and fills the temples where the Ten Commandments are blazoned on the walls, with idols which poor ignorant souls are tempted to bow down to instead of to Him.

The history and philosophy of idolatry is too large a subject to be treated, even in outline, in such a discourse as this. But if we consider steadily this act of idolatry of the Jewish people, we shall discover some principles which will help us to understand its history and manifestations in the wide world.

The common conception of idolatry is, that it is the refuge to which the soul betakes itself in utter ignorance of God, and when too debased and blinded to form any higher conception of His nature than the visible forms of creation can set forth. The idolater recognizes in nature the

12—2

workings of a life which he cannot understand, which fill him with wonder, and which he gladly bows down to as divine. The idols of the heathen are mostly either dull imitations of the forms of nature; or the result of an effort to express symbolically, by a combination of natural forms in one unnatural image, the idea of a power dwelling and working in various forms, but not to be identified with any particular creature. And this is in fact an effort of the human intellect to free itself from the mere creature worship, which in the long-run is the inevitable end of a turning away in spirit from the Lord.

But let us consider it more closely; we may find occasion to modify this view. I observe, taking this history for my guide,—

I. The very essence of idolatry is, not spiritual ignorance and obtuseness, but a wilful turning away from the spiritual knowledge and worship of God.

I have already said in effect, that to understand idolatry you must not go to the stupid savage, the aboriginal Australian, or the South Sea Islander, who, knowing no better, takes a bit of stone or wood and makes it, or gets it made, into a god. Idolatry has degenerated into this, and it is its native tendency to bring men to this; but its essence is quite other than this, and must be sought for in the higher region of man's being and the nobler strata of man's history. You could never understand man by studying the savage form of him, by supposing that the savage is his original and typical image, and that the higher forms of human life present to us what man may grow to by culture and civilization. The savage is a degenerate man. The earliest records of the human race, in all countries, are "golden" legends : man in a golden age, man as we find him in Genesis, with much of the divine original about him, which in the savage is almost wholly lost. Civilization, society, moral and mental power and dignity, these present the normal status of man. You must study him under these his highest conditions, if you would understand his lowest ; Adam explains both Plato and the savage ; the savage explains not even himself. And the principle of these remarks bears directly on idolatry. The gross forms of it, to which it has sunk during the lapse of ages, must be explained by the finer and subtler, but equally fatal form, which is to be met with in the records of the historic races and the nobler times. Of all these records, unquestionably the most important, the most pregnant, is this. Let us study it, and get from it what light we may.

1. This act of idolatry was in the very front of the majesty and splendour of Jehovah, revealed on Sinai. It was in the very face of the mount that might be touched and that burned with fire, and the sound of the trumpet, and the voice of words, by which the Lord God of Hosts was declaring Himself to them there.

Let me beg you to note these words:—

"And it came to pass, on the third day in the morning, that there were thunders and lightnings and a thick cloud upon the mount, and the voice of the trumpet exceeding loud; so that all the people that was in the camp trembled. And Moses brought forth the people out of the camp to meet with God; and they stood at the nether part of the mount. And Mount Sinai was altogether on a smoke, because the LORD descended upon it in fire: and the smoke thereof ascended as the smoke of a furnace, and the whole mount quaked greatly. And when the voice of the trumpet sounded long, and waxed louder and louder, Moses spake, and God answered him by a voice. And the LORD came down upon Mount Sinai, on the top of the mount. And the LORD called Moses up to the top of the mount, and Moses went up."—Exod. xix. 16–20.

"And all the people saw the thunderings, and the lightnings, and the noise of the trumpet, and the mountain smoking : and when the people saw it, they removed, and stood afar off. And they said unto Moses, Speak thou with us, and we will hear : but let not God speak with us, lest we die. And Moses said unto the people, Fear not : for God is come to prove you, and that His fear may be before your faces, that ye sin not. And the people stood afar off, and Moses drew near unto the thick darkness, where God was."—Exod. xx. 18–21.

Now it was in front of all this, while the splendour still shone, while the cloud still lowered, while the thunders still echoed through the gorges of the resonant mountains, and the ground still quivered beneath their feet, "*that the people gathered themselves together unto Aaron and said unto him, Up, make us gods which shall go before us ; for as for this Moses, the man that brought us up out of the land of Egypt, we wot not what is become of him.*"

We have here a mental condition, at any rate, far removed from ignorance. They had heard the Divine Name ; they had entered into a solemn, explicit, binding covenant with God ; " all that the Lord hath spoken will we do." Their elders had "seen the God of Israel." Nor could they have forgotten it. That dense shroud over the brow of the mountain, from whose deep recesses

ever and anon flashed forth the glory of the
Lord, was, we may be sure, a sufficient memorial;
and yet filled with fear—that fear which is terror
and "hath torment"—they made to themselves a molten image and sang, "These be thy
gods, O Israel." It is a very awful chapter of
man's history; incredible, but that its comment
is in our own hearts. It is the history of the
genesis of all idolatries. Idolatry has not been
born, after ages of degeneracy, to fill up a dread
chasm in man's circle of knowledge, with some
images which, at any rate, may stand as signs of
the divine. We meet with idolatry in the morning age, and in the morning land of history.
Terah was idolatrous; Laban was idolatrous;
Egypt was idolatrous; Assyria was idolatrous; and
that at a time when the echoes of the Divine Name,
as it had been proclaimed to Noah, had not sunk
in silence, and the traditions of divine truth had
not faded from the memory of the most careless
of mankind. God wrote His name over the
temple of creation; man's art has blotted and
obscured it. But while it was yet fresh, and
man could read it reverently, idols were set up,
and "the glory of the incorruptible God was
changed into an image made like to corruptible
man, and to birds, and four-footed beasts, and
creeping things." Not more magnificently was

the name of God emblazoned there in the heart
of that mountain wilderness, than in the grandeur,
the beauty, and the brightness of the world.
" The heavens declare His glory, and the firma-
ment showeth His handiwork. Day unto day
uttereth speech of Him, and night unto night
showeth knowledge." And the early idolaters
heard it. The eye was not closed to the divine
glory of creation, the ear was not shut to the
tones of the divine voice which still lingered in
the silent places of the world, when men " darkened their foolish hearts " into idolatry.

Paul's argument on the origin of idolatry distinctly asserts that it was when men " knew God,
they glorified Him not as God," and sank into
this deadly sin.—Rom. i. 18, 23. St. Paul's
profound moral analysis of idolatry expounds this
chapter, and this chapter of history sustains the
conclusions of St. Paul. Neither the visible
manifestation of the glory of the Lord in a specially awful and impressive form on Sinai; nor the
declaration of the Divine Name as the wise and
good One, the Author of order, the Fountain of
blessing—in the harmony of the heavenly motions
above us, in the grace, the sweetness, the brightness of the melodies of the earth around us,
which bathe us in their atmospheres, and lift the
spirit in joy to the footstool of the King who

makes such music in His palaces, for the delight and instruction of His sons—can struggle against this prone tendency of the human heart to worship idols, which first broke out in the very face of the revelation of Jehovah in His temple of creation, and has wrought on until it has rendered man by nature incapable of a pure knowledge of and communion with Himself.

Remember, the people saw the glory of the God of Israel, and while the vision was there, and all its impressions fresh on their hearts, they made themselves a molten calf and sang, " *These, O Israel, be thy gods.*"

2. The second remarkable and characteristic feature of this scene which I notice is, that after Aaron " had fashioned the molten calf with a graving-tool," and the people had said, "These be thy gods, O Israel, which brought thee up out of the land of Egypt," " *he built an altar before it ; and made proclamation, and said, To-morrow is a feast to the Lord.*"—Exod. xxxii. 5.

With the idol before him, the priest proclaimed a feast unto the Lord ; and the people evidently entered into his thought, and with some dim notion that they were celebrating a divine festival, " they sat down to eat and drink, and rose up to dance." So this people, like the Samaritans in after ages, pleased themselves with the thought that they were "fearing the Lord, while they served their own gods." And I believe that the real heart of idolatry is here laid bare. It is, in plain terms, an effort to bring God within reach ; to escape the trouble, pain, and weariness of spiritual effort, and substitute the effort of the eye, hand, and tongue for the labour of the soul.

You may find idolaters in throngs up and down the world, whose conception of God is no higher than the bit of stone, brass, or mud which they worship. But a missionary to the heathen would make but little way with them, if he were to presume, in his appeals to them, that they imagined their idol to be God. The more thoughtful and earnest would testify that they have no such idea of God ; that God is above and beyond all representations ; that He is above even all particular deities ; but that this unknown Being connects Himself with certain places and images, so that the worshipper through them finds a way to Him. There are thoughtful men among idolaters in all ages, and this is what they say that they mean by their idol : that it is a thing with which God has connected Himself—through which He may be addressed, and by which He communicates with man. The "winking Virgin" and the fetish of the Gold Coast are on a level here ; each is conceived of as an agent or instrument—a means of manifestation of the Divine. As we study the history of the earlier idolatries, tracking back the stream of time, this fact comes out with increasing clearness, until we meet with men who seem to have had a considerably intelligent belief in Jehovah, and yet to have sought to help that faith by images. A very remarkable instance and proof of this, the following passage will supply:—

" Then Jacob rose up, and set his sons and his wives upon camels; and he carried away all his cattle, and all his goods which he had gotten, the cattle of his getting, which he had gotten in Padan-aram, for to go to Isaac his father in the land of Canaan. And Laban went to shear his sheep : and Rachel had stolen the images that were her father's. And Jacob stole away unawares to Laban the Syrian, in that he told him not that he fled. So he fled with all that he had ; and he rose up, and passed over the river, and set his face toward the mount Gilead. And it was told Laban, on the third day, that Jacob was fled. And he took his brethren with him, and pursued after him seven days' journey; and they overtook him in the mount Gilead. And God came to Laban the Syrian in a dream by night, and said unto him, Take heed that thou speak not to Jacob either good or bad. Then Laban overtook Jacob. Now Jacob had pitched his tent in the mount: and Laban with his brethren pitched in the mount of Gilead. And Laban said to Jacob, What hast thou done, that thou hast stolen away unawares to me, and carried away my daughters, as captives taken with the sword ? Wherefore didst thou flee away secretly, and steal away from me ; and didst not tell me, that I might have sent thee away with mirth and with songs,

with tabret, and with harp ?   And hast not suffered me to kiss
my sons and my daughters ?   Thou hast now done foolishly in so
doing.   It is in the power of my hand to do you hurt : but the
God of your father spake unto me yesternight, saying, Take
thou heed that thou speak not to Jacob either good or bad.   And
now, though thou wouldest needs be gone, because thou sore
longedst after thy father's house, yet wherefore hast thou
stolen my gods ?   And Jacob answered and said to Laban,
Because I was afraid : for I said, Peradventure thou wouldest
take by force thy daughters from me."—Gen. xxxi. 17-31.

Again : the Egyptians were the worst, the most
complete idolaters, in the ancient world.   Perhaps it was at them that St. Paul was specially
glancing in the passage which I have quoted from
the Romans ; for a Roman satirist, of about the
same age, assails their multitude of idols with
his keen scorn.   Now, in Exod. iii. 1, Mount
Horeb is styled "the mount of God ; " and in all
the communications between Moses and Pharaoh
it is taken for granted that Pharaoh would understand their allusion to that mount of God, and
their desire to sacrifice there.   There is strong
reason to believe that Mount Serbâl, the nearest
mountain of the Sinaitic chain to Egypt, was an
old Egyptian sanctuary, and sacred to a more
awful name than those of their domestic and
municipal gods.   I do not press this, but it is
worth noting.

Let me turn your attention to 2 Kings,

xviii. 1–6. I extract the most important verse:
—"Hezekiah removed the high places, and brake
the images, and cut down the groves, and brake
in pieces the brazen serpent that Moses had
made ; for unto those days the children of Israel
did burn incense to it : and he called it Nehush-
tan,"—that is, a piece of brass.

This piece of brass the Lord Himself had expressly appointed to be looked to. His name
was associated with it. It is impossible that the
history of it could be quite forgotten; and yet the
people made it an idol, and Hezekiah ground
it to powder.

The preceding chapter, 2 Kings, xvii. 24–41,
gives us the history of some idolaters who do not
seem to have been very far from Laban's state of
mind. The whole passage is of deep interest.
But this is the leading point:—" Then one of
the priests, whom they had carried away from
Samaria, came and dwelt in Beth-el, and taught
them how they should fear the Lord. Howbeit
every nation made gods of their own, and put
them in the houses of the high places. . . So
these nations feared the Lord, and served their
graven images, both their children, and their
children's children : as did their fathers, so do
they unto this day."

These are deeply important and instructive

chapters in the history of idolatry; and they sug-
gest the principle which lies at the heart of it,
which explains at once the idolatry of the ignorant savage, and that of the enlightened Church,
which, knowing God, is prone to this deadly sin. It
is the endeavour of the weak and faithless human
spirit to connect God with something which he
can handle and possess, so as to have a perpetual
and palpable assurance of the presence and favour
of Deity. In fact, it is an attempt to deal with
that, by means of the senses and understanding,
which only reveals itself to the spiritual faculties
of the soul. I cannot too strongly impress upon
you my conviction that the essence of idolatry is
not the saying, "I do not care for the God of
heaven; I will not have the God of heaven to be
my God, but will worship these." It is the saying, "I do not know the God of heaven; I do
not know what He is, or where He is; and I
thankfully believe that He has associated Himself
with this object which I do see and know, and
that I hold this pledge of His presence and care."

It .is impossible to suppose that Israel had
forgotten, intellectually, the Lord who had led
them. They had seen His wonders in the land
of Ham; they had been fed by His bounty every
morning in the Wilderness; they had the most
terrible manifestations of His power at that moment

before their eyes. Had Aaron wished them to
declare themselves traitors to the Lord, to believe
that their deliverance and guidance was all a mistake, and that the Lord God of their fathers was
all a delusion, I believe that they would have
risen up and stoned him before the mount. They
thought, in their ignorant and sensual hearts, that
they were helping themselves to believe in Him ;
and their old Egyptian memories rising up, they
took the sacred image of Memphis, the bull
Apis, and made that the image of their Lord.
Moses, while he had been with them, had been
their channel of communication ; God had visibly
been with him, and he had been to Aaron and to
them in the place of God. But his long absence,
leaving them there shut up in the terrible wilderness, destroyed their confidence ; with Moses, God
seemed to have abandoned them ; or rather, what
knew they of God apart from him ? Moses was
marked out to them as the man of God, by many
infallible proofs ; and when he was gone, God
faded into a mere name. It was the blackest
ingratitude and faithlessness. The God who had
led them thus far, could not have led them out to
perish. Clouds and darkness were round about
Him ; but within those clouds they might be well
assured that He was at work for them, devising
fresh purposes of mercy, and perfecting fresh mini-

stries of love. But it has its parallel in our history.
You have been fed and guided in a way not less
wonderful by the Lord's hand ; yet in some wilderness, when your guide has for a moment left you,
and darkness has settled on the plain, I hear you
crying, "The Lord has forsaken me, and my God
has forgotten me ;" and I see some of you setting
up a golden image and saying, "Let this be to
us instead of God." How much of what is called
"rest in the Church"—rest in some infallible
human guidance—springs out of this root? So
Aaron made them their molten calf, and proclaimed through the host, "To-morrow is a feast
unto the Lord."

3. In God's sight, that is, in reality, this is a
turning away from Him.

They meant this bull to be an image of God,
their Leader. God saw that it was an image of
their own idolatrous and sensual hearts. They
had, as every man has, the means of knowing the
mind and will of God. From none who seek Him
in faith will He hide Himself; none who cry, in
believing supplication, can be sent empty away.
But faith and prayer, involving purity, come not
readily to human hearts. It is easier and plea-
santer to the flesh to have some nearer and
morally cheaper guide : to have something which
will at once allow us to choose our own course,

13

and yet appear to lend to it the sanction of the Divine name. Idolatry is just the act of a man who declines to seek the Lord in faith, and says, "Let the Lord be made plain to sense, and meet me in my daily customs, in the habits of my sensual life, that I may believe." It is a dull recognition of God, so far. The man does not dare to go on with his life unless he can believe that God goes with him; but he dreads the Lord, and, like Rachel, takes the image with him instead.

Does not this explain the idolatry of Judaism, where God was known—the idolatry of Romanism, where the God-man is known—the idolatry of Protestantism, where the Church, the letter of the Word, or the traditions of the religious world, are idols to careless, ease-loving, and sensual hearts? The heart of man yearns after a fuller knowledge of God than our own intellectual searchings can give us. But God reveals Himself only to faith: and faith is a power; it changes the heart, it purges the life, it sets a man's back to the world, while it sets his face to God and heaven. But, suppose the face of the heart is turned to the world still, and the pure Lord, the pure Christ, only reveals Himself to those whose faces are set the other way? Then man makes gods of saints and martyrs; "they

are more pitiful to sin and weakness; they are
men like us, and we shall be able, worshipping
them, to keep a feast unto the Lord, and rise up
to dance." " These be thy gods, O Israel."

To us the temptation to idolatry presents itself
in a more subtle form. We dare not take any
image and treat it as a god. Protestantism lives
to protest against all that. But there is a habit
of thought about God, which grows up in a mind
not momently awake to the spiritual presence—a
way of conceiving of Him as He looks upon and
deals with us—the direct effect of which is to sus-
pend the free, fresh, and constant spiritual communion with Him, by which alone can we come to
know Him; and to reduce spiritual life to a mere
habit of thought or action, which, like a golden
calf, may be made to go with us in any track we
please. This habit of thought about God and
divine things, which comes between the eye of
the soul and the living God, may be embodied in
elaborate church institutions, or it may reign
among those who protest against elaborate church
institutions, in the popular sentiment and judgment of a community; which of all spiritual des-
potisms is perhaps the most formidable, because
the least visible and avowed; but reign where it
may, its work is everywhere the same, and its
fruit.

The advantage of an idol is, that we can take it with us, and its way becomes very pleasantly our way. God will not go with us, we must go with Him; and the multitude, who see not the issues of either way, their own or God's, cleave to their idols even before His face. Thus men take their own course, and get, as they fondly hope, a divine benediction upon it, till the prophet appears, and their idol gets ground to dust.

II. Let us consider the contrast between the prophet and the priest.

The priests and the prophets divide the spiritual empire of humanity between them. The priest's function is to conduct *for* man his divine relations and transactions; the prophet's, to speak *to* man the truth of God. The priest's office here supposes a system of intercourse between man and God already established and recognized; the prophet's pre-supposes nothing but the two beings —the human soul and God. The priests have, in all ages, been the willing ministers of idolatry; at least, as an order, they have rarely lifted up their voice against it, unless inspired by the prophets of truth. There is something in a formal official duty which identifies a man with the customary and common, which gives him a direct interest in the *status in quo*, which is never the best. If the people are set on idolatry, they can always find priests to help them, and to lend the sanction of their great authority to the dishonour of the Divine name.

But God has a band of men upon earth—they are not an order, they wear no badge, and know no traditions—through whom He speaks to mankind. They are men whom the cloud and the fire do not drive to a distance; whose eagle sight can pierce the cloud and gaze on the glory, and who can bear the "burden" of the Lord's word in trust for their fellow-men. The man who professes to conduct man's transactions with the spiritual world, and the man who has to declare God's truth to men, rarely, in any age, are at one. The prophet becomes the censor of the priesthood; while the priesthood marks the prophet as a man to be silenced, and, if possible, put down. The perfect Mediator is both priest and prophet: He reveals God to man in conducting man to God. The Christian priesthood—in the only sense in which I understand the term, the whole body of those who are kings and priests to God through Christ—partakes of this double character. But what age has found it up to the mark of the idea of God? Aaron led the people, or rather helped the people—the professional priest is rarely leader in anything—into idolatry. Moses rescued them, at what cost we will briefly trace.

Idolatry dishonours God doubly. It disobeys Him, it tramples in the dust His most solemn commandments; and it dishonours the faculties which He has endowed man withal, that he may be able to know and commune with Himself. Its fruit in all countries, in all ages, and under all forms, is bitterness and death. As a symbol of this, Moses ground their calf to powder, and made them drink it with their daily food. And the world is drinking still the dust of its idolatries. There are few who are not expiating some creature-worship, whereby they have robbed the Lord. Man, disusing the god-like faculty, ceases to be god-like; his holiest powers shrivel, and he becomes at last the mere shell or husk of himself. The penalty of making an image of God to the sense, instead of seeking God with the soul, is the destruction of all in man which has affinity with the Divine. The soul, turning from its true activity, is palsied; the senses take possession of the man, and make havoc at their will. The connection between idolatry and the grossest sensuality is universal: there has never been an idolatry which has not borne this fruit. I am not saying that idolaters have never struggled against this; some have struggled against it heroically. Pagan Revivals, too, have a history. But the pressure has been too strong for them; and the sensual passions have, in the end, never failed to drag down whole peoples, a whole world, to wallow in the grossest sin. This is no accident. The soul expands and grows to strength and mastery in the sunlight of the Divine presence ; let that be shaded, and the man, like the children of an Arctic winter, becomes inevitably gross and carnal as the brutes. Greece and Rome were drinking the very dregs of the cup of the idol when Paul went forth to preach to them. Words of man cannot describe the bitterness, the heart-sickness, of the whole pagan world when the Lord appeared. And man's lower nature is bloodthirsty. " Whence come wars and fightings among you ? Come they not hence, even of your lusts ?" And whence come lusts ? Come they not of this effort to set the creature and the creature-god in the place of the Lord ? The bloody tragedy in which this brief idolatry ended, is a most significant picture. Man's idols have gathered his hosts to fields of ensanguined slaughter, have led the shock of his armies, and heaped up the trophies of his slain, from the day when Levi made himself a name by his zeal in the work of retribution, to the day when the nations shall close in vengeance on the seat of the idolatrous church.

III. I said that the central principle of idolatry is the shrinking of the spirit from the God of

heaven; which soon passes into spiritual ignorance, and utters itself in the cry, "I do not
know the God of heaven; give me some form,
some visible, tangible shape, to persuade me He
is near." It is the glory of the incarnation, that
it presents that image of the invisible God, "the
express image of His substance," which is not an
idol; that it gives into the arms of the yearning,
straining spirit a man, a brother, a husband of
the heart, and declares that He—the man Christ
Jesus, the man of sorrows and sympathies, the
brother born for adversities — is the God of
heaven. Moses longed for such a revelation
when he cried, "*I beseech Thee show me Thy
glory.*" God recognized the need of the people
in the ark and the mercy-seat, and in the visible
glory which dwelt among them. But the true
glory is man. Man, the image of God, is the
true shekinah; and the cry grew strong and passionate through the ages, which uttered itself by
the lips of Philip, "Lord, show us the Father,
and it sufficeth us." Jesus answered, "HE THAT
HATH SEEN ME, HATH SEEN THE FATHER;" and
put away that ground of idolatry for ever.

It is to deny Jesus, to rob his incarnation of
reality, his brotherhood of tenderness, his communion of completeness, to set up a mediator
between man and the Brother of every human

heart. The Romanist thinks that the Virgin, the
woman, will be nearer and more pitiful than
Jesus, and makes her his idol; if she seems too
far, too pure, he has his saint. But to turn to an
idol is to deny, not the unknown King of heaven,
but the man Christ Jesus. "It is to trample
under foot the Son of God, and to count the
blood of the covenant wherewith He sanctified
Himself an unholy thing, and to do despite to
the spirit of grace." To turn from the splendours
of Sinai, which revealed the Lord Jehovah, to
worship a golden image, was corruption ; to turn
from the God-man, the true shekinah, to worship
an image, or to interpose a second mediator, is
death.

Sermon ix.

Sinai: The Dispensation of Law.

" And the Lord commanded us to do all these statutes, to fear the Lord our God, for our good always."—Deut. vi. 24.

THE dispensation of law! The unfolding to man's intelligence the inner principle of all the concords of the universe—the thoughts of the mind of God. This is what a dispensation of law means, if we look into its depths. The idea of the Divine mind is the principle of the exquisite concord of creation. It shaped itself, or rather, it lay from eternity shaped and compacted in His mind, so perfect in its composure that the expression of it in form would be music; and so, when God's eternal thought clothed itself in creation, the melody floated upward, and all the morning stars, it is pictured, sang together for joy. Each thing on the earth and in the heaven was fashioned according to the pattern in the sanctuary of the heaven of heavens—the mind of God. And each thing received, with its form, the principle of its relations and movements,

the observing of which, through the ages, is the
condition of the beauty and order of the world.
The rhythm of the march of the forms and forces
of creation was then established ; the axis of the
earth with its very nutations, the orbits of the
stars, the tint and fragrance of the flowers, were
then decreed. These—the inner principles and
methods of the life of the universe, expressed in
forms cognizable by the understanding—are the
laws of creation ; to know them, as we have come
to know the truth of the movements of the starry
heavens, is to be within the council-chamber of
the Eternal, and to be able to think out, after
Him, the thoughts of God. To know the laws
which inhere in all things is the highest glory,
the completest triumph of the intellect ; as the
glory of a spirit is to know, by spiritual senses,
and commune with God. We have a fashion of
thinking and speaking of law at large, as though
it were a humiliation, to the spirit at any rate, to
deal with it—as though, to be under the law, even
to God, were the badge of serfdom instead of the
condition of freedom, as it is, and shall be through
eternity. "Under the law to Christ" is Paul's
description of the freest Christian life to which
man has ever attained. That is, under the law,
not to a code written on tables, but to a Being
whom the heart knows and loves, whom the spirit

recognizes as its centre and its sun; and this is the secret of glorious life.

Law to a transgressor stands out in a new relation; it acts as a constraint from without, not as a life moving the muscles of action from within. This is a degradation, but the degradation is in the transgressor and not in the law. The law is still holy, good, and beautiful; it is still God's thought expressed. It represents what the transgressor was made to be, and should be, in order to enter into God's concord, and fill his appointed space in the scale of creation. Let the transgressor take the law into his heart and love it, and it will move him as blessedly, as the sun-quickened sap in the veins of a plant stirs the buds to bursting, and presses out, with soft compulsion, the leaves, the branches, the flowers, the fruit. We have this guarantee about God's law. Its principle is harmony, order, perfect blessedness. His law is not strange or arbitrary. None can obey it and be still out of concord with the universe and with Him. If He says to a child, "Honour thy father and thy mother," and to a parent, "Provoke not thy child to wrath," He says that which, if fulfilled, is the secret of the concord of homes. If He says to the merchant, "Thou shalt not go beyond nor defraud thy brother in anything," He says that which, if fulfilled, will make order in the jarring world of commerce. Nothing which he ordains can be of the nature of a peremptory or despotic command, the only reason of which is the despot's will; the doing of which may lift us into his favour and buy his benediction, but which adds no blessing or riches to our inner life. Every word which He speaks man can live by. Let him take the word into his heart, and its fruit must be concord; it must bring the life into harmony with the universal life and with Himself. This is the point which the Jews quite missed. They lost the key to their dispensation, and turned it into a yoke which neither they nor their sons were able to bear. Instead of feeling that there was a grand reality in it, that this was the form of a perfect life, sketched out by God's own hand, for a people in a mental, moral, and social condition like theirs, and that living it would make exquisite order in their homes and hearts, they set themselves wearily to do it; as you would do a despot's will, seeing no reason in it and having no hope, save that you might win the despot's favour and secure his rewards. And thus it became a bondage, a yoke of serfdom; not because of its own bright nature, but because of the corruption of the nature out of which it had to bring forth its fruits.

Imagine, if you can, the automatic processes of our body suspended, and that we were commanded to expand and contract the heart by a distinct volition, and to distend and exhaust the lungs; what a fearful bondage would our existence become! Life carries on these operations gaily; it halts not, it wearies not; it is conscious of no stress or strain through the years. So the Jews made to themselves a yoke of bondage out of the living and loving commandments of the Lord. They lost the vital principle of fulfilment; the life within, becoming cold and feeble, refused to work out the complete idea of God. Then having it as a mere commandment, having lost the reason and love of it, they made ghastly spasmodic efforts to fulfil it, and became the most lifeless of formalists, the most abject of intellectual and spiritual slaves.

But I cannot consent, for one moment, to the idea that God's law, as proclaimed on Sinai, was other than good and beautiful—most germane, in every jot and tittle of it, to a noble personal and national life. We often speak of it hastily, and with a certain outward truth—as when we say that the sun rises and sets—as a system of bondage. It became so; with such a people it could not fail to become so; but in itself it claims to be handled reverently. There was a sensual-hearted people before the face of God, a mere rabble of enslaved souls ; and the law which they heard from Sinai was the complete deliverance of the mind of God, as to what would make them a nation of noble freemen, and secure order, harmony, and blessedness in their personal, domestic, and national life. Very sublime are the words of Moses, God's great witness to this view of the law :—"For this commandment which I command thee this day, it is not hidden from thee, neither is it far off. It is not in heaven, that thou shouldest say, Who shall go up for us to heaven, and bring it unto us, that we may hear it, and do it ? Neither is it beyond the sea, that thou shouldest say, Who shall go over the sea for us, and bring it unto us, that we may hear it, and do it ? But the word is very nigh unto thee, in thy mouth, and in thy heart, that thou mayest do it. . . . I call heaven and earth to record this day against you, that I have set before you life and death, blessing and cursing : therefore choose life, that both thou and thy seed may live : that thou mayest love the Lord thy God, and that thou mayest obey His voice, and that thou mayest cleave unto Him : for He is thy life, and the length of thy days : that thou mayest dwell in the land which the Lord sware unto thy fathers, to Abraham, to Isaac, and to Jacob, to give them."—Deut. xxx. 11–14; 19, 20.

I. Let us examine a little more closely the popular idea as to the excessive severity and formality of this law. To a transgressor who had not in him the living principle of obedience, it was, without doubt, fearfully formal and stern. So is our statute-book to a felon, while on you and me it sits lightly as the air. We are quietly, without being the least conscious of it, living out a whole statute-book every day. If you talk of formality and severity, consult the statute-book of the starry heavens; conceive the order of the procession of the planets written out on tables— each movement, through orbits the units of whose measures no brain can carry, defined to the breadth of a hair. There is form, sublime in its formality, severity, awful in its righteousness and constancy. Equally overwhelming, as we have already hinted, would be the revelation of the laws of bodily, domestic, or political life, in the form of a statute-book. We should start with horror to find what formalists we are in our freedom; how prescribed are the motions of the most complete and royal faculties of sense and soul. In fact, to find the law is to find freedom. A flower, ordained to the sunlight, is a serf in the darkness; a soul, ordained to holiness, is a slave in sin. Outlaws are

ever outcasts ;—out of law, out of fellowship,
order, happiness, as long as the outlawry lasts.
St. James speaks of a perfect law of liberty, and
he utters deep truth.   Liberty is perfect, in perfect obedience to the perfect law.   The powers
are free, and have free play, when they find their
full expression and action in harmony with the
mind of Him who fashioned them, and touched
them to that particular use.

The Jewish system, as I understand it, is the
complete statute-book of a life under those particular conditions; not for you and me in all its
details, but for you and me wherever it deals with
that common human nature wherein they and we
are one.   But in its details it is for them—a
people in a particular country, climate, and stage
of development ;   and it contains in these spe-
cialities the sentence of its own abolition when it
had done its appointed work.   Most formal it
would be to us, in such a state of development
as we have reached to ; to us it could but be, in
its sacrificial system, for instance, an arbitrary
and despotic law ; but to them most perfect in
its adaptation ; the one condition then and there
of a complete national life.

Many seek the key to it in the future.   They
say that it was provisional and preparatory, and
that the Jews were shut up under their law as in

14

a kind of prison-house, until the emancipation day of the Gospel. There is a great truth in this way of representing it, and a great untruth. God sees the end from the beginning, and everything which is, has relation to something which is to be. What else does "natura" mean? There is strict concatenation in nature; all things are knit by golden chains, of which the links deeply interlace, to the throne of God. There would have been no Judaism if there had been no Gospel; but we dare go further, and say that there would have been no Eden, no Man, if there had been no Gospel. The Gospel underlies the whole of man's history; and wherever the interest of that history deepens and becomes concentrated, as at Sinai, be sure that its relation to the Gospel will come out with singular fulness and force.

But it is false to conceive of any age as merely a stalking-horse for a future age. It is a mistake to conceive of the Jews as laden with special burdens, sacrificial or otherwise, that we in the fulness of time might better understand and profit by the Gospel. It is fatal to all just thought, thus to interpret the equal ways of the Lord. Judaism was given from Sinai to that people, for that people's good. There was no forethought, no afterthought—except as the Divine reason

looks ever before and after. It was God's best
gift to them as they stood there before the mountain ; and there was nothing in it which was not
a good gift to them there. Its relation to the
future was their relation to the future; in training, educating, and developing them, it was
making a future possible to their nation and to
the world.

I observe—

II. That the very heart's core of a dispensation of law is duty, and duty is the master-key
to life.

God led them forth to give them a law in
Horeb—that is, to train them in duty, to make
them servants of duty, and lead them thus into
the inner sanctuary, the Holy of Holies of life.
That is what is meant by a dispensation of law.
I say the very core and kernel of the idea of law,
in its relation to a moral agent, is duty. Law is
the buttress of right : its object is to fortify the
dutiful soul. There must be a precedent right
in the claim which the law makes, or it is
immoral, and tends to confusion in the soul
and in the world. The real object of law is to
help men to do right, and thus most effectually
restrain from wrong; unless there be a sentiment
of duty latent, which the law can appeal to and
elicit, it is heartless and hopeless work. Law,

14—2

explicit and mandatory, declares the right, and man's heart and conscience respond Amen.

To bring forth that Amen, a manly, outspoken consent to the law, that it was good, God led that people forth from Egypt into the heart of those sublime and magnificent mountains; where, like as on another mountain, after a yet diviner fashion, He opened his mouth and taught them out of His law. It was the first clear revelation of duty to them. There are laws which are right by a higher sanction than the voice of our own hearts, which but echoes the sanction. The echo we can trifle and tamper with; we can make it by our cunning babble folly or false-hood; but who shall dare tamper with the word of Him who speaks by that awful thunder, whose words glow and glare in that blazing lightning, the sight of whose glory, the touch of whose hand, is death? Those lightnings of Sinai lit up a whole heaven of duty. From the first word of the law to the last, there was not a letter which did not demand attention and obedience on grounds deep as infinity, lasting as eternity, and sacred as the name of God. They became the soldiers of duty from that hour. They gave instant consent to the covenant of God. "And Moses came and told the people all the words of the Lord, and all the judgments: and all the

people answered with one voice, and said, All
the words which the Lord hath said will we do.
And Moses wrote all the words of the Lord, and
rose up early in the morning, and builded an
altar under the hill, and twelve pillars, according
to the twelve tribes of Israel. . . . And he
took the book of the covenant, and read in the
audience of the people : and they said, All that
the Lord hath said will we do, and be obedient.
And Moses took the blood, and sprinkled it on
the people, and said, Behold the blood of the
covenant, which the Lord hath made with you
concerning all these words.—Exod. xxiv. 3, 4
—7, 8.

They felt that there was a right, all-pervading
as the air of Heaven ; and that their lives had
become sacred to duty.   Not as men who accepted
a law which they could not help submitting to,
but as men who said Amen to a law which they
heartily believed, which they knew to be right,
and which they accepted as spiritual beings because of its rightness, they sealed their covenant
with God.   It was duty which God preached
from Sinai ; and duty is, as I have said, the
master-key of man's life.   Let a man live for
duty, and he lives nobly ; his life will be a benediction to men.   Let a man live carelessly, aim-
lessly, walking in the sight of his own eyes, and

the imagination of his own heart, and he lives weakly, shamefully; his life becomes a snare and a curse to himself and to mankind.

Sinai was to the world the revelation of duty, which grows out of the revelation of the name of God. Earth knew the meaning of duty from that hour, for she knew the name of her King. The vague convictions of righteousness and sanctity which floated through pagan consciences, and ever and anon wrung such fearful sacrifices from agonized pagan hearts, have received form and certainty from the declarations of Sinai. The words which were then written on tables of stone with God's own finger are still, and ever will be, the commandments of the world. Life dies down in a soul, in a people, when the sentiment of duty is not matured into a principle, and does not rule the conduct. A life which has no duties, no offices of trust and obligation, which has simply to expand itself in bland enjoyment, wearies at last the most weak and babyish heart.

Man, out of the bond of duty, explains all the world's disorders, all its frustrated hopes, all its withered, ruined lives. Man, the servant of duty, explains all noble, manlike, beautiful deeds and ministries—a life bright as the sunlight, and musical as the symphonies of heaven. Our lives mean nothing, and produce nothing, till the revelation of duty breaks on us; till we, led forth to some silent wilderness, see a form and hear a voice, which makes us the bound servants of righteousness to the end of our days. All life's real concords and true pleasures spring out of its duties. The soul set to this key is in that presence, " where there is fulness of joy and pleasures for evermore."

To some, duty, like law, seems a cheerless and rayless thing. The sun thinks not thus, when he "rejoiceth as a bridegroom coming out of his chamber, or a strong man to run a race." There is a sunny joy in the motion, the life, of all creatures, which to the tuned and attentive ear is music—which is but the hum of duty in the acting. The song of the creation is the hymn of duty. Every bird that sings, every bee that hums, every flower that lifts its tremulous voice of praise to Him who has made so good a world, every star,

> " Which in its motion like an angel sings,
>   Still quiring to the young-eyed cherubins,"

bears its part in the great flood of harmony which floats the tributes of the duty of creation before the Eternal throne. For man, duty in the doing is glory in the winning. "To them who by patient continuance in well-doing"—the complete picture of duty—" seek glory, honour, and immortality, eternal life." Duty stands watching like the guardian spirit, with folded wings and eyes dewy with tears, over the cradle where an infant sobs and gasps into life. Duty, in the mien and dress of a mother, feeds the young nursling with self-forgetful tenderness, and guides its feeble steps as it explores the limits of the kingdom to which the child believes himself heir. Duty, when he steps out of his charmed home into life's highway, leads him by the hand into the great forum, and there leaves him to his heaven-appointed work. He may turn his back and slink through life, with craven branded on his brow; or he may face it manfully, giving open-hearted welcome to a man's cares and sorrows, knowing that they bring with them in their train a man's consolations and joys. Such an one will find that the most costly services are richest in blessing; the self-denials and deeds of duty which have scared the very root of self in the soul, and racked him with sharp agony, have become, when the agony was over, perennial bubbling fountains of consolation and bliss. Which are your richest memories, your most living springs of joy and hope? Those, I well know, which you opened in some hour of solemn sadness, when you yoked yourself to a duty to which you did not easily tame a rebellious heart.

Perish gold, fame, knowledge! but leave me my memory of duty—those tablets, blotted with tears, but precious, inexpressibly precious, to my soul through eternity! Are there any echoes to this in the inner chambers of your being, or have you yet to be led out to the wilderness to listen to the law? It is the first step into life, to see the heaven of duty, and, clear shining in its zenith, beaming down on us with unutterable benignity, ineffable serenity, as of one who, though the Lord of duty, had "learnt obedience by suffering," the face of Emanuel, God with us. The people had learnt to exist by the flesh-pots of Egypt; but they must go forth into the wilderness, and stand before the Lord in Horeb, to learn to live.

III. The receiving of a law was the first step of the people in a new and glorious career of personal and national development; which, though they have missed the crown, has left them the most notable, powerful, and capable race in the world.

In other words, it opened a noble man's career to them; it will open the same to you.

They came out of Egypt a straggling, disorderly throng; they broke up and marched from Sinai in orderly array—an army, a nation, a church. The key to their transformation was this dispensation of law. It gave them a standard;

thenceforth they had unity, and a history. When
a man says, " this is right; I am very far from
fulfilling it, but I believe in it, I will work up to
it;" his life has a meaning and a result which
the mere child of the world, however brilliant his
talents, never attains.   In this case the whole
people had a law of conduct, a standard of action,
remaining changeless through the ages, with
which the national character and life might compare itself; and by which the nation attained to
a completer liberty than has ever been realized
by any nation upon earth, except, perhaps, our
own.   Let the character of the legal dispensation be tested by its results in the history of the
people, and it will appear, as Paul says, to be
glorious.   Formal as it appears to us, burden-
somely minute in detail and severe in discipline,
yet it made incomparably the most noble, free,
deep-hearted, and fruitful people in the ancient
world.

The real liberties of man, the real dignity of
woman, the nature of the home, the state, the
church, were never so well understood and so
fully set forth in the life of a people, until that
most heaven-ordained and fruitful of all marriages
was consummated, the marriage of the Anglo-
Saxon race to Christianity.   The Jews were the
Anglo-Saxons of the old world.   The nation was

a community of freemen; each with his allot-
ment of land—a freeholder whose rights were
guarded with most jealous vigilance, who was
forbidden to sell or alienate his land under the
severest penalties: and thus they were able to
maintain the political freedom of each member of
the nation, against that fearful propension to
slavery, which we see destroying, in turn, every
great empire of the ancient world. The world,
in old times, gravitated towards slavery. The
Greeks and the Romans saw the fatal tendency,
but found no remedy. The real cancer of the
Empire was slavery; this was the fell disease
which preyed upon its vitals and dragged it down
to perdition. The Jews alone bore up against
the temptation heroically. They remained a
nation of freemen, even to the very last. So
deeply was this passion for political liberty rooted,
that the Romans found it necessary to deal with
them more cautiously than with the other conquered nations; and to respect the form, at
any rate, of freedom, until the nation, by suicide,
asserted its freedom in death.

These words, in Deuteronomy xv., implanted a
seed which bore fruit in the national history for
1,500 years:—

"And if thy brother, an Hebrew man, or an
Hebrew woman, be sold unto thee, and serve

thee six years; then in the seventh year thou
shalt let him go free from thee.   And when thou
sendest him out free from thee, thou shalt not let
him go away empty: thou shalt furnish him
liberally out of thy flock, and out of thy floor,
and out of thy wine-press: of that wherewith the
Lord thy God hath blessed thee, thou shalt give
unto him.   And thou shalt remember that thou
wast a bondman in the land of Egypt, and the
Lord thy God redeemed thee : therefore I command thee this thing to-day.   And it shall be, if
he say unto thee, I will not go away from thee
(because he loveth thee and thine house, because
he is well with thee); then thou shalt take an
awl, and thrust it through his ear unto the door,
and he shall be thy servant for ever.   And also
unto thy maid-servant thou shalt do likewise.   It
shall not seem hard unto thee, when thou sendest
him away free from thee ; for he hath been worth
a double hired servant to thee, in serving thee six
years : and the Lord thy God shall bless thee in
all that thou doest."—Deut. xv. 12–18.

I wish you would carefully contrast the history
of their tumultuous and disorderly exodus, with
the history of their breaking up from the encampment before Sinai, and resumption of the Canaanward march.   It is wonderful what their law
had already done for them.   There is something

sublime in the order with which that band of
fugitive bondmen arranged themselves around
their tabernacle, and took their way through the
dreary wilderness.   In the midst of the vast
wastes, with many temptations to stray or to tarry,
they took their march in the exactest order, and
encompassed, with a resolution which could not
be vanquished, the shrine of their national faith.
When settled in Canaan, and scattered at first in
tribes, and even in families, amidst a hostile
population—engaged much like the Anglo-Saxons
in England, in hand-to-hand conflicts with the
former masters of the soil—one thing alone pre-
served their unity, and brought them forth from
this stage of national trial and temptation—their
law, and the ark of the testimony and the Tabernacle in Shiloh.   That was the centre of the
scattered bands of Israel, the heart which maintained vital communications with the remotest
members of the national frame.   Settled at length
more completely, and organized as a nation, their
law set them on high above all the nations of the
earth, in every point which is material to national
greatness.   It stirred the deep fountains of their
deep hearts, and produced a literature whose
influence at this day, through the length and
breadth of the civilized world, is incomparably
the mightiest motor of the human intellect and

spirit; and which, in the breadth and depth of human passion which it awakens, and human power which it wields, casts the rarest productions of classical antiquity into the shade. Plato's Republic may be a store of political wisdom for the accomplished scholar; there is rare honey stored there for the use of even modern society. But Isaiah's prophecies—Isaiah's glowing picture of what a State must be to fulfil the idea of God, and develop instead of dwarfing its citizens—is a book which you should keep in your counting-house in the heart of the bustling city, and is at this day as true and fruitful for Cheapside and Clapham, as it was for the traffic and the homes of Jerusalem.

When I consider the history of this great people, constituted a people there before the rock of Horeb; their gallant conquest of Canaan; their heroic victory over the temptation to scatter themselves and be lost to history during the era of the Judges; their deep-thoughted prophets; their wise-hearted kings; the freedom of their political, and the sacredness of their domestic life; their hatred of serfdom; their noble defence of their mountain home against the massive strength of the two greatest monarchies of the earth; their splendid and profound literature; their world-renowned hymns;—and consider further that by

God's law they were what they were—I magnify
the grace and wisdom which led them forth to
the shrine of that sublime and awful temple of
Sinai; and I join reverently in the hymn of the
heavenly temple, which blends the song of Moses
and of the Lamb, " Great and marvellous are Thy
works, Lord God Almighty; just and true are all
Thy ways, O thou King of saints."

I wish I could make you feel more deeply, that
putting yourself under the law to God, is the first
step out into a true man's life. " Man lives and
works in the Idea," says a deep thinker. Unless
a man has set himself a standard of action, and
made a covenant with his soul that he will make
it the work of his life to fulfil it, his life is aimless,
hopeless, " without understanding, and like the
brutes that perish." If a man has an inward idea
of duty, and daily seeks strength to deny and
conquer himself, that he may come nearer to it,
there is a true growth and progress—that man
has a character and a history. I say to you,
come under the law to Christ, " for the grace of
God that bringeth salvation hath appeared unto
all men, teaching us that, denying ungodliness
and worldly lusts, we should live soberly, righte-
ously, and godly, in this present world ; looking
for that blessed hope, and the glorious appearing
of the great God, and our Saviour Jesus Christ,"

(Titus ii. 11, 12) —because this is the standard,
and here the true idea· of life is to be found.
Hereby shall every conviction cherished by your
spiritual nature be nourished, and herein shall
every passion of your soul rejoice. Your man's
life, buried in dust and darkness in Adam, comes
forth and aims at glory in Christ; to whom it
passes under the law, and through whom, " the
righteousness of the law is fulfilled in us, who
walk not after the flesh, but after the spirit."
The first step out into life is to put yourself under
the yoke of duty to the Lord Jesus; and to make
it the aim of your being to live up to your covenant with Him.

Alas ! what a dreary, aimless, joyless, hopeless
life many of you are living, who have never found
courage to get out into the wilderness, and there
in silence and solitude make covenant with God.
Your days are slipping away, and you are gaining
nothing; many a battle you have had, with here
and there a victory; many a resolution has been
formed, acted on for a space, and then forsaken;
and you are as far from a real Christian life and
the kingdom of heaven as at first. Why, what a
life is this ! Like the sands through the hour-
glass your days flow on, and then you turn it and
the sand flows through again, but no fruit—
nothing that remains, endures, and must endure

through eternity. Build on the rock, course by course, with calm and patient courage, that the edifice of life may grow stronger and stronger against the marauding temptations which throng this wilderness, and promise to stand fair and stately amid the last wreck and crash of all things, and to be a habitation of the soul for eternity. No longer let Egypt waste and spoil the treasures of your being, after this vile fashion; say now in heart, I will play at living no longer, I will go out into the wilderness and be awhile there, alone with God.

IV. But, however we may magnify it, and however justly, the law is not a Gospel, and can in nowise supply the place of a Gospel to the world.

The legal dispensation was, historically, the great stage of preparation for the fulness of times, and for the advent of Him who "is the end of the law for righteousness to every one that believeth." And the dispensation of law, in our individual histories, is but "a schoolmaster to bring us to Christ." Man can only be blessed by being brought into the peace of God; into harmony with God's constitution of things, and with God Himself. The Gospel is the instrument of the reconciliation which the law declares to be needful, but cannot secure. If you want to

15

master the relations of Law and Gospel, study closely the passage from Romans vii. 1 to viii. 4. You will see there how a man, who has seen the solemnly serene and beautiful aspect of law, repelling him from God, revealing the awful sacredness of the divine constitution of things, which he profanes and tramples on every hour, cries out in ecstacy when he hears the name of Jesus, "I thank my God through Jesus Christ my Lord." To that man the righteousness of the law becomes a solemn reality. Without righteousness he will not dare to appear before God, and he joys in Him who is the "Lord our righteousness;" whose righteousness by faith is *in* us as well as on us, for "the righteousness of the law is fulfilled *in* us, who walk not after the flesh but after the spirit."

No man who has not felt the sacredness of duty, the divine strength and glory of law, understands all that is in the Gospel. Those who have stood before the mount, see most of the glory of the cross on Calvary. The ear that is harassed and oppressed by the roarings of the thunder of the mount of testimony—and it becomes terrible to the sinner—catches joyfully the ineffable sweetness of the voice of the Redeemer, "And I, if I be lifted up, will draw all men unto me."

We talk familiarly of the abolition of the law of commandments. Let us understand what it

means.   I know but of one way of abolishing
law—hiding it in the heart.   Let it be read there
in living characters, and the law is abolished, as
I hope you have abolished it.   Abolish it by so
hiding it within that your whole nature is instinct
with it, and fulfils it calmly and noiselessly, as a
sensitive-plant shrinks from contact, or an angel
shrinks from sin.   But let no man dare to think
that the Gospel loosens the tightness of our moral
obligation, or lowers by one half-tone the pitch of
that concord into which the Saviour calls us—
such heap to themselves a double damnation.
But blessed be the God and Father of our Lord
Jeses Christ, that while the law remains as a
witness, the Gospel is preached as the means of
reconciliation ; " For God is in Christ reconciling
the world unto Himself, not imputing our trespasses unto us ; for He hath made Him to be sin
for us who knew no sin, that we might be made
the righteousness of God in Him."

𝔖ermon x.

The Gospel under the Law.

"And thou shalt put the mercy-seat above upon the ark; and in the ark thou shalt put the testimony that I shall give thee."
—Exod. xxv. 21.

GOD is one. There can be but one Gospel of God. There is but one way of salvation for man, every when and every where. Unity of dispensation, is a conception imperatively demanded by the unity of God. If dispensations appear to us to be diverse and progressive, establishing, in successive ages, various terms of relation between man and God, the progress is in the apprehension of the beings who are the subjects of the dispensation, and not in the Divine idea. God's basis of intercourse with the fallen sinner, in all countries and in all ages, and in all stages of his culture, is ultimately one and simple—Himself. In God Himself is, and ever has been, that on which the reconciliation of the sinner to the Divine holiness rests. That eldest word of promise, which lit the first steps of the weary march of man—the pilgrim of the ages, and the last

word of benediction when the pilgrimage is over,
spring from the same fountain, rest on the same
basis, and express the same fundamental purpose
—a great moral necessity to a being who loves
as God loves — to redeem man by sacrifice to
Himself.

Speaking more closely to the truth of things,
there could have been no basis of reconciliation,
no justification, peculiar to the patriarchal or the
Jewish ages, differing essentially from that which
was reserved for revelation to these Christian
times. If a patriarch, or a Jew under the law,
received forgiveness of· sins, and walked as a
friend, a child, in holy fellowship with God, it
must have been on the same ground, and by the
same way as that by which a Christian walks with
God, and receives and exercises the power to
become a son. For God remains One through
the ages; and the relation of man to Him being
a spiritual thing, is a simple and absolute thing,
and must, likewise, remain one : so that the
faith by which Enoch, Noah, Abraham, Moses,
and David walked, is the identical faith by which
St. Paul lived his life in the flesh; and the salvation at which they aimed, and which, by faith,
they realized, is essentially the same salvation as
that in which St. Paul gloried, " the receiving the
adoption of a son." Spiritual things do not

change, die, and reappear. Their dress changes, their form of manifestation changes, the measure in which they are apprehended by the intellect, and the mode in which they are set forth, change; but the thing itself, the spiritual state of a being reconciled, and in living fellowship with God, does not change; that abides one, as God is One, through all time, through all eternity.

To discern the principle of man's reconciliation with God in one age, is to discern it for all ages. The Gospel can but unfold explicitly what was enfolded implicitly—not in the formal words and institutions—but in the whole dispensation of the law. God's promise to Adam, was God's Gospel to Adam. God's covenant with the Jewish people, was the Gospel to the Jewish people; and it is substantially the same Gospel, springing out of the same fountain in Himself, and resting on the same basis in His work, as that which reveals the whole heaven of His redeeming wisdom and love, in the redemption which is by Christ Jesus.

God cannot alter His terms of relation with human beings. A Jew cannot be saved on one ground, and we on another. It is confusion to imagine that there was a basis of a more formal and narrower kind open to them, which is open no longer; a new ground having been revealed in Christ, as that on which alone, in these Chris-

tian ages, a man can rest. Discover the ground
of relation between man and God anywhere, and,
like the plutonic bed of the earth, it is universal.
It is the Gospel of all ages which the Bible unfolds to us; and I think that its selectest and completest symbol is the image presented in my text
—a mercy-seat above an ark of testimony. Law
looking up to enthroned and regnant mercy;
mercy guarding, cherishing, and glorifying law.

In studying, as I feel it is very important to
study, what was presented as a Gospel to the
Jewish people, and which, if my position be true,
must contain substantially the broad truths of the
universal Gospel, the Gospel which is preached
also unto us, I observe—

I. We have here the very core of the sym-
bolical ordinances of the Jewish Church.

I have no call to enter here into the general
question of ecclesiastical symbolism. Neither is
it needful to dwell at length on the special significance and worth of the symbolism of the Jewish
dispensation. Probably we are all agreed that
the worth of a sign is the measure, of the thing
signified, which it presents to the mind or soul.
We shall be equally agreed that, organized as we
are, clothed spirits, the contemning of symbols—
the resolution to deal with what we may choose
to consider the naked reality of things—is a con-

temning of the counsels of God; who, whatever
He has made us, has not made us naked spirits in
a naked world.

The word of God, the essential truth of things,
has forms in which it presents itself, according
to their several natures, to body, mind, and spirit.
The whole visible creation is a garment, or body,
in which God presents what of Himself can be so
presented, to the touch of the senses, and the faculties which correspond with the senses, in the soul.
The unity of Him, whose thought runs through
the whole scale of creation, fills the universe
with analogues. Each note contains the chord,
and the octaves carry it forth beyond our bounds.
Truth, again, consents to take shape in formal
propositions, that it may furnish matter for the
exercise of the intellect,—the final function of
which is, not to know as if knowing were the
end of being, but to enlarge and lift the spirit;
that, by its own royal faculty, *it* may know truth,
by knowing Him who is the truth, whom to know
is life. But the propositions in which the truth
unfolds itself to the cognizance of the intellectual
faculty, though true, are not the Truth. That
ever transcends them; that inheres in a Being.
And only by that in a man which is capable of
knowing a spiritual being, can the Truth be
known. But it is when ideas, which have to

do directly and absolutely with the spiritual in man, clothe so much of themselves as can be clothed in sensuous forms, and address him by the methods by which creation addresses him on behalf of God, that the difficult question arises—How far is such symbolism helpful or hurtful to the spiritual faculty, whose direct and healthy action on the realities of spiritual truth it seems to supersede? And there is no general form of answer. The question of milk or meat as food for children, cannot be answered in generals; it is entirely a matter of wise discernment, whether the higher form of nourishment will clog the immature digestion, or, whether the continued administration of the lower form will keep in chronic impotence the maturing powers of the frame. One thing let us note, that meat, material and spiritual, demands the higher effort; and as man is indisposed to high effort in the upper hemisphere of his nature, there is a standing danger lest the religious symbol should become the downy sleeping-bed of the indolent and faithless soul.

The Jewish dispensation was largely symbolic. It dealt in tropes, figures, pictures, suited to an avowed infancy of mankind. But that which we seek to convey to a child by pictures, is surely not a thought or a fact which is true for children

only, and has no truth for a man. It is the very
thing which is hereafter to occupy his manly hours,
which you are seeking to impart to him in ways
suited to the feeble insight and weak digestion of
an infantile soul. The question is, after all, not
of the sign, but of the thing signified : how much
of that can in any way be made known? Let
men's supreme attention be bent on that—the
end of the symbol, and they will cease wrangling
about the forms. Any dress, any speech, any gesture, will do to bring a much-loved friend into
the presence of the soul. There were those in
Judaism to whom the milk of the symbol was
almost more than they could take in. There were
those, in various grades of development, whose
spiritual concern was but slight with the signs of
their dispensation : "Thou desirest not sacrifice,
else would I give it; Thou delightest not in burnt
offering" (Ps. li. 16), said one when he fell into
the depths. The forms of the dispensation, at such
a moment to such an one, were no more than are
the garb and manner of the friend in whose clear
eyes one is reading the responses of a devoted
heart.

We speak familiarly of the dispensation as a
symbolic dispensation. The symbols were there;
they are here ; they are everywhere. There were
those who, under that order of things, lived life-

long in a world of shadows; there are such here,
under this. While there were those to whom the
veil, so opaque to others, was translucent, they
saw a vague light beyond it; to some, again, it
was fully transparent, and they (call them patriarchs, Jews, or what you will) were the free citizens of the kingdom of heaven. Read St. Paul,
in 2 Cor. iii. The whole chapter is full of light
on this subject. In the 14th verse he says:—
"*But their minds were blinded. . . . . Even
unto this day, when Moses is read the veil is upon
their heart.*" The veil was not on the things, but
in the heart of the people; if we see more purely,
it is because we bring an open face to behold the
glory—because, through Christ, the veil is lifted
off our hearts.

We have, as I have said, the very core of the
ritual dispensation here. There was a tabernacle
—a holy place; then there was a portion shut off
by a veil, and called the most holy place; (shall
we say that these correspond, the one to the whole
mass of the called nation, and the other to the
inner circle of those who were walking humbly
and lovingly with their God); and then in the very
centre—the core and marrow of the whole—there
was the ark, with its mercy-seat above, and the
veiling cherubim of glory, presenting that which
was in the heart of the Jewish nation, the one

essential principle of its moral vitality—the merciful, righteous God.

At this point all the interest of the dispensation is concentrated. The days of that people's life as a spiritual community all array themselves around that day, when their high-priest, their daysman — who represented their nation in shadow, as Christ, in substance, represents the world—entered that inner sanctuary with the incense of his people's prayers and the blood of his people's sacrifice, and received commission from the Lord God who dwelt between the cherubim, to lay the sins of the nation on a victim, who should bear them into the wilderness away. Here, then, is the focus of the spiritual power of the dispensation, I mean its power to order man's spiritual relations with all things and with God. And hither, to this mercy-seat above the ark, we are to look—if my principle, that this is a typical people, typical of you and me, be a right one—for those elements of the good word of God to the men of that dispensation, which relate it to the universal Gospel of God to man, and to all worlds —God's method of "reconciling all things to Himself."

II. Let us pass within the shrine, and behold what it has to reveal.

"*And thou shalt make an ark of shittim wood;*

". . . . *and thou shalt overlay it with pure
gold. . . . And thou shalt put into the ark the
testimony which I shall give thee. And thou shalt
make a mercy-seat of pure gold. . . . . And
thou shalt make two cherubims of gold . . . in
the two ends of the mercy-seat . . . And thou
shalt put the mercy-seat above upon the ark; and in
the ark thou shalt put the testimony that I shall give
thee. And there I will meet with thee, and I will
commune with thee from above the mercy-seat, from
between the two cherubims which are upon the ark
of the testimony, of all things which I will give thee
in commandment unto the children of Israel.*"—
Exod. xxv. 10–22, *passim.*

1. What is the supreme symbol here?

The last, the highest, the crown of the whole,
is the mercy-seat.

And this appears to me to mean more, infinitely
more, than a promise of forgiveness, upon certain
terms. The fact that with the mercy-seat God
completed and crowned the symbolism of the
Jewish dispensation; that He only felt it fit to
be His habitation and organ of expression when
that mercy-seat was set there over the ark; that
till then it was a mere shell of a dispensation—as
Adam's body was a mere shell of a man until
God had breathed into his nostrils the breath of
life—but that when the mercy-seat was set, it

became capable of entertaining the Divine glory, and became, in fact, inspired; this fact, I say, is the broad, grand declaration to Judaism of the essential nature of God. It was the utterance to that age, of the word which by ten thousand half-articulate voices has been uttering itself to man since the first days of the creation, and has now become fully articulate in Christ,—GOD IS LOVE.

The mercy-seat being the chosen place of God's presence and manifestation, seems intended to declare solemnly something about God Himself, His name, His nature, that out of which all His purposes and operations proceed. It proclaims not the mercy of God, but that God is merciful; not that God will love, but that God is Love. It associates, as indissoluble, the name of God with the quality of mercy. Righteousness is His attribute; law is His utterance; they are there within the ark which His glory shrouds; but He, the living Lord, is on the mercy-seat—He *is* Love.

I believe, brethren, that we shall be very far from the true teaching of this passage if we understand by it, that God was willing, at times, to appear on that mercy-seat, as a monarch on his throne, in benignant mood, to hear and answer the prayers of His people. It means much more than that: it means that God is merciful, that God ever was merciful, that God must be merciful;

that there is in His heart that deep fount of mercy, deep as His own being, out of which all actual forgivenesses and reconciliations spring.

The mercy-seat *above* the ark. I dwell specially on that. Not *beyond* it, not *behind* it, so that the ark was the only approach to it; but above it, crowning it as a flower crowns its leaves, or a head its limbs.

Understand that God's mercy, God's great love to man, goes before all acts of forgiveness. God does not forgive on conditions, when men seek Him. He forgives because it delights Him to forgive. The conditions, as they appear to us, prescribe the way in which alone, in the very nature of things, His forgiveness can be bestowed, on the one hand, and enjoyed on the other. Mercy is precedent to forgiveness. The knowledge of the essential love and mercifulness of God kindles the desire and hope of forgiveness in the sinner's heart. It is the sight of the mercy-seat as God's dwelling-place which makes sin dreadful to the awakened sinner. " *With Thee there is mercy that Thou mayest be feared,*" cried one who had fathomed the depths of the subject. God shows Himself in Christ, reconciling the world unto Himself, as His strong appeal to the world to be reconciled to Him. God has proclaimed before humanity in all generations His merciful name;

it is the primeval fact on which the life of
humanity rests.   Man's uprightness perished
from beneath him, melted like a wave from under
his feet, in the hour of the first transgression ; he
had plunged down then and there into the nether
abyss of darkness to which gravitate all waste and
wreck, but that God spread beneath his feet in
that hour, firm and strong as the pillars of His
eternal throne, His own merciful name.   There
man's redemption begins.   The Lamb was slain
in that hour, on the true altar, the Father's heart.
And there redemption completes itself, in the
satisfaction of that merciful heart of God.

In the ordering of the mercy-seat, then, above
the ark of the testimony, crowning the ritual of
the dispensation—the special seat of the manifestation of the Eternal—I discern the proclamation
of that foundation truth of the universal Gospel
out of which all redemption springs,—God is Love.
The truth is the same for them and for us ; the
substance of the proclamation is the same ; the
difference lies here, they heard the word, and
saw the glory, but "HEREBY KNOW WE THE
LOVE OF GOD, BECAUSE HE LAID DOWN HIS LIFE
FOR US."

2. Beneath the mercy-seat, within its bosom,
as it were, was the ark of the testimony, and in
it the word of the law.

It would be a great mistake to imagine that the two tables of stone are exclusively referred to, when we meet with the words "testimony" or "law" in the Old Testament scripture. The two tables are but portions of a legal code, it may be the very essence of the code, the whole summed in brief—though the Lord teaches us that it is capable of a yet briefer summary—but still to be looked at and dealt with in connection with the whole system of commandments, of which they were the most prominent features. When we speak of the mercy-seat as above the ark, and in inseparable connection with it, we regard the whole Jewish system as ministrant to that mercy which the mercy-seat declares. The image here reveals a harmony—the tables of stone *in* the ark, the mercy-seat *above* it, crowning it, and the glory of the Lord enveloping the whole. The two ideas are inseparable—mercy and righteousness—when we connect them with the Divine name. "Mercy and truth have met together, righteousness and peace have kissed each other," in every manifestation of the love of God to man.

In order to enter fully into this idea, we must remember that the declaration of the mercifulness of God, the assertion, however solemn may be the form, that God is Love, is not a Gospel to

16

man.   The Gospel is "a way of salvation;" the
way in which that pure love and man's impurity
may be brought into relation with each other;
the way in which a lost image may be recovered,
a lost harmony restored, a lost home regained.
And therefore, within the bosom of the ark, over
which the Mercy brooded with outstretched wings,
was hidden the testimony of God.   The mercy-
seat declares His love, it reveals His essential
nature, as the fundamental basis on which the
Gospel rests, or rather the root out of which it
springs.   But we must turn to the testimonies, to
understand the way in which alone the mercy
which is reigning there can work towards its
victory.

i. The first aspect which the testimonies present to man in his present moral condition is, as
a witness against sin.

This is not in their essential nature, as we
have seen, but it is inevitable in the present moral
condition of mankind.   The very first aim of
God's testimony to the Jewish people was to force
home on their consciences the conviction of sin.

God is merciful; God is Love.   But until you
have added to that, the confession, " I am sinful,
I am alienated from that Love," the Gospel is
still hidden from your heart.   The law, full of a
benign meaning to the obedient soul, is full of

deadly menace to the corrupt and erring. "The law is holy," says St. Paul, "and the commandment holy, and just, and good;" but to me, the convicted sinner, it becomes the minister of death. And God set His testimonies beneath His mercy-seat, that they might convince us, convict us, and terrify us, if we will not be drawn, into an intense concern about our spiritual state; that they might probe the depth of our nature, lay bare the diseased centres of action, and bring us to cry, crushed down to the very dust in an agony of self-abasement and despair, "O miserable man that I am, who shall deliver me from the body of this death?" It is between man, the sinner, and God, the Saviour, that those most blessed relations have to be established, which are to fill heaven with glory and bliss. To show man as the manifest sinner, and to show Himself as the manifest Saviour, is the deep purpose of God: and he begins—under the law, under the Gospel, the method is one—by laying bare the deadly, and, out of Him, the hopeless malady of the human heart. Any other Gospel, any Gospel which began its work by making light of the transgressions which it undertook to cure, man's conscience would spurn.*

* I have treated this subject much more at large in the earlier portion of a former volume, "The Divine Life of Man."

I say that the method is one under the law and under the Gospel. Here are the burning words of the commandment, flashing the light of heaven in upon the sinner's heart and life ; and there, under the Gospel, the very first work of the Holy Ghost, the Comforter, is conviction, for " He, when He is come, shall convince the world of sin, of righteousness, and of judgment." The first Gospel sermon filled men with an awful terror. They thought of the deed which they had done— and it was not their private deed, it was man's ; had we been there we had done it—and they trembled and quaked to the innermost chambers of their hearts. We may say that one great object of the death of Christ was to reveal what sin was capable of, and to drive the conviction home. Never till the world had slain the Holy One and the Just, and exposed the Divine love to the shame and torture of the Cross, did sin reveal to man its deadly, damning character ; never till then were the deepest fountains of contrition unsealed in human hearts. The law was there, under the mercy-seat, that the sinner, self-convinced and self-condemned, might stand there, and know, as such only can know, the depth of the riches of the love of God.

But we must explore the testimonies further.

ii. No man can study the commandments of

God to the Jewish people, without coming across the idea of sacrifice; without the blood of a victim, without an offering of atonement, the high-priest of the Jewish people, their mediator, durst not lift that veil, or stand before that throne, lest the splendour should wither him away.

" And Aaron shall take of the congregation of the children of Israel two kids of the goats for a sin offering, and one ram for a burnt offering. And Aaron shall offer his bullock of the sin offering, which is for himself, and make an atonement for himself, and for his house. And he shall take the two goats, and present them before the Lord at the door of the tabernacle of the congregation. And Aaron shall cast lots upon the two goats; one lot for the Lord, and the other lot for the scape-goat. And Aaron shall bring the goat upon which the Lord's lot fell, and offer him for a sin offering. But the goat, on which the lot fell to be the scapegoat, shall be presented alive before the Lord, to make an atonement with him, and to let him go for a scapegoat into the wilderness. And Aaron shall bring the bullock of the sin offering, which is for himself, and shall make an atonement for himself, and for his house, and shall kill the bullock of the sin offering which is for himself: And he shall take a censer full of burning coals of fire from off the altar before the Lord, and his hands full of sweet incense beaten small, and bring it within the veil: and he shall put the incense upon the fire before the Lord, that the cloud of the incense may cover the mercy-seat that is upon the testimony, that he die not: and he shall take of the blood of the bullock, and sprinkle it with his finger upon the mercy-seat eastward; and before the mercy-seat shall he sprinkle of the blood with his finger seven times. Then shall he kill the goat of the sin offering, that is for his people, and bring his blood within the veil, and do with that blood as he did with the blood of the bullock, and sprinkle it upon the mercy-seat, and before the mercy-seat: and he shall make an atonement for the holy place, because of the uncleanness of the children of Israel, and because of their transgressions in all their sins: and so shall he do for the tabernacle of the congregation, that remaineth among them in the midst of their uncleanness. And there shall be no man in the tabernacle of the congregation when he goeth in to make an atonement in the holy place, until he come out, and have made an atonement for himself, and for his household, and for all the congregation of Israel. And he shall go out unto the altar that is before the Lord, and make an atonement for it; and shall take of the blood of the bullock, and of the blood of the goat, and put it upon the horns of the altar round about. And he shall sprinkle of the blood upon it with his finger seven times, and cleanse it, and hallow it from the uncleanness of the children of Israel. And when he hath made an end of reconciling the holy place, and the tabernacle of the congregation, and the altar, he shall bring the live goat: and Aaron shall lay both his hands upon the head of the live goat, and confess over him all the iniquities of the children of Israel, and all their transgressions in all their sins, putting them upon the head of the goat, and shall send him away by the hand of a fit man into the wilderness: and the goat shall bear upon him all their iniquities unto a land not inhabited: and he shall let go the goat in the wilderness."— Levit. xvi. 3–22.

This shedding of the blood of the appointed sacrifice, was the condition of the manifestation of mercy from the throne. And here we open up questions which it is easier to bury under platitudes than to solve. My object in the present

series of discourses is to consider, what the
wilderness history presents to us; the human
conditions and experiences of those who are
brought into a relation to God like that of the
Jewish people, rather than to analyze the conditions and methods of the self-manifestation
of God in reconciling His rebellious children to
Himself. This is a book of experience rather
than of theology. I therefore do not enter into
any elaborate argument on the subject of sacrifice
generally. Indeed there is little need that I
should do so, as in a recent pamphlet on the
"*Divine Fatherhood in Relation to the Atonement,*" I have expressed my views upon that
subject fully.

But in glancing at this subject, the Jewish
sacrifices, shall we say that God has many kinds
of sacrifice, which, under various conditions, He
holds to be acceptable and sufficient? that the
terms of His relation with men vary in successive
generations; that a people in old time, who
sprinkled the blood of a slain bullock, offered to
Him a sufficient and acceptable atonement; while
from us, if we offered a hecatomb, He would turn
sternly away. This is a notion about God's ways
largely entertained in some theological schools,
but it seems to me most full of peril. I believe
that there is no more fertile source of wrong

thinking about Divine things, and its fruit,
unbelief, than the notion that there is "yea
and nay," about a matter as fundamental and
essential as sacrifice, with God.

Must we not say, that before God there is,
there can be, but one sufficient sacrifice for sins?
That from the hour when Adam fell, to the hour
when the last of the redeemed shall be gathered
home, there is but one simple, absolute, sufficient
ground of the justification of souls. That every
transaction of God in relation to man's transgression not only rests on it, but springs out of
it.   That every act of forgiveness, every promise
to the transgressor, seeks its justification there.
So that for Jew, for Gentile, for patriarchal,
legal, and Christian dispensations, there is but
one atonement before the Father, one Daysman,
one Mediator, one High Priest, who, through
death, has become also King.   I believe that this
is the simple, absolute truth; and that we shall
get into utter confusion if we suppose, as the
whole truth of the matter, that God forgave the
Jewish penitent on the ground of his animal
sacrifice, as being the thing enjoined on *him*,
while he deals upon deeper grounds with us.
The truth is, that God looked upon that Jewish
penitent and his bleeding victim, and dealt with
him on the ground of His own great sacrifice,

which even then was before Him ; and that all
the feelings, thoughts, and associations which
clustered around the Jewish institution of sacrifice, drew all their virtue from the unseen fountain of the perfect sacrifice, as moons absorb the
lustre of an unseen sun.

The sacrifice of Christ, when offered visibly on
earth, was at once to justify—that is, to reveal
the unseen basis of—past forgivenesses, and to
show to the future the ground on which all its
divine relations must rest. God had this before
Him from the first, as the deep ground of His
acts of mercy; and revealed it in progressive
measures, as it could be borne by the strengthening spiritual vision of man.

I say, "in progressive measures." Nothing
can be further from the truth of things, than
to maintain that the Jew who derived any vital
help from his sacrificial institutions, must have
been intellectually conscious of the real basis on
which his justification rested, and been thus a
conscious prophet of the suffering of our Lord.
He was a prophet, but a mute one. There were
men who from · the height of their prophetic
eyrie looked over the gulf of ages, and "spake
beforehand of the sufferings of Christ, and the
glory that should follow." But the Scripture
assures us that they themselves saw but dimly,

and understood but feebly, that whereof they
spake; and we may be sure that the multitude
of their countrymen understood still less.   But
God understood it—that was the great matter.
God offered the sacrifice; God accepted it; and
on the ground of it justified every Jewish worshipper who put himself into spiritual relation
with Himself.   This last point is essential.   To
justify is a spiritual act; to be justified is a
spiritual reception of an act.   A careless, sensual soul can no more appropriate the virtue
of the sacrifice of the Lord Jesus, than can a
shut eye take in the daylight, or a stopped ear
the concord of sounds.   But just as light may
flood the atmosphere and gladden watching eyes,
though the sun be hidden; so did the light of
the great Atonement gladden all waking hearts
in the old time, before its form was visible in
our world.

I regard, then, the offering of sacrifice by the
Jewish worshipper as a spiritual act.   If I am
to regard it as a formal act, the mind of the
man having nothing to do with it, I should find '
it impossible to disentangle the confusion into
which such a view would plunge the whole
counsel of God.   The act, to have been worth
anything, must have been spiritual; that is,
must have exercised the spiritual faculties of the

worshipper by whom, or on behalf of whom, the sacrifice was offered.

The connection of the atonement for sin with the life of a victim, had most important teachings, as WE more fully understand. All that was meant by that, they only can comprehend who have seen " the Lamb of God, who beareth away the sins of the world." But to the thoughtful Jew there would be much solemn suggestion in the institution. The blood is the life : life is sacred—the life even of the meanest creature— and life is offered. Sin, then, touches the life ; it tinctures the very blood: by the shedding of blood only can it be purged away. The sign can only be fully understood when the thing signified appears. The types were dim, till that which they mutely prophesied was revealed. Then, and not till then, was it understood,— though the awful form of some of the pagan sacrifices shows terribly that the blood of bulls and of goats brings no real release to man—that the true atonement cannot be a life which God can claim, a creature life, but a life which God can offer—Himself. Some dim glimpse of this thought would be caught by the more earnest worshippers under the law, but to many it would be quite veiled, as is the depth of Gospel truth to many believers now. But this truth about sin was really, however dimly, expressed to and by the worshipper, whenever the high-priest passed with the blood· of atonement before the mercy-seat, and proclaimed to Israel the Lord's passover of sin.

And the Jew was specially taught to connect his forgiveness, not with a basis which he could improvise, which he could either invent or create; but with a work which was God's ordinance, which was God's appointed way of access to Himself. It was by God's way, and not by his own, that the Jew sought to be justified; and this renunciation of his own way and acceptance of God's, was an act of obedience essentially spiritual. What if it appeared to lead him but into the outer court of the tabernacle? the spirit which led him thither was that same spirit of faith, by which, when the way to the inner court, the Holy of Holies, was laid open by the blood of Christ, he would enter with reverent boldness, and bow with open face before the throne.

Here, then, are two fundamental principles of God's universal way of reconciling sinners to Himself, unfolded to Judaism by the Divine testimonies; principles which are meaningless utterly, delusions, mockeries, snares to souls, if there be no great propitiation, whose work of atonement was at length in full measure to be revealed to the world. Thus it appears that the milk of the children contained all the essential principles. of the nutriment, which was to feed the intelligent manhood of mankind.

3. The third lesson of the symbol, perhaps the highest, is to be gathered from the contemplation of its unity.

We have considered it in its parts, but. it is essentially one. An ark, with a mercy-seat above it, the cherubim shadowing both, and the Divine glory, the light which was the sign of God's personal presence, bathing the whole.

I have spoken of the truth which is thus set forth, at large, in my discourse on law. It tells us that mercy only crowns us fully with its benediction, where the Divine testimonies are hidden within the heart. Man is the true Shekinah. The glory shines from him when the Word is enshrined within him. "Christ is the end of the law for righteousness to every one that believeth." In Him it is no law of words addressed sternly to the understanding, but a law of life shrined lovingly within the soul. We talk of the abolition of the legal dispensation, but, as I have said, there is but one way of abolishing the law—hiding it within the heart. Abolish it there, and thus: "Sin shall not have dominion over you, for ye are not under the law but under grace."

There were Christians in the apostolic age, as there are in all ages, who thought that it was abolished otherwise; to whom Gospel liberty was the proclaimed saturnalia of sin. How terribly does the apostle warn such, that through Christ they were more absolutely bound to God's law than ever: "Not without law to God, but under the law to Christ." And if any one wishes to know what that includes within its range, let him read it here, Col. iii. 5–17. And let him learn that to have within the heart such delight in the testimonies of God, that His statutes become our songs in the house of our pilgrimage, was in old time, is now, and shall be through eternity, life, liberty, glory, and bliss.

Sermon xi.

Alone: yet not alone.

" *And he said, My presence shall go with thee, and I will give
thee rest.*"—Exod. xxxiii. 14.

THESE are the words of God's assurance, in
answer to an almost agonizing supplication of
Moses, "Except thy presence, my God, go with
me, carry us not up hence." The prayer was
uttered on the edge of the great wilderness,
when he was about to loose his hold on his last
familiar resting-place, and commit himself and
his people to its unknown wilds. All the magnitude of his grand undertaking was pressing on
him at that moment. "Who is sufficient for
these things," he cried, like one who, after the
lapse of ages—a pilgrim of Sinai, too—set his
hand to the conversion of a world. And the
prayer is a high exemplar for us. The Divine
guidance was the one question which to them,
to us, is absolutely a question of life or death.
Thus far the ground over which they had passed
was familiar marching-ground to their great
leader. Moreover, their march had been a tri-

umphal exodus from bondage. Up to Sinai,
Egypt was behind them, and they had the joyous
sense that they were escaping from hated and
tyrannous foes. From Sinai, Canaan was before
them, and the grand difficulties and perils of
their enterprise began. It was the great critical
point of their course. Verily they had need of
a vision of a Divine leader, whose pillar of flame
should shine, not on their march only, but in
their hearts. I have said already that Moses
was the Man of Israel, the man in whom all
the higher life and aim of the whole community
expressed itself. We study Israel through him ;
and I am persuaded that we shall get nearer
to the heart of this great matter—the Lord's
guidance of the host—if we listen to his wrestling
supplication, in which the intercessor was uttering the cry of a whole people, and catch the words
of the answer of God, than if we were to study,
as we might, the external form of the guiding
angel, marvellous, miraculous, and richly symbolic as it unquestionably is. "And the Lord
went before them by day in a pillar of cloud, to
lead them in the way ; and by night in a pillar
of fire to give them light ; to go by day and
night. He took not away the pillar of cloud
by day, nor the pillar of fire by night, from
before the people." A grand, sublime, symbol—

amongst the greatest things in history.   What a
picture is this !   " And on the day that the tabernacle was reared up the cloud covered the tabernacle, namely, the tent of the testimony : and at
even there was upon the tabernacle as it were
the appearance of fire, until the morning.   So it
was alway : the cloud covered it by day, and the
appearance of fire by night.   And when the cloud
was taken up from the tabernacle, then after that
the children of Israel journeyed : and in the place
where the cloud abode, there the children of Israel
pitched their tents.   At the commandment of the
Lord the children of Israel journeyed, and at the
commandment of the Lord they pitched : as long
as the cloud abode upon the tabernacle they
rested in their tents."—Numb. ix. 15–18.

Imagine that mighty host winding through the
dreary paths of the desert, lonely there as a
people among peoples, as their Lord became
lonely as a man among men ; cut off utterly from
all national associations and sympathies ; the
strongest people in the world behind them, ani-
mated by the most deadly hatred, and powerful
nations in front, armed to receive them, and to
dispute with them every inch of the inheritance
they were resolved to win ; marching on along
those solemn desert pathways, with the visible
sign in the midst of them of the presence in

person of the Lord God of the whole world.
There, under the blazing rays of the burning noon,
a soft cloud spread its cool shadow on the weary
plain, and refreshed imagination at any rate—and
what pure refreshment that is—with the picture
of the shadowing love of the Lord God Almighty
over the whole wearying pilgrimage and battle
march of life ! And then, as evening fell, and
the glooms of night began to drop their awful
shroud—for nightfall is awful in the lonely waste
—over the weird forms and hues of those beetling
cliffs, or the gaunt outlines of the desert palms,
the cloud began to glow and lighten, till it cast a
broad flood of living lustre, such as we see on
earth only in dreams, on the whole scene of the
desert encampment. It touched the spurs and
peaks of the mountains, till they stood glowing
like angel sentinels around the camp of God's
redeemed, and filled the night watchers—and let
us be sure that there were a multitude, and not the
least earnest-hearted of the people—with some
vision of what might be seen, if, as at Elisha's
prayer, the veils were lifted, and all the heavenly
armies appeared attending the path of God's
host through battles and perils, through foaming
seas and dreary deserts, to their glorious rest.
But magnificent as was the sign, the thing signified transcended it. In vain had the Divine

presence been shewn to them in that miraculous
cloud and glory, if there had been no inner sense
of the Divine presence in their hearts. It is in the
communion between Moses and the Divine Leader
of the host, that we are admitted into the true
sanctuary of that people's strength.   Just so far
as their spirits went with Moses in this prayer, in
this yearning for the inner presence and guidance
of God, did they march joyously and triumphantly
on their way; and when that failed, the visible cloud
of splendour helped them no longer; they dropped
like blighted fruit from the living tree, and their
carcases fell in the wilderness.   So we will enter
with Moses within the cloud that sweeps round
Sinai, and consider our sources of strength and
guidance for the pilgrimage of life.

Remember that Moses was about to quit the
familiar ground, the old home of his exile, the
mountain region of Horeb.   The path onward
lay through unknown deserts, and would most
surely be beset by daring and experienced foes.
It was a prospect before which even a soul of such
heroic mould might faint.   Would God go with
him, not in a pillar of cloud, as the national
leader, but as friend, companion, comrade of
his spirit ?   Let him have that promise, and he
would bravely on.   But well he knew that the
loftiest sphere, unlit by God's presence, is but a

sunless world; that a life of the grandest orbit,
unquickened by His smile, is joyless, barren, un-
blessing and unblessed. We moan sometimes,
or maunder, over the uncongenial scenes·into
which duty leads us, the distasteful tasks to which
we seem to be yoked by the will of God. When
you next make your moan, try to realize that man's
life. Scholar, statesman, profound and accomplished thinker, used to mix as a master in the
foremost circle of the foremost society of the world
in his day, God had cast his lonely lot amongst
a people utterly uninstructed and unintelligent,
unable to understand, indisposed to reverence his
thoughts, and ever breaking in on the meditations
and communings on which the fate of unborn
ages was hanging, with their sensual outcries,
"Hast thou brought out this whole nation into
the wilderness, that it may perish with hunger?"
A man, moreover, who had deeper thoughts about
the Divine nature and character than any other
man of his day; to whom the meaning of life and
the sacredness of duty were more plain. For,
had he not entered into the inner court of the
Divine presence, and gazed on the glory which no
eye but his had prevailed to look upon, and talked
with God face to face, as a man·talketh with his
friend? And see him there, among a people who
clung to the outer court, for it was less dreadful

than the inner; who had no conception of the solemnity of a Divine command, except when it was enforced by plagues, and who assailed him, when he came forth from this Divine communion, with the very glory on his countenance, full of that "favour" which is the life of men and peoples, with scornful questions about graves! Never, perhaps, was man so lonely. Not Elijah, when he flung himself in fierce wrath on the floor of the cave of Horeb, and the very ravens rebuked his despair; not Paul, when he stood, aged and friendless, before the bloody tribunal of pagan empire; not Alfred, when alone in the neat-herd's hut, that winter when, in Asser's simple words, "he lived an unquiet life in the woodlands of Somerset," and the destinies of England rested in his single hand; not Columbus, with the weary waste of waters still round him, and the land which God had called that pious and patient captain to discover, still far away: none of them, perhaps, ever felt so utterly lonely as Moses at that moment; and yet not alone —not alone—for God was with him. Servants of duty, pilgrims of discipline! others, greater than you, have passed through it all before you; others have laid on that altar a sacrifice which you cannot mate; others, the world's elect spirits, have accepted this word of the Eternal—"My presence shall go with thee,

and I will give thee rest," as the mariner accepts
the pole-star, as the world accepts the sunlight, as
an army accepts a renowned leader, as an age
sick of revolution accepts its king.

I cannot see that this choice of Moses, to walk
in God's way, if but assured of God's presence,
differs in anywise from the choice which that
people was called on to make at that moment,
and which God is ever pressing upon us all.   In
considering it in its broad human aspect, I
observe—

I. Here are two ways on which the choice is
to be exercised—two paths, which very plainly
diverge.

It is the old, old choice—worldliness, godliness—duty, pleasure—God's will, self-will—the
passions and appetites of the flesh or of the
mind, the convictions of conscience and the
word of God.   We may fence with these questions concerning right, truth, and duty; but
every man in his secret soul knows full well what
they mean. - And there come great crises in the
history of our lives in which the two ways lie very
plainly before us, and when, by our own delibe-
rate election of the one or the other, our life-
course gets shaped, and our eternity.   It was
such a crisis in the history of Israel.   They stood
there before God an independent nation, capable

of national action and national choice. No longer slaves, driven in gangs by a taskmaster's lash, but conscious freemen, with all the dignity and all the burden of the freeman's lot upon them, they stood there in the heart of the great wilderness, through which lay the path to beautiful and wealthy lands. Straight over the desert a Divine guide pointed their way. He had hidden from them nothing of the toils, perils, battles, famines of their pilgrimage; there, before the Mount of God, He had unveiled to them Himself, themselves, and their future. They had had a full taste of what a desert life must be, as they journeyed thither, and He gave them no hope that it could be otherwise to the close,—as He passed the word of command once more through their host, "set forward." On the other hand, in soft contrast to this stern and awful desert, lay Egypt, swimming in the sunlight; her wanton beauty and lavish plenty wooed them eagerly to return. Unholy passions and longings, never so fierce as when they tremble for their sway, flashed up to frenzy; and the old cry, " Better, far better, slavery with food and pleasure, than liberty with God and death," trembled on their lips. Here were the two paths : Divine duty, with privation and suffering; worldly pleasure, with bondage and degradation : the one, on through the wilderness to Canaan; the other, back, one step, one brief step, to Egyptian bondage and night. They went on, but half-hearted. Moses alone went on believing; they, compelled by an overmastering awe; their hearts went back to Egypt, and in the desert, not in Canaan, they found their graves.

And now let me show forth the same history in yourselves. These Jews are our exemplars; God wrote this page of their history for us. To every man who has a soul to be saved or damned God opens at some time, in some way, the question of duty and life, or pleasure and death. And it is often after this fashion : He takes you, by some striking visitation or overpowering influence, a step out of the Egypt of your daily natural bondage; shows to you the wilderness, tells you of Canaan, and whispers the assurance, "My presence shall go with thee, I will give thee rest." I cannot analyse your experience. I state the matter broadly. In some way, at some time—and it is now in the broad daylight of memory—God makes you hear His vocation, and asks for the possession of your hearts. It may have been by some preacher, who seemed that day to speak with the power and truth of an angel to your spirits ; it may have been by some stroke which shattered your idols round you, and bowed you down mute before the footstool of

your King; it may have been by the lips of some
dying saint, or by the holy and beautiful life of one
who has gone to walk in white before the Lamb.
I know not, but God knows, and you know.
For the time, a strange change came over all your
feelings, thoughts, and hopes. God took you out
one step from the drudgery, the circle of slavish
tasks, the reeking flesh-pots, and the tyrant's
lash; out into the clear air, the bright heaven,
the free earth of the wilderness—and what was
the world to you then? what the wealth of
Crœsus, the throne of Cæsar? Another world
enveloped you with its atmosphere, and ravished
you with its music—a world where Crœsus is a
beggar, and Nero a slave. You caught some
gleaming of its splendour, some echoes of its
choral hymns. You learnt there, that all God's
universe is not as dark as the sin-begotten gloom
of this world; that all man's being is not earthly;
that all man's life need not be consuming and
degrading toil; that there is a world open to him
in which the longings of his spirit—that aspiration which kills the pleasures of sin, though it
wins not the joys of virtue—can find free play
and progress, and, gaining power from Christ to
master flesh and world, make the very air around
him musical with loud hosannas and shouts of
victory; a world in whose sphere, though sense

may pine, spirit rejoices ; though gold may waste,
riches grow ; though the outer man with its
infirm purposes and vain passions may perish,
the inner man is renewed daily, stands up in
freedom, rejoices in discipline, and exults in hope
of the glory of God.

All this, at such moments—and to all at some
time is the vision sent—God shows to us ; and
He calls us to make our final election ; to go on
with His pillar of cloud and flame through the
desert, conscious freemen, or if the flesh-pots are
too sweet, to go back to Egypt, conscious slaves.
Thus God calls you, claims you, stirs you up to
the great enterprise of life ; and I dare not mock
Him by supposing that He does not wish or
mean you to go on.   But then, just as you are
realizing the truth of these impressions, the
majesty of eternal things, and the glory of
spiritual conquest, and are about to commit
yourself to the Divine hand, you bethink yourself—the devil takes care that you shall not
forget it—of the sacrifice it demands, the dangers,
wanderings, and difficulties which it will entail,
the dear associations from which it will sever
you, the loved companions it will compel you to
forsake ; you look on, the drear, dread desert
sweeps out before you, you hear the night wind
moan through its desolate wastes ; you know

that its farther bounds are thronged by foemen armed for your destruction ; you ask, how
many in fulfilling the will of God have found not
kingdoms, but graves, and forgetting for the
moment that the bosom of Jesus is their sleeping
bed, you let the sensual cry break forth once
more, " It is better for us to serve the Egyptians
than that we should die here in the wilderness."
The cry of the spirit is choked and silenced ; the
choice is made.

I do not ask you whether this be a chapter of
your experience ; I know it is. God has not
formed each human spirit to be the heir of immortality, laid on it responsibilities of fearful
moment, and sent it forth to a probation in which
sin is the harbinger of death eternal, without
coming to that soul, whose destiny He has so
fearfully interwoven with its duty, to talk to it of
duty, to urge it to action, to kindle its aspirations for freedom, life, and glory, ere He leaves
it to its carnal, earthly passions, to bury it in
eternal night.

" O Jerusalem ! Jerusalem ! thou that killest
the prophets, and stonest them which are sent
unto thee ; how often would I have gathered thy
children together, even as a hen gathereth her
chickens under her wings, but ye would not ! "
is Christ's lament over every self-immolated soul.

II. The cry of the human spirit for rest.

The longing of man's spirit amid all these strifes, discords, and confusions, is for rest. We are made for rest, and have a right to cry for it, if we do but understand what it really means. Nothing can eradicate man's conviction that strife and discord have no right in the universe; that they are abnormal : that the normal condition of things and beings is harmony, and that harmony is the music of rest. God must rest—rest even in working; and all that is of God and from God, has the longing and the tending to rest. I believe that some dull notion that they will have more rest in the life of the world, that they will escape many cares and distractions, and, at any rate, be at peace in sin, lies at the bottom of many a backsliding to Egypt in human hearts. No man at first is content to let the question alone—to leave the riddle of life unread. The inward and the outward carry on the conflict, and refuse to settle it on the cheap terms of sin. Hence arises the long discord in him who has not found the principle of the Divine harmony : "the flesh lusteth against the spirit, and the spirit striveth against the flesh, and the two are contrary the one to the other." We long to find some truth which shall release us from the agony, and make some kind of harmony in our lives.

We find this battle of life inexplicable; it sometimes shakes our faith in the wisdom and goodness of our God. We shout into the Sibyl cave
and listen for the responses; we take the whispers of sense for the answer, and then we go on
our way. But the conflict again begins, the
perplexities again return; again and again we
cry, each time in a more frenzied mood, "Who
will show us any good?" "Who will give us
rest?" Now, to find peace, we are willing to
abandon the world for God, for Christ, for a holy
life, and the rest of heaven. But then the
magnitude of the sacrifice appals us; we fall
back again, and take to shouting, "Peace, peace!"
where there is no peace, instead. At times, in
the full flood of the reaction, we blasphemously
pray that the Spirit may be withdrawn, that the
Light may be quenched: "What have we to do
with thee, Jesus, thou son of God; why art thou
come to torment us before our time?"

We search passionately after a true philosophy
of life; we ask to understand the reason of this
conflict, and to see on to its end. Is there no
truth which can cast light for us over these
troubled waters, and show us, though from afar,
that all is not rough and dangerous—that beyond
them is a calm ocean, a Pacific unswept by
storms, and studded with the peaceful islands

of the blessed. Or is all to be darkness, and for ever ? Are we to wrestle all night with the moaning surge, until morning casts us shattered on the strand of eternity? Tell us why these storms are raging ; why only through that deep dark sea and howling wilderness lies the path to the better land. Above all, show us a light which can guide us through the glooms and lead us into rest,

Listen : there is such a word of guidance, and but one. Amid all the storms which duty calls you to brave, all the sacrifices that God calls you to make, the perils, pains, and battles through which your heavenward path may lead you, voices come down, calm and clear, from those who have fought and suffered, and are at rest with Christ,—

> Mortal, they softly say,
>   Peace to thy heart :
> We too, yes ! mortal,
>   Have been as thou art ;
> Hope-lifted, doubt-depressed,
>   Seeing in part ;
> Tried, troubled, tempted,
>   Sustained as thou art.

While, above all the voices of the creature, from the midst of the glow of glory which surrounds the throne, the word of the Son of God, the great Captain of the human host, comes down to every earnest, struggling spirit : " MY PRESENCE SHALL GO WITH THEE, I WILL GIVE THEE REST."

We pass on, to complete the subject, by considering—

III. The Divine assurance, which was to Moses, and should be to us, an all-sufficient warrant to leave the world and the pleasures of sin, and commit ourselves to the desert under God's guidance, as the path to the heavenly rest.

"He endured as seeing Him who is invisible." Such only can endure. We have talked hitherto of the two lives, the two paths, mainly in their present aspects, as they seem to man, not as they are before the eye of God. We have spoken of sacrifices, struggles, and sufferings; of earth, to the child of God, as a wilderness, and life as a long and weary night. Now let us lift our eyes and see with what stars of God this night is illumined, what arms of Divine love enfold the pilgrim, what heavenly voices, amid the storms of life's wild sea, the surgings of passion, and even the wreck of our sensual existence, can hush the pilgrim to rest. "My presence shall go with thee." Now there arises a light in the darkness. There is compensation, yea, infinitely more, something for which earth has no name, " a far more exceeding, even an eternal weight of glory." Not by striking out pains and strifes, but by crowding in conquests, joys, and glories, do we set our fraction of life square with the measures of the Eternal. "For the joy that was set before Him, he endured the cross, and despised the shame." He is the ensample unto us. With all that we have pictured of the aspects of the wilderness, there is a Divine presence with the soul, which is its joy, its strength, its life, its heaven—yes, even on earth its heaven. "The best of all is, God is with us."

I shall speak briefly of the reality of this Divine presence, and its fruits.

1. Its reality.

We can come nearer to the heart of this great matter than even Moses can lead us. "Jesus answered them, do ye now believe? Behold the hour cometh, yea, is now come, that ye shall be scattered, every man to his own, and shall leave me alone; AND YET I AM NOT ALONE, BECAUSE THE FATHER IS WITH ME. These things have I spoken unto you that in me ye might have peace. In the world ye shall have tribulation : but be of good cheer : I have overcome the world." John xvi. 31–33.

Let me ask you to study, in the light of this train of thought, this passage of our Lord's history—John xviii. 28—xix. 12.

Is this the strongest reality or the deepest delusion known to man ? It is one or the other. We are here in the presence of an awful fact, or a more awful lie. You may use fine words about " the Divine idea," " the higher self-consciousness of Jesus," "the subjective reality of a Divine presence with him there ;" but I confess that all such talk seems to me blank blasphemy when intruded into such scenes as these. Either there was One, above the world, who was with the Lord in that hour, whose word represented to Him all truth, whose touch represented to Him all power, whose ministries represented to Him all love ; or the arch-delusion triumphed in that hour, and for ever, over man. He who stood there unarmed and friendless before Pilate, had One to stand by Him, in whom all power, wisdom, truth, and life were centred. The roots of the witness to the truth which the Lord then bore, were deeper than the everlasting mountains, deeper than heaven, deeper than hell ; they were firm in the Being of the Living God.

I have no other key to this awful transaction. If the Lord mistook His own idea for that Living God, and gave an " objective" reality to what was but the phantom of a longing and aching heart, then there is no reality anywhere around us or above us ; nothing to justify, purify, and

18

lift us out of ourselves.   He who is enamoured of
or content with himself may find this a gospel ;
but for me, if there be no living God my Saviour,
to redeem me from myself, to inform me with His
truth, and inspire me with His life, why then,
"Let us eat, and drink—and die, and let it be
soon." No! the one real thing in this universe
is God's presence with the human spirit; having
that we have all things, missing that we lack all
things; all things collapse, and vanish like a
dream away.

Think you that *he* did not find it a rock, who
stood up before kings and an angry world, and
said, "This is God's word.   I can speak no
other.   Here stand I, God help me."   What to
him were kings and popes and hostile armies?
What, as he said himself, all the devils in hell?
And what did they do to harm him!   He finished
his course with joy, he died peacefully in his bed,
a conqueror, and filled the world with his immortal
fame.   And I would rather see the weakest and
most trembling being that I loved, in the right
path, following Christ through tribulations, than
lapped in ease and worldly indulgence, and lulled
by soft strains to voluptuous repose.   And why?
Because I believe that all blessing is compre-
hended in the promise, "My presence shall go
with thee, and I will give thee rest."   Pray for

this, for your children and for your dearest : give
God no rest till He has promised to guide them,
and then leave them in His hand for life and for
eternity.

Let God appear, and light rises on the troubled
pilgrimage with soft healing wings. The dark
drear night flushes with auroral splendour, herald
of the celestial dawn. In the fiercest fires that
man can kindle, a grand and godlike form is by
the martyrs, and the tyrant world shudders as it
sees that the flame touches nothing but their
bonds. The Captain of the Lord's host is ever at
the right hand of the child of duty, covering him
with his shield in all deadly perils, and in sorrows
drawing him closer to his heart. And moments
there will be, when the moaning surges of the
stormy life-sea around him are silenced, and he
hears with strange joy and wonder the calm but
mighty heavings of that eternal ocean, which
bears the rushing tides of being back to their great
fountain, God.

2. The fruits. *" I will give thee rest."*

I have already said that the longing of the
human spirit amid all this is for rest. There are
two kinds of rest, or rather what goes by the
name of rest, within reach of man. The secret
of the one is, escape from trouble ; the secret of
the other is, entering into life. Life is the harmo-

nious balance of conflicting forces, the calm control of all opposite powers. Escape from trouble
is not permitted to man, though he thinks it is.
"This same shall comfort us concerning our
work and toil of our hands, because of the ground
which the Lord hath cursed," said Lamech,
on the eve of the deluge. Even thus saith the
worldling, "Peace, peace," while "there is no
peace, saith my God, to the wicked." It is a wonderful feature in man's constitution that he can
find rest only in his highest, in the full culture
and activity of all his powers. He tries to rest in
a luxurious home, in a feverish orgy, on a wanton's
breast. But who shall paint the anguish of the
rest of the wicked? How many a man has gone
out from a scene of uproarious merriment, to
blow out his brains, in blank despair! There is
no rest but in God. Man rests only in the fulness of his existence, in the completeness of his
life. Moses found no rest in communion with
earthly natures, but there was rest for him—it
bathed his soul like the dewy moonlight the
flowers—when he entered into that which is within
the veil, and talked "of things unspeakable" with
God. "Brethren, they which believe do enter
into rest." Having faith in the blood of atonement, in the God and Father reconciled in Christ
Jesus, the conscience rests in the sense of recon-

ciliation. Having faith in the Saviour's power
and love, the spirit rests amid the severities of
discipline, yea sleeps sometimes, as Jesus did
while the storm was highest ; for ever when the
danger is imminent, and the foaming surges are
parting to engulf their prey, the Divine presence
within shines forth around, and immediately there
is a great calm, and the spirit rests still. "And
I heard a voice from heaven saying, Blessed are
the dead which die in the Lord from henceforth :
yea, saith the Spirit, that they may rest from
their labours; and their works do follow
them."

To that world we must carry on our gaze, if
we would see the issues of the divergent paths,
whose various courses on earth we have attempted
to scan. The believer, he who "endures as
seeing the invisible," is led by the Divine angel,
the angel of the presence of God, through a storm
of conflicts to a glorious rest. The lover of
pleasure is led by his angel, the angel whose presence he loves, through the sensual joys which
are but the painted mask of the inward miseries,
to the outer darkness, "where the worm dieth
not, and their fire is not quenched for ever." In
life the believer has the assurance, "My presence
shall go with thee, I will give thee rest;" in
death, "Yea, though I walk through the valley

of the shadow of death, I will fear no evil, for
Thou art with me, Thy rod and staff, they comfort me." " As for me, I shall behold Thy face
in righteousness; I shall be satisfied when I
awake, with Thy likeness."

Then, having done the will of God, he rests in
the bosom of Jesus, midst the unveiled splendours
of the Eternal Light, and the full outflowings of
the Infinite Love, until the trumpet of the arch-
angel summons him to exchange that rest for
glory.   And then, what eye hath not seen, what
ear hath not heard, shall be disclosed in that
last great day of God ; when the redeemed spirit,
fresh from the rest of Paradise, shall put on the
radiant form, immortal as itself, and know all
that the Divine love, which saved the helpless
sinner, can show to the glorified son, through all
the ages of eternity.

Sermon xii.

Kibroth-hattaavah: the Graves of Lust.

"*And there went forth a wind from the Lord, and brought quails from the sea, and let them fall by the camp, as it were a day's journey on this side, and as it were a day's journey on the other side, round about the camp, and as it were two cubits high upon the face of the earth. And the people stood up all that day, and all that night, and all the next day, and they gathered the quails: he that gathered least gathered ten homers: and they spread them all abroad for themselves round about the camp. And while the flesh was yet between their teeth, ere it was chewed, the wrath of the Lord was kindled against the people, and the Lord smote the people with a very great plague. And he called the name of that place Kibroth-hattaavah: because there they buried the people that lusted.*"—Numb. xi. 81-34.

THE eleventh chapter in the Book of Numbers is one of the gravest and saddest in history. The tenth chapter shows to us the people developed into a nation and a church, before the face of the Lord in Sinai. They set forth, with a grand orderliness and courage, on their Canaanward march; I call it grand, for the root of it was in heaven, with God. The tumultuous throng had found its relation to God, and understood, through Him, itself and its

vocation. Full of a new dignity and bravery, full
of a high sense of the sacredness of its mission,
it marshalled itself as an army, and marched
on to victory. Doubtless the people felt, in their
intense and lofty emotion, that the follies and
lusts which had erst defiled and dishonoured them,
were done with for ever. Which of us has not
felt it, and been disenchanted, perhaps that very
day, in bitterness of soul? They would have a
brief march, a sharp conflict, a swift conquest, a
glorious possession of their promised land. But,
alas! quite another future was before them : aspiration is not achievement, hope is not endurance.
But two of that mighty army ever trod the sacred
ground.

It seems that they had a "mixed multitude"
among them. "*And a mixed multitude went up
with them.*" Exod. xii. 38. There is sure to be
trouble with that mixed multitude. These con-
cessions through indifference, weakness, or mere
softness of heart, rarely fail to breed mischief in
companies and souls. They are the alloys in
the pure metal of life, and, like the tin in the
silver, make it brittle and apt to flaw. They were
pleased, perhaps proud, to take a great company
with them. Lovers, mistresses, servants ; all
bound to them by some tie, but not that tie which
bound them to God and to each other, their

calling to the promised land. That which we tolerate in the coasts of our homes and hearts, too good to expel, too bad to assimilate, and which we suffer therefore to lodge with us, rarely fails to make havoc in our lives.

I think it probable that this mixed multitude felt that there was something unsatisfactory in their position, after the organization of the nation before Sinai. The children of Israel marched thenceforth by tribes under their banners, arrayed in a grand order around the shrine of the national faith; while the mixed multitude struggled on as they could in their tracks. Be that as it may, they fell a lusting, the host caught the infection, and there fell a multitude before the fire of the Lord, ere the murmuring and lusting were stayed. Then follows an intercession of Moses with God, or rather let us call it a remonstrance, so bold and outspoken that we hear it with awe; but so honest, so simple-hearted, so full of a thorough willingness to bear the burden if there was no help for it, as to draw forth from the Lord a compassionate and sympathetic answer. Then follows the communication of the spirit of wisdom and guidance to the seventy elders, the Pentecostal baptism of the Old Testament dispensation; then the prophesying of Eldad and Medad in the camp, whereat the bold young spirits, jealous for official dignity, were indignant; but the wise and careworn elder, eager for help from any quarter, nor thinking that a single man or order can contain a blessing large enough for a nation or a world, was glad. And then came flights of quails from the sea, and fell in showers around the camp, juicy and nourishing meat, meat by acres; that they might know how little the Lord's arm was shortened, how little His store was spent when it pleased Him to open His hand and give. The rest our text reveals: *"And while the flesh was yet between their teeth, ere it was chewed, the wrath of the Lord was kindled against the people, and the Lord smote the people with a very great plague. And he called the name of that place Kibroth-hattaavah; because there they buried the people that lusted."* KIBROTH-HATTAAVAH; THE GRAVES OF LUST.

Now, this is a most rich chapter of human history. We will stand by those graves, and listen to their teachings; they may save us from standing by the graves of the idols of our own hearts.

I shall endeavour to illustrate this subject by dwelling on three principles :—

I. There are perpetual resurrections of easily besetting sins.

II. The time comes, in the history of the indulgence of besetting sins, when God ceases to strive for us against them, and lets them have their way.

III. The end of that way is inevitably and speedily a grave.

I. The perpetual resurrections of easily besetting sins.

This lusting was no novelty in their experience; it was the besetting temptation of the desert, and the besetting sin of their hearts. But they ought to have known. They ought to have viewed the first rising of its ghastly shape in their camps with horror; there were graves enough, in the path from Egypt, to remind them of its deadly work. God had been at great pains to teach them the lesson of dependence, that "man doth not live by bread alone, but by every word which proceedeth out of the mouth of God doth man live."

"*And when Pharaoh drew nigh, the children of Israel lifted up their eyes, and, behold, the Egyptians marched after them; and they were sore afraid: and the children of Israel cried out unto the Lord. And they said unto Moses, Because there were no graves in Egypt, hast thou taken us away to die in the wilderness? wherefore hast thou dealt thus with us, to carry us forth out of Egypt? Is not this the word that we did tell thee in Egypt, saying, Let us alone, that we may serve the Egyptians? For it had been*

better for us to serve the Egyptians, than that we
should die in the wilderness. And Moses said unto
the people, Fear ye not, stand still, and see the salvation of the Lord, which He will show to you to-day :
for the Egyptians whom ye have seen to-day, ye shall
see them again no more for ever. The Lord shall
fight for you, and ye shall hold your peace. And
the Lord said unto Moses, Wherefore criest thou unto
me? speak unto the children of Israel, that they go
forward : but lift thou up thy rod, and stretch out
thine hand over the sea, and divide it : and the
children of Israel shall go on dry ground through the
midst of the sea." Exod. xiv. 10–16.

"And they took their journey from Elim, and all
the congregation of the children of Israel came unto
the wilderness of Sin, which is between Elim and
Sinai, on the fifteenth day of the second month after
their departing out of the land of Egypt. And the
whole congregation of the children of Israel murmured against Moses and Aaron in the wilderness :
And the children of Israel said unto them, Would to
God we had died by the hand of the Lord in the
land of Egypt, when we sat by the flesh-pots, and
when we did eat bread to the full; for ye have
brought us forth into this wilderness, to kill this
whole assembly with hunger. Then said the Lord
unto Moses, Behold, I will rain bread from heaven
for you; and the people shall go out and gather a

certain rate every day, that I may prove them, whether they will walk in my law, or no. And it shall come to pass, that on the sixth day they shall prepare that which they bring in; and it shall be twice as much as they gather daily." Exod. xvi. 1-5.

"*And all the congregation of the children of Israel journeyed from the wilderness of Sin, after their journeys, according to the commandment of the Lord, and pitched in Rephidim: and there was no water for the people to drink. Wherefore the people did chide with Moses, and said, Give us water that we may drink. And Moses said unto them, Why chide ye with me? wherefore do ye tempt the Lord? And the people thirsted there for water; and the people murmured against Moses, and said, Wherefore is this that thou hast brought us up out of Egypt, to kill us and our children and our cattle with thirst? And Moses cried unto the Lord, saying, What shall I do unto this people? they be almost ready to stone me. And the Lord said unto Moses, Go on before the people, and take with thee of the elders of Israel; and thy rod, wherewith thou smotest the river, take in thine hand and go. Behold, I will stand before thee there upon the rock in Horeb; and thou shalt smite the rock, and there shall come water out of it, that the people may drink. And Moses did so in the sight of the elders of Israel. And he called the name of the place Massah, and Meribah, because of*

*the chiding of the children of Israel, and because
they tempted the Lord, saying, Is the Lord among
us, or not?"*   Exod. xvii. 1–7.

And now, with firmer assurance than ever that
God was in the midst of them, to bring them
into the place which He had prepared, they resumed their march through the unknown desert
paths.   The tabernacle, the ark, the order of the
camp, the pillar of cloud and flame, were all
among them, the pledge of His presence.   But
all in vain.   They must have flesh, or they would
give up the enterprise, and die in despair.   And
they had flesh; they were fed, were crammed
with it to nauseation, and with it "God sent
leanness into their souls."

I dwell on two points of large importance for
the understanding of this history.

1. The side from which the temptation came
to them.

2. The special season at which they were
assailed.

1. The side from which it came.

" *And the mixed multitude that was among them
fell a lusting: and the children of Israel also wept
again, and said, Who shall give us flesh to eat? We
remember the fish, which we did eat in Egypt
freely; the cucumbers, and the melons, and the leeks,
and the onions, and the garlick: But now our*

*soul is dried away: there is nothing at all, beside
this manna, before our eyes."* Numb. xi. 4-6.

This mixed multitude corresponds precisely to
the troop of disorderly passions and appetites,
with which we suffer ourselves to march through
the desert of life. Passions, desires, ever mad
for indulgence, and reckless, scornful, of Divine
law. The mixed multitude was but loosely
attached to them. They had no call, no ancient
traditions, no national hopes, no right to call
Canaan a home. They might have won all these.
Judaism was ever benignant to the stranger.
God's elections are ever inclusive and not exclu-
sive; but the title was not to be won by lust.
They were a loose, coarse, common company,
with nothing to dignify, elevate, inspire.* No
wonder they fainted, murmured, lusted; and
thought flesh for to-day was better than Canaan
to-morrow, and heaven beyond. They had come
into the wilderness with the people, perhaps
to escape from bitter bondage, perhaps to make
what they could out of the people's necessities in the desert; the camp-followers of the
great army, greedy, vicious, disorderly, and liable
to all sorts of senseless panics, which not seldom

* It is noteworthy, that the strangers, after the long common experience and discipline of the wilderness, are spoken of
in much higher terms, as " the strangers that were conversant
among them."—Josh. viii. 35.

imperil the whole host. I say, again, there
was no ban upon them, because they were not of
the heirs of promise; a nobler sympathy with a
great people's destiny had won them a nobler
place in history. There was one once, one of a
mixed multitude, "a Syrophœnician woman,"
who would take no denial. Even " It is not meet
to take the children's bread and cast it unto the
dogs," would not drive her away. "Yea, Lord,
yet the dogs eat of the crumbs which fall from
the master's table," was her faithful response.
The word, "O woman, great is thy faith, be it
unto thee even as thou wilt !" received her into
the elect circle of those who had power with
God and with man to prevail.

But this mixed multitude was of another sort,
an ignoble rabble, to whom uncleanness was
native, like the disorderly rout we lead about
with us through life's pilgrimage ; and rarely
does a day pass that they do not drag us into
mischief, and expose us to burning shame.

The question was not one of sustenance. It
rose not out of the healthy action of the appetites
which God had implanted for the nourishment of
the bodily life. " God gave them bread from
heaven to eat." It was distinctly a question of
lust. Enough for appetite was there ; enough
for all the uses of life, guaranteed by God ; " but

they wept again, saying, who shall give us flesh
to eat; we remember the fish which we did eat
in Egypt freely—the cucumbers, and the melons,
and the leeks, and the onions, and the garlic;
but now our soul is dried away "—they meant
their fat, their notion of a soul lay there—" there
is nothing at all beside this manna before our
eyes." Lust was strong in them, the love of the
satisfaction of the bodily appetites for the sake
of the momentary pleasure they bring. And
appetite runs swiftly into lust in every one of
us; each act of indulgence opens a fresh mouth
which craves to be fed. And till this troop of
desires is taken in hand and curbed with an iron
bit by a resolute will, there is no orderly march
for us, no manly progress; there are the seeds
of panic and confusion in our array, and the
devil's own terminus, a grave, awaiting us, before
our pilgrimage is half done. The moment you
take pleasure in the indulgence of appetite beyond
the use for which it was ordained by God, you
take an element into your life which will humble
it, and drag its glory in the dust. Look back
and see what deadly humiliation lust has already
brought you; what ulcerous sores, through which
wells out so much of the pith and life-blood of
your being. It is the grand battle of life, to
teach lust the limits of Divine law, to break it

19

in to the taste of the bread of heaven, and make
it understand, that "man doth not live by bread
alone, but by every word that cometh out of the
mouth of God."

2. The special season when the easily besetting sin rose up and again made them its slave.

We have all of us a shrinking from a life-long
struggle.   One sharp battle we can stand; yes,
and one sharp pain—however sharp.   Oh, could
we but gather up our sins to one head, and sever
it by one sweep of the Spirit's sword !   No matter
how keen the agony, no matter if we bleed
inwardly, and have to cauterize the wound; we
can stand all that, if we might but feel that sin
was done with, was slain to rise again no more for
ever.   So strong is the passion for this complete
deliverance, that we easily persuade ourselves
that it is accomplished.   The wish is father to
the thought which sometimes, in moments of
high and rapturous vision, visits us.   Well, we
say, that sin which has haunted me like a spectre,
attended me like my double, is slain at last.   I
have laid it in its tomb; other battles I may have
to fight, but that slain foe I shall see no more.
Look round ! yes, while the word is on your lip
and the glad thought in your heart, look round.
There, close by you, is the ghastly shape, ghastlier
than ever, with a wicked Mephistopheles grin of

satisfaction, that its clutch is tight upon you still. Oh, the sickening thought which then fills us! Am I ever to be thus haunted? Shall I ever shake off this infirmity? Will it follow me to my grave, will it rise with me, and make a hell of my heaven?

Look at this orderly and gallant host. They had been baptized as God's soldiers by the splendours of the Mount of the Law. Full of Divine joy, zeal, courage, hope, they set forward; their hearts bounding with gladness, as the sound of the silver trumpets rang through the desert air and marshalled them on. "Scant fare, hard marching, fierce battles, but exhilarate us. The flesh-pots, the melons, the garlic, they belong to the days of our bondage; we are free men now, and their power to tempt us is gone." And so many a gallant young spirit, having heard the trumpet-call of the Gospel, having girt on the armour of godly battle, and joined the glorious company of the soldiers of the Cross, the pilgrims of eternity, feels in the first pride of strength and flush of joy that the flesh is so bruised as to be broken and crushed for ever. There seems but to remain a merry speedy march to the possession of the goodly land. While the first flush of excitement lasts, it is so. You could pass then quite calmly through scenes of temptation which once would have set your passions in a blaze. But dread the hour when the glow begins to die down; when the practical burdens, pains, trials which you still meet with, prove to you that the Divine life on earth is no paradise regained; when you find your strength barely equal to the demands made upon it, and see stretching on through long years a path of struggle, denial, and mortification of the flesh, the end of which is not yet in sight. A chill despondency is wont at such a time to take the place of the glow of exhilaration; and wonder not if in that moment the old demon of temptation returns. And dread lest the rush of old associations, long repressed, should burst forth, and sweep you from your firm standing-ground into what may prove worse than the grave of your lust—the grave of your soul.

It is a fact which all close students of human character must have observed, that there is a back-water of temptation, if I may so speak, which is more deadly than its direct assaults. You may fight hard against a temptation, and fight victoriously. You may beat it off, and crush it down; and then, when, weary with the conflict, you suffer the strain of vigilance to relax, it shall steal in and easily master the citadel, which lately it spent all its force in vain to win. Beware of your best moments, as well as of your worst; or rather the moments which succeed the best. They are the most perilous of all. Just when the consciousness of a triumph seems to permit and justify disarmament for a moment, the subtle foe with whom you have to deal will steal in on you, and win a treacherous victory.

Never relax the strain. Never allow temptation within arm's-length. Never forget that each new victory opens a new danger, and gives fresh call for vigilance and courage to keep what has been won. Never believe that the devil is asleep; never believe that a besetting sin is eradicated; never boast of a crowning victory: lest Kibroth-Hattaavah, the graves of lust, be written on the head-stones that mark the chief stations of your pilgrimage; but "lay aside every weight, and the sin that doth so easily beset you, and run with patience the race that is set before you. Looking unto Jesus." Like Him, "resist even unto bloodstriving against sin."

II. There comes a point in the history of the indulgence of besetting sins, when God ceases to strive with us and for us against them, and lets them have their way.

Remember, this was not the simple appetite for flesh, it was *lusting* for flesh, against the

provisions of the wisdom and love of God. Quite
otherwise did God respond even to their faithless
murmuring for water and for bread, as we have
seen. Bread and water He had provided out of
His store with generous hand. But they *would*
have flesh in spite of Him, and He let them have
their way to its only end—the only bourne of
self-will—a grave. It is worth our while to
study closely this spiritual history, and to analyse
the conditions out of which its catastrophe springs.

1. God has great patience with the weaknesses
and sins of the flesh. No one can read this
history, and the life of the Saviour, without
feeling how mercifully God deals with those who
are overtaken in sin which springs out of the
infirmities, appetites, and passions which belong
to the bodily life. But it is a dreadful mistake
to suppose that therefore He thinks lightly of
them. He regards them as sins that must be
conquered, and, no matter by what sharp discipline, extirpated and killed. He knows that, if
tolerated, they become the most deadly of spiritual evils, and rot body and spirit together in hell.

2. Hence all the severer discipline by which
the Lord seeks to purge them, the various agencies by which He fights with us and for us against
their tyrannous power.

What is life but one long discipline of God for

the cleansing of the flesh? Are not the after-
pains of departed sensual joys among its chief
stings and thorns? God has made a sure link
of connection between such sins and their penalties. The body itself is made the index of its
indulgence; and the man and society are so
organized, that their transgressions of God's laws
bear a rapid harvest of sorrow and shame. Does
He not give us the bread of heaven, that He
may waken within us a taste for purer pleasures,
and lead us out of the coils of the fleshly
tempters by giving us the food of a Diviner life?
Doubtless the manna was something very different
from the flesh-pots of Egypt; purer, fresher,
more like the heaven from which it came. Less
palatable probably to a gross taste, used to
gorging; more sweet to a fine and disciplined
palate, to the man who ate simply to strengthen
himself for higher things. Perhaps it symbo-
lizes the whole of the higher interests and pur-
suits of men as social and intellectual beings,
which God supplies to wean them from gross
feeding of the flesh; as well as the true heavenly
bread of righteousness, which if a man eat he
hungers no more. It is only when a man *will*
not enter into his Father's counsel in this; *will*
not suffer the higher tastes to develop themselves,
and the higher appetites to indulge their cravings

with the bread of God ; *will* grovel when God
gives him wings to soar; *will* go on the belly,
snake-like, when God lifts him and sets his front
face to face with heaven ; *will* clamour for flesh
when the bread of God is in his very hand : it is
only then, when the evil becomes deadly, and
deepens into spiritual sin of the darkest dye and
most incurable malignity, that God stays His
hand, closes His witness, withdraws His guardian angel, and leaves the will to itself.

Some into whose hands this book may fall are,
I fear, being let alone by the Lord. He has
witnessed, striven, smitten ; and all in mercy.
There is a grave-stone in some churchyard which
He has reared as a witness against lust and self-
will in your life. Many an ill-gotten heap of
gain He has scattered; many an idol He has
broken ; many a picture, sermon, book, He has
brought before your eyes to scare you, just when
hot passion was in full pursuit of the prize; but
He does not seem so busy with you now. With
a kind of easy assurance you now walk freely,
where once you stepped as on a thin crust, which
might crack and let you into an abyss. Beware,
beware ! God is letting you alone; and if "it
is a fearful thing to fall into the hands of the
living God," it is more awful to be left by Him,
to take your own road to death.

3. Let alone by God.

"Ephraim is joined to idols, let him alone!" is to my mind among the most awful sentences in the word of God.

How often does it happen, in the history of these wilful sinners of the flesh, that after a while all things seem to smile upon them and prosper them according to their heart's desires. Are they mad for gold? gold seems to roll in upon them. Are they mad for pleasure? their seductive arts are successful, and victims come readily to their lure. Are they mad for drink? those around them, kindred, friends, cease to strive with them, and give it up as hopeless; shame, too, abandons them, they may wallow in beer or gin, nobody cares. It is very wonderful to see how often, if a man is bent on an end which is not God's end, God gives it him, and it becomes his curse. God does not curse us; He leaves us to ourselves; that is curse enough, and from that curse what arm can save us! We *will* have it, and we shall have it. We leap through all the barriers which He has raised around us to limit us, yea, though they be rings of blazing fire, we will through them and indulge our lust; and in a moment He sweeps them all out of our path—perhaps roses spring to beguile, where flames so lately blazed to warn. "Flesh,

give us flesh to eat! This manna does not tickle
the palate nor fire the blood. We will have
flesh!" "Yes! here is flesh. You shall have it;
see here, in this blank wilderness, the flesh is
falling round you in showers. Kill and eat;
there is nothing to hinder you; gorge yourselves,
here is plenty; and then lie down to sleep—the
sleep of sated lust shall be your grave." This
leads me on to observe—

III. The end of that way is, inevitably and
speedily, a grave.

The grave of lust is one of the most awful of
the inscriptions on the head-stones of the great
cemetery, the world.

The words in Psalm cvi. 13–15, "*They soon
forgat His works, they waited not for His counsel;
but lusted exceedingly in the wilderness, and tempted
God in the desert. And He* GAVE THEM THEIR
REQUEST, BUT SENT LEANNESS INTO THEIR SOUL,"
cast much light on this passage. There the lust
is spoken of as the grave of the soul. And I
believe that it is the common form of God's judgment. Where He buries one in the wilderness,
He suffers a thousand to bury themselves in their
lust. It is the inevitable end of all wanton self-
indulgence; either a sharp judgment, or that slow
pining of soul which makes the body its grave.
Graves! why there are a hundred before me at

this moment. Where is the promise of your youth, sensualist! where the resolution of your manhood? Where is the purpose which that night on bended knees you uttered, and asked to have registered in heaven? where the protestations and vows to live "a godly, righteous, and sober life, looking for that blessed hope, the glorious appearing of the great God, and our Saviour Jesus Christ?" Where?—dead as the leaves of summer! And where are the graves? I need only look on that sensual face, that bloated form, that dull and glassy eye, that brazen brow, to tell. They are buried there, deep down in the flesh you pamper; and there they rot, and rot the flesh that shrouds them, and will rot on till the last great burning day. How many of us are growing in wisdom, pureness, nobleness, charity, and grace, as the years roll on; more Christlike, less disfigured and flawed by the blemishes of the flesh? In how many do we now search in vain for fruits whose flowers once bloomed there; for generous emotions, swift responses to the appeals of sorrow, unselfish ministries, and stern integrity? How many have learnt now to laugh at emotions which once had a holy beauty in their sight; to fence skilfully with appeals which once would have thrilled to the very core of their hearts; to grasp at advantages which once they

would have passed with a scornful anathema, and
to clutch at the gold which was once the glad
instrument of diffusing benefits around! Yes!
there are graves enough around us—graves of
passion, graves of self-will, graves of lust.

There is that pompous and impressive mil-
lionnaire, a man whose word is good for millions,
to whom the leaders of commerce pay deference,
as to a great power in their state. He is most
admirably correct in all his transactions; a good
giver, too, liberal by repute, his name is against a
large sum in all *public* subscriptions. Go to him
with a case which the rulers and Pharisees believe
in, and you will never be sent empty away; but let
a poor wretch cross his private path and whine for
a morsel, a dog would hardly get such a brutal
rebuff. Let a servant in his employ yield in a
dark hour to temptation, wrong him, and throw
himself on his mercy, you may get blood out of a
rock sooner than one compassionate word from
that ruthless heart. There is a whited sepulchre
of a soul! Once he was a poor boy; he had but
a crust in the wide world, and he shared it with a
poorer comrade, without a regret, without a care.
Once he loved, too, and was beloved. His heart
was large, warm, genial. He valued life for its
friendships and relationships; its claims gladdened him, its duties inspired. But that has

long, long been buried. A cold sneer, whenever
he thinks of it, is its epitaph. One day, when he
is dead, and they bear him pompously to his
splendid tomb, there will be lawyers and heirs at
his strong-box, to rifle the secrets which he has
so jealously and successfully hid. Pile on pile of
papers and securities is arranged there in admi-
rable order. But there is an inner cabinet, a
secret drawer—surely the sum of the whole is
treasured there, the coveted balance-sheet of his
affairs. No key is found, no spring can be discovered; they burst it open at length, and find
there—a faded letter, a withered flower, and a
lock of a woman's hair! He buried them there
years ago, when he buried his higher nature, of
which they are the memorial, in—himself.

There is a brilliant woman of society; so gay,
so witty, so genial, so friendly, the life of her
circle, the idol of a crowd of empty friends. At
home—and she is rarely to be found there—there
is a chill, bad atmosphere. The children are
made over to a careless governess; the mother
cannot bear their worry. The husband is simply
the sponge which she squeezes with ruthless constancy for her expenses, and casts aside as ruth-
lessly when that one end is gained. Society is
her idol; a place, a name, an influence, she will
have, at any cost; and she is digging another of

the Kibroth-hattaavah—the graves of lust.   Once
there was a warm, wifely, motherly heart in her;
once she looked up fondly in that man's face, and
vowed to be the joy and sunlight of his life.   Once,
beautiful, holy tears filled her eyes as she gazed
down on her first-born on her bosom, and vowed
a mother's love and tenderness to the little nursling of her heart.   But that was all buried long
ago.   The world possesses her wholly; she is the
mere charnel-house of a soul.   The finer natures
feel it already, and avoid her; and soon all will
see it and shrink from its corruption.   Your worn-
out woman of the world looks more like a
sepulchre than anything else upon this earth.

There is another man; a father, let us say,
with a cheerful home, wife, children, and sufficient comforts round him, who persuades himself
that misfortune has marked him for her prey.
His son, the pride of his heart, may have dishonoured his name, or his daughter sullied the
purity of his home; his circumstances have become embarrassed; he struggles hard to keep
pace with the time, but finds himself falling slowly
but hopelessly into the rear.   He struggles all
the harder because the process is a slow one, and
he can fight against ruin inch by inch.   But the
battle is against him.   At home he has no joy;
abroad no hope.   Little by little he begins to find

some comfort in the passing exhilaration of drink; for the moment it enables him to laugh, and to snap his fingers at fate. The habit, once established, becomes tyrannous. He has no resources of mind or spirit to fall back upon, and no will to cry to Him who, when "all His waves and billows" were surging over David, "commanded His loving-kindness in the daytime, and His songs in the night." He begins to come home in the evening excited; he stutters out his requests; often he is plainly intoxicated; they have to lead him to bed like an idiot. Then he sits boozing alone by his own fireside, till his children get sick at heart, perhaps fierce against him; perhaps they fly his home to escape the atmosphere of misery he has created there. His wife, well-nigh broken-hearted, begins to seek refuge in the same excitements. They sit drinking together in their abandoned home; they exchange drunken caresses, or curses, as the case may be; they abuse each other's vices, they swear, fight, clutch each other by the throat, and their neighbours or children part them; they are overwhelmed with shame for the moment, but soon bury shame, too, in lust. The scene recurs, it gets talked of in the neighbourhood, whispered among friends; acquaintances cut them, friends remonstrate in vain, and forsake them, and their home becomes fairly a hell. The

accursed lust sets its mark on their forehead.
Bloated features, trembling limbs, stuttering
speech, and a mad thirst that goads them on to
deeper orgies. Friends, let us drop the veil.
God keep us from the temptation to bury misery
in a grave of lust!

Beware, young men; young women, beware!
The grave-diggers began their work far back, in
those wretched histories. The first step was the
really fatal one : the first flying, in sorrow and
heart-ache, to any refuge but God. Beware! for
the dead things buried in these graves will not lie
quiet; they stir and start, and ever and anon
come forth in their ghastly shrouds and scare you
at your feasts. No ghosts so sure to haunt their
graves, as the ghosts of immolated faculties and
violated vows. That purpose, that prayer, that
ennobling friendship or love, sacrificed to interest,
that high ideal of relationship abandoned for lust,
they are dead, but they have their resurrections.
The memories which haunt the worn-out worldling's bed of impotence or lust, are the true
avengers of Heaven. The brain loses power to
repel them, but retains power to fashion them.
Once it could drive away thoughts and memories;
now it can only retain them, and fix them in a
horrid permanent session on their thrones. Each
act of indulgence makes the grave wider and

deeper, where the whole breadth of God-like faculty will at length lie buried; and it fixes in the brain a memory which will one day turn tyrant, and be the dread avenger of a murdered hope. I know that the thought, "Rejoice, O young man, in thy youth," is strong in the young heart. "God is merciful to these young follies," you say; "age will give soberness, and repair the waste." If ever the devil is tempting you to believe that, and to break down the barriers which you have built up against the impetuosities of passion and the ragings of lust; if ever you feel that the firm hand is trembling, and that the reins of control are slipping from the strong grasp of the will, then open the eleventh chapter of Numbers; go out alone into that desert; look at those mounds which break its weary monotony, and spell out the word which is burnt into their headstones, sharp and clear at this moment as when the finger of God inscribed it, "KIBROTH-HATTAAVAH—THE GRAVES OF LUST!"

Sermon xiii.

The Common Levels of Life.

"And thou shalt remember all the way which the Lord thy God led thee these forty years in the wilderness, to humble thee, and to prove thee, to know what was in thine heart, whether thou wouldest keep his commandments, or no."—Deut. viii. 2.

TINIEST insects build up loftiest mountains. Broad bands of solid rock, which undergird the earth, have been welded by the patient, constant toil of invisible creatures, working on through the ages unhasting, unresting, fulfilling their Maker's will. On the shores of primæval oceans, watched only by the patient stars, these silent workmen have been building for us the structure of the world. And thus the obscure work of unknown nameless ages appears at last in the sunlight, the adorned and noble theatre of that life of man, which, of all that is done in this universe, is fullest before God of interest and hope.

It is thus too in life. The quiet moments build the years. The labours of obscure and unremembered hours edify that palace of the soul, in which it is to abide, and fabricate that organ whereby it is to work and express itself, through eternity. It is of these common places, or common levels of life, that I have now to speak to you, the obscure records of long wanderings through dull and dusty pathways in our wilderness world.

The history of this people must again be our guide. We left the Israelites mourning beside the graves of lust: we find them on the very borders of the promised land. The Desert behind them, bright Canaan before them, God's angel in the midst of them, waiting to lead them to victory and glorious rest. The fact that they are there, speaks an inspiring word to all of us. Blessed be Christ, we are none of us doomed to lie moaning by graves. Forth from the heart of the deepest darkness that ever settled over a grave, even of lust, the word of Him who is the resurrection and the life cometh unto the mourner, *" He that believeth in me, though he were dead, yet shall he live: and whosoever liveth and believeth in me shall never die."* It is well that we should stand by our graves and feel their awfulness; it is well that we should taste the agony of the chastised and smitten soul. But that man is false to Christ, and faithless, who suffers himself to be tempted to say, " There in that grave lie buried all my treasures; hope is bankrupt; a grave

20—2

henceforth is the sanctuary of my spirit; that headstone epitaphs my life."

I know that the temptation often presses heavily. In the first anguish of chastisement, it seems to us as if hope were fairly killed. But just as Kibroth-hattaavah was near to the border of Canaan, so are the graves by which our bitterest tears are wept, near to the bounds of heaven. The saddest and most hopeless case before man, is when a man has made a grave of himself, and has buried deep down in the slough of a worldly or sensual nature every bud and promise of his soul. Yet even these deep graves can be broken by the Saviour's voice. Even these dead men can rise. His hope is deeper than man's despair, for His arm is stronger than man's destroyer. You have but to cry to Him with the long strong outcry of a soul ready to perish, sinking into the graves of lust, and even thence His arm can snatch you, and set you in front of the promised land.

To me it is full of the grandest meaning. And oh! what a gospel it should be to you, who feel the soul well nigh buried in some sensual tomb, that the angel who led them did not destroy them there in the mass, every man of them, while the flesh was yet between their teeth, and passion was mad; he but smote them sharply, and then led

them on to the vision of the land of rest. It was
a weary march on from Kibroth-hattaavah to
Kadesh, probably as far as we can identify the
stations, the dreariest of the whole route, (it is
never a bright path, that onward march from a
grave) : but their next station set them actually
within sight, within reach of rest. Their merciful God did not accept their lusting for flesh as
their final decision. One act of sensual lust,
dark, deadly as it was, was not to be the turning
point of their lives. Once more they were to go
forth one step out into a clearer air than that
which steams around the fleshpots, and under a
brighter heaven; and then it should be settled,
and settled finally. Shall it be a brief stern
battle march to Canaan and triumph, or a shameful rout to the wilderness and death? Whatever
may *seem*, it is never on one hasty act of passion
that destiny hinges; it is on the broad, calm,
decisive elections of the soul. Men curse the
passionate acts, or the unpremeditated moments
which seem to cast a shadow upon the whole of
their life course, and give a new character to their
future. The roots of the acts lie in the depths
of their being, and such unpremeditated moments
are the fruits of the meditations of years. It is
the whole aspect of the soul, as its vision ranges
over the field of life's enterprise, counts the costs,

measures the perils, and balances the chances of
defeat or victory, that Christ is watching. The
vision is then clear, bright, enchanting. " The
land is a good land," cry the heavenly voices;
" surely it floweth with milk and honey, and thou
art well able to overcome it." " Nay," cry the
earthly, " but the Anakim are there; the cities
are walled and strong; the battle must be long
and desperate, and we are but as grasshoppers
in the presence of those gigantic foes. The case
is hopeless, the strain of the battle is harder than
we can bear; even Canaan is not worth winning at such a cost. Back! back! We are not
fit for great enterprises. Sadly enough we feel
it; the fleshpots must be our portion, and Egypt
must be our grave."

There is one grand damning sin of man—
unbelief. That people " believed not, and their
carcases fell in the wilderness." It is not on any
isolated sin or even crime, but on the deep unbelief
of our hearts, broadly, strongly, finally expressed,
that the angel sets our faces decisively to the
wilderness, and trains us there in long marches,
wanderings, and conflicts, for a glorious possession
of the promised land. This is the root sin of all
of us. A comparison of the topic of the eleventh
chapter of the Hebrews, with the first verse of the
twelfth, will show that this is the sin of which the

apostle is speaking, when he warns us of the sin
" which doth so easily beset us." It is just this
faithlessness. And it is when this root sin of our
nature is laid bare, as it is laid bare in every one
of us before the eye of God, that He turns us
back into the desert from the very edge of the
land of rest. " *And thou shalt remember all the
way which the Lord thy God led thee these forty
years in the wilderness, to humble thee, and to prove
thee, to know what was in thine heart, whether thou
wouldest keep His commandments, or no. And He
humbled thee, and suffered thee to hunger, and fed
thee with manna, which thou knewest not, neither did
thy fathers know; that He might make thee know
that man doth not live by bread only, but by every
word that proceedeth out of the mouth of the Lord
doth man live. Thy raiment waxed not old upon
thee, neither did thy foot swell, these forty years.
Thou shalt also consider in thine heart, that, as a man
chasteneth his son, so the Lord thy God chasteneth thee.
Therefore thou shalt keep the commandments of the Lord
thy God, to walk in His ways, and to fear Him.*"
(Deut. viii. 2—6.)

The forty years' wanderings! What remains
of them? A list of unknown names, no more.
The dust of time has settled on the stations;
and the events, big at the time with interest to millions, are without a note in history.

What weary years of plodding marches through a dark unheavenly country; what dreads and dangers, what wants and distresses, what keen agonies and fierce complaints, that oblivious silence covers! They are all there, days of fighting, nights of weeping, years of trudging. They seemed at the moment as if they were burning an indelible mark deep into life records; as if things were done and suffered there, the memory of which would ache or glow through eternity; but they are already behind us, dim in the distance, a softening veil has fallen over the whole pilgrimage: a broad sense of pain conquered, shame endured, duty done; the consciousness that we have come out of the wanderings richer, braver, stronger, more earnest, but sadder, than when we entered the Desert, is all that is left to us. And this is the heritage which the obscure paths and hours hand down to all of us, to bear with us, if found faithful, into the inheritance of the promised land.

And this brief abstract of the wanderings is a chapter out of your life and mine. Who knows anything about ninety-nine out of every hundred of the moments which make our lives? Do we know much about them ourselves? Very many of the most important of our bodily movements are automatic. We contract the heart, expand the lungs, exhale the breath, without the slightest consciousness that we are at work in the very laboratory of life; and that if that work were stopped for an instant, this fair fabric would fall straightway into waste and death.

And how much of our higher activity, as intelligent and moral beings, is automatic too! It is no very conscious or noble act of volition which takes us down daily to our accustomed tasks, seats us at the accustomed desk, marches us through the same wearisome waste of figures, or yokes us to the same dull mill-wheel, where we grind, grind, grind, and make grist for the hungry mouths at home. It is just matter of strong and stern compulsion, as with those Israelites of old. We should like, when the reality of the life forces itself on us, a shorter and swifter path to our end. " Nay, but we *will* go up." We will storm fortune by a bold stroke, we will seize by a spurt of enthusiasm what will give us rest and plenty, and spare ourselves this monotony of toil and trouble all our days. But we are not fit for rest and plenty. It would be but indolence and surfeit ; we have shown our faithlessness too lately to be trusted. God will not let us go. He leads us out into the desert, where we *must* wander till our lusts, at any rate, are killed, where we *must* work and wait till the appetite gets tamed, where we *must* watch the bands of robbers who prowl around our encampments, till vigilance become perfect, and we are thus prepared by the daily habit of energy and patience to wield nobly the sceptre of the kingdom which we shall win. How much of our lives is hard dull duty, blank, bare, and dust-stained as that level plain—the El Tih, the vast dry limestone plateau of the desert which I have described to you * — contrasting so strangely with the rich interest of the Sinai desert—the dreariest scene of wanderings that can be conceived! It answers to the common levels of life; the unremembered years of undistinguished toil. The years of work to which we were bound, pining the while for nobler, and thinking that we were fit for it, though God did not; kicking under the yoke—something like the poor camels in those wastes, moaning and shrieking piteously under their burdens—but on the whole struggling on, bearing them manfully, not daring to unbind them, but pining—oh, how longingly!—for the hour when God should release us, and lead us, inured to duty, into the sunny pastures, by the living waters, of the long-lost, long-sought home!

Nothing of all these marches survives but a

* The name by which this dreary region of the Desert is known is El Tih, which means " The Wanderings."

vague memory of pain, patience, and hope. Those stations of our journey which stand out against the common background of life, the touches of form and colour which light up its neutral tints, —the Marahs, Elims, Rephidims,—are clear in memory at this moment, after the lapse of years, and will be clear through eternity. There I buried Rachel; there I wrestled with the Angel, and prevailed ; there the angels of God met me ; there I took my father's blessing ; there I sealed my covenant with God ; there my vows were shamefully broken ; there I grovelled in penitence, and was uplifted in prayer ; there I fainted under the burden of my cross ; there my soul sweat blood-drops in its Gethsemane, and there appeared unto me an angel from God strengthening me ;—we recall them all, clear as though the sunlight were on them, defining their outlines and blackening their shadows. These are the sacred treasures—these memories—which we bear with us weeping through our life-course here, and these are the fruit which shall enrich, the trophies which shall glorify, eternity.

In order that we may better understand the method of God in ordering our wilderness marches, let us consider—

I. The reason of " the wanderings." Why is so large a portion of our years spent under the

yoke of undistinguished duties, leaving no record
but " the wanderings" behind ?

Briefly, because a few critical experiences do
not make a character ; a few impassioned, enthu-
siastic moments do not make a life. We must
remember that this people had passed through a
series of exciting and impressive scenes, unparalleled in history. There had been crowded into
their last months, events which have made an era
in the history of eternity. They had lived rapidly
through the stages of experience which mark the
development of a life. They had passed from
infancy to manhood at a bound. The " stations"
had succeeded each other in swift succession; and
on each they had spent a treasure of thought and
feeling which, if husbanded, would have formed
the wealth of years. Higher and deeper experiences they could not have. Providence had
exhausted the art of impression, and the people
had exhausted the power of being impressed.
They had been awed, affrighted, warned, instructed, guided, inspired, but they had not had
time to live ; that is, to work the fruit of these
extraordinary moments of vision or suffering into
the common texture of their lives.

We are all, in fact, unconscious poets, and live
in the ideal. The commonest lover, after some
fashion, sings. We all dream our dream of Utopia.

We have all our Atlantis there across the waters; or visions of an Eden, contrasting strangely with the dry and dull daily wastes of life. We have our moments of high excitement, when the spirit is stirred, and asserts its mastery. Thick films seem to fall from the eyes of sense, and the nerves are strung to catch the most tremulous vibrations of that finer fluid, which is the channel of all the higher communications of our world. It seems, at such moments, as if the organ of capacity had grown within us to grand proportions; as if we had but to will, to throw off the fleshly clog for ever, and step forth into a world in which the soul's volitions, sympathies, and elections should be supreme. We dream a poet's dream of life, and we awake, thinking for the moment that we hold what we touched in dreams. The day of duty disenchants us. We find that the glow of the spirit, fired with momentary passion, is not strength; that the vision of what life may be, is not life.

The children of Israel there before the Mount, saw the vision. The glorious splendour, the thunderings, lightnings, and the voice of God, so overawed their spirits, so crushed down their sensual lusts and choked back their faithless murmurs, that it seemed for the moment the most glorious and noble life, to serve such a Lord

Jehovah as this. "All that the Lord hath said
unto us that will we do," they cried to Moses,
when he rehearsed before them all the Lord's
commandments; and they meant it heartily, as
you have meant it, when the spell of the world
has been broken for the moment, when under the
word of some inspiring preacher, or under the
shade of some terrible calamity, or in some of
those high moments of visitation, which—how,
why, we know not—do at times bring the reality
of God and heavenly things most blessedly near
to our hearts. You have then lifted your heart
to God with a passion of supplication that He
would take you to be His pilgrim, and lead you
by His own good path to His home. How long
was it before those Israelites were dancing around
their golden calf, and singing, " *These be thy gods,
O Israel, that led thee out of the land of Egypt.*"
And where are your vows? Where the sword and
shield which you then girt to you? Where the
crown which was then in sight? May God help us
not to live by dreams! We have our moments of
vision, blessed be God, before the pilgrimage
begins; clearer, brighter, more blessed moments,
like Moses, like Paul, we have before the pilgrimage ends. But a moment's intense vision, high
resolution, earnest endeavour, glorious victory,
will not expand into a grand Eternity. God will

try us, what metal we are of within ; what lies under all exceptional experience ; what He can rely upon to maintain in constancy a high, full pulse of life.

Hence we are taken forth to Kadesh. The whole country is spread before us ; God's vocation reaches us,—clear, solemn, decisive ; He calls on us to go up to possess the land. To every human spirit the vocation comes once at any rate. "Go up and possess thy land of promise ; make real thy dreams. Thou hast had a vision of this to sustain thee through many an earlier desert march ; and now it is here, go up and take it. Have done with sin, with tremor, with murmuring, for ever ; live a divine man in a broad and wealthy land." And none of us is able. No man lives up to the level of his young resolutions and aspirations ; no man keeps his heel firmly on the lusts and passions which in moments of divine visitation he scorned. Who is able to square his life by the heavenly rules which at such moments seem so grand and fair ? The moment comes when the senses fire again, and grow mad after their idols ; when the heavenly rules have a veil dropped over them, they are too pure for a world like this ! And at last the vision comes to be remembered with a kind of contemptuous wonder,

" Was I ever fool enough to entertain in earnest such a dream of life ! "

The inevitable falling off of the common hours and experiences, from the level of the moments when our life gets up into the world which was made to be its home, seems to me to be the great teaching of this passage of Israel's history. It is a broad fact in the history of every life ; in a measure, of every day's life, for the great cycles repeat themselves in little, as the organs of the body are present potentially in every part. But these narratives gather up the scattered incidents of our moral life into one grand incident, and show us with a large dramatic point and emphasis, what we are daily doing under the eye of the great Leader, which makes these long, dry, unnoted wanderings inevitable ; what it is which compels Him to impose what I have called the yoke of undistinguished duty, and to lead us up and down in the wilderness, that we may, if we will yield ourselves to His hand, work the sublime lessons, which we cannot learn and practise in a moment, into the common daily texture of life, that is, of eternity. We will now pass on to consider,

II. The purpose of the wanderings.

Briefly, again, to work godly principles of action into the common texture of our daily lives. To make it a matter of perpetual, quiet choice and habit to square every action by the rule of the mind of God.

There are two states of mind possible, and more than possible, about these wanderings. There are two states of mind with which we are constantly meeting, with regard to the commonplace character of so much of our daily lives. We may say, " It is weary work, but we must do it ; God yokes us to it, and there is no escape from Him. But we have no call to put anything into it but submission. Submit we must, and will ; but we have no need to do more, for the thing we hate. We must just go through with it, if God compels us,—by those modes of moral compulsion which preserve our liberty, and yet necessitate action in the direction which He has decreed—to waste almost the whole of our lives in a round of busy occupations which simply wearies us ; to which, perhaps, by some act of a half-awakened nature, we bound ourselves in youth, by a bond which we have to honour sorrowfully with matured sympathies and developed powers. We must just go through with it. We shall not flinch. The work shall be done, the round shall be tramped as speedily as may be, and then we will give ourselves up to thoughts, reminiscences, or longings, which will embody the true aspiration and bias of our hearts." Or we .

may say, " God has bound us thus, because He
loves us most tenderly; not to compel us by His
bare will, but because He is Himself compelled by
His great love. Not in bitterness, not in wrath,
not even in judgment, if we could fathom the
deepest springs of His will, has he relegated us to
this wilderness. It is before Him, less a judgment
on the past than an education for the future,
though it partakes of both characters : it is
because of the great world—a good land and a
large—into which He will bring us out, and the
God-like work He has for us in eternity, that He
has sent us hither, and bound us to tasks which
fret and exhaust us. We shall be in the way of
blessing in doing them heartily, in exercising our
noblest faculties on our most common duties, in
making the sphere of our daily toils and frets
illustrious by heavenly strength, patience, and
hope : content, if we miss the fruit in the present,
if, like seed-corn cast on the waters, it vanishes
from touch and sight, to believe that we shall find
it again—the fruit of every grain with royal increase—in the long day of eternity."

I say there are these two states of mind possible
about those wanderings—the first common, the
last, alas! more rare. There are no records to
tell us, but I know well which this people elected.
I can see it in their gallant courage when they

stood again before the gates of Palestine ; in their prompt submission to every divine behest ; in their brave endurance of the toils and perils under which once they fainted; and in their manly resolute adherence to their covenant with God, in the face of all the discouragement which drove their fathers into the desert, and made them ready to fly to Egypt, to fly anywhere, if they might but escape from a God who seemed to demand so much of them, — who seemed to expect of poor weak mortals that they should aim, at any rate, at that lofty life which would liken them unto Himself.* The following passage out of the book of Joshua will amply sustain my words, and show how much this people had gained :—" And if it seem evil unto you to serve the Lord, choose you this day whom ye will serve : whether the gods which your fathers served that were on the other side of the flood, or the gods of the Amorites, in whose land ye dwell : but as for me and my house, we will serve the Lord.   And the people answered and said, God forbid that we should forsake the Lord,

---

* It is no answer to this view to say that those who went into Canaan were the sons—the sires fell in the wilderness. We have a right to speak of the nation as a unity ; and more than this, if the fathers had continued in a slavish or murmuring mood, their sons had never been nursed to such godly manhood.

to serve other gods ; for the Lord our God, He it
is that brought us up and our fathers out of the
land of Egypt, from the house of bondage, and
which did those great signs in our sight, and pre-
served us in all the way wherein we went, and
among all the people through whom we passed :
and the Lord drave out from before us all the
people, even the Amorites which dwelt in the
land : therefore will we also serve the Lord ; for
He is our God. And Joshua said unto the people,
Ye cannot serve the Lord : for He is an holy God ;
He is a jealous God ; He will not forgive your
transgressions nor your sins. If ye forsake the
Lord, and serve strange gods, then He will turn
and do you hurt, and consume you, after that He
hath done you good. And the people said unto
Joshua, Nay ; but we will serve the Lord. And
Joshua said unto the people, Ye are witnesses
against yourselves that ye have chosen you the Lord,
to serve Him. And they said, We are witnesses.
Now, therefore, put away, said he, the strange
gods which are among you, and incline your heart
unto the Lord God of Israel. And the people
said unto Joshua, The Lord our God will we serve,
and His voice will we obey. So Joshua made a
covenant with the people that day, and set them
a statute and an ordinance in Shechem. And
Joshua wrote these words in the book of the law

of God, and took a great stone, and set it up there under an oak, that was by the sanctuary of the Lord. And Joshua said unto all the people, Behold, this stone shall be a witness unto us ; for it hath heard all the words of the Lord which He spake unto us : it shall be therefore a witness unto you, lest ye deny your God. So Joshua let the people depart, every man unto his inheritance." —Josh. xxiv. 15–28.

There is the fruit of the forty years' wanderings, the commonplaces, the common events of their lives. They became noble, daring, patient soldiers of the Lord God of Hosts, who was able to speak to them with a plainness, and wield them with a force, unparalleled in any other period of their or the world's history. And how did they attain to it ? We can answer absolutely, by repeating, day by day, day by day, day by day, the lessons which they had learnt in those high moments in which they had seemed to be exalted above the human level, and to be admitted within the veil to God. Daily, during those forty years, we may be well assured, the Lord was repeating the lessons of Marah, Elim, Rephidim, and Sinai ; not under the high excitements which lifted those stations so far above the ordinary human ranges of experience, but in the quiet hours of daily pilgrimage, daily hunger, thirst, sickness, temptation, and terror of foes. Each day of their obscure wanderings was a high day in miniature; nay, perhaps more blessed than a high day, because the Lord could come nearer to the common levels of their experience, and edify there the structure of a noble and godly life.

Brethren, if our holy days are to shed no sacredness on our work days, we are better, far better, without them. Better Egypt, the flesh-pots, the fish, the melons, the garlic, and the slave's carelessness about his daily bread, than a life with visions of Heaven which remain ever no more than dreams. If you keep all the richer interest of your spirit for the holy days of life, if you concentrate all your thought and fervour in the moments when you seem to be lifted into the empyrean regions, and breathe the air of a diviner world than this, you are doing your best to turn into foolishness God's counsels about your wanderings in the wilderness of life. You can do it if you will. Man *can* turn God's wisdom into foolishness. He may make his forty years' wanderings—the term of an average manhood— a weary, hateful drudge, and fall ignobly at the end of it, leaving his bones to bleach on the sand. But this people judged more nobly of their vocation. They learnt bravely, in their years of toil and trudge, the lessons which, in the high

days of their wilderness career, had slipped so
swiftly out of their hearts. They accepted the
daily discipline; failed often, murmured often,
repented often, and renewed their way; but
always with a clear growth of strength and wisdom,
a higher spring after each recoil; until God saw
that they were fit for the enterprise at the sight
of which their fathers fainted, and led them up to
the swift conquest and armed possession of the
land.

And now tell me, brother, is the wilderness a
loathed and soul-wearying pilgrimage, or a grand
training-ground of God? Are you despising your
daily tasks, or magnifying them? Do you cry
wildly, "Why does God tie me here to tasks which
I abominate? Oh! for some work which will meet
and satisfy the finer appetites and subtler sympathies of my soul; but this wholly expends my
higher faculty: it makes life a waste, and the
future a blank." Or do you say, "God, my God,
has bound me here, because He knows what
eternity means, and what I have to do there.
Because of the grandeur of my future, He is not
ashamed to make the scene of my present discipline so bare and poor. He is training me to be
faithful in the few things thoroughly; to rule the
little that is under my power with the bold, free,
royal hand of the heir of a kingdom; then He

will lift me to a throne. Be my one work here to
make the commonplaces and levels as full of His
presence as the Holy of Holies, where His glory
dwells ; so to beautify earth's dull paths by
heavenly patience and joyfulness, that the angels
of God may frequent them ; and to handle the
commonest tools and materials as a man who is
daily building up a character and a destiny, which
will rise, stately and fair, not among the perishing
fabrics that shall share the wreck of earth's dissolution, but in the calm heaven of eternity.

This leads me to speak of—

III. The "wanderings," in view of their eternal
results.

They, obscure and unprofitable as they may
seem, are the builders for eternity. It is easy to
say that the great crises make the common experiences of our lives, and determine both their
track and character. There is a surface truth in
such an impression. It is at the great crises that
the changes in character and course become manifest ; and we are ready to believe easily that the
reasons of them, too, are there. The grand direction of our life-course seems to be determined
by what transpires in critical moments, in which,
as far as our consciousness is concerned, our
will is well nigh powerless, while the current of
external influence eddies around us, and whirls us

away. True enough : it does seem just to seize
us and sweep us away. But what makes the
"us?" What makes that within us which will
yield to it, and be swept along pleasantly by its
current, lulled by the soft music of its waters, till
they cast it up, a wreck, on some rock-bound,
eternal shore ; or which will battle against the
current, will sooner or later make some landing,
it may be but on some dreary, marshy islet, and
will begin at once to edify there a fortress of life ?
What makes that ? First, fundamentally, effectually, the Spirit of the living God, the Holy
Ghost, who "worketh in us to will and to do of
His own good pleasure." "Not by might, not
by power, but by My Spirit," saith the Lord, and
saith the awakened human conscience, of every
effectual stand against evil, of every fortress of
life which is edified against sin. But there must
be concert of the clinging and trusting human
will with the victorious force of the Spirit, in order
to the realization of the fruits of spiritual life.
That the faithless multitude in all ages is swept
away by the current, must have some other reason
than that the Spirit—who with the Father and
the Son is Love—is not willing to put forth effectual power to save them. Those men there, before
the gates of Canaan, settled their own destiny,
against the commands of God and the testimony

of His witnesses. Stephen testifies that this was
a resisting the Holy Ghost; and against the same,
the multitude are settling their destinies still. And
it appears to me most important that we should
understand that no mere moment, no isolated act
of choice, under a pressure of temptation, settles
destinies. The quiet, undistinguished years decide
the matter for the moments when the election is
finally and openly made. It takes years to give a
form and bent to a character. Temperament we
are born with, character we have to make; and
that not in the grand moments, when the eyes of
men or of angels are visibly upon us, but in the
daily quiet paths of pilgrimage, when the work is
being done within in secret, which will be revealed
in the daylight of eternity.

Habits, like paths, are the result of constant
actions. It is the multitude of daily footsteps
which go to and fro which shapes them. Let it
light up your daily wanderings to know that there—
in the quiet bracing of the soul to uncongenial
duty, the patient bearing of unwelcome burdens,
the loving acceptance of unlovely companionship
—and not on the grand occasions, you are making
your eternal future. It is the multitude of little
actions which make the great ones. I mean this
absolutely. Tell me the habit of a man's soul in
his daily undistinguished wanderings, and I will

tell you the part he is destined to play in the great crises of life. As I have said, they appear to be independent of the common hours. As if a man were lifted out from among the looms of time, above their rush and din, into the calm presence of the Eternal. It may be so. God has wondrous power to lift us out of ourselves, to set the naked spirit before His face ; but the man has already settled it in his quiet years of wandering whether, like the Israel of the old generation, he shall sink down from that lofty height to grovel among the fleshpots, or whether that moment of vision shall lift his whole life nearer to heaven and to God.

And much of the work of these quiet hours will never appear on earth. It lies deep down in the very framework of the being; or is gathered as nourishment around its germ—the albumen of the seed of the everlasting future. Much discipline appears to be wasted even in God's elect pilgrims. Had we seen that host as they approached the term of their wanderings, I doubt if we should have estimated them as God estimated them—fit for a conquest and a kingdom. Much of the work was done in them, is done in us, where no eye sees it but God's. The deeper it lies, the less it often shows on the surface. The exterior habits of the life, and the customs of the dull, unheavenly world, may hide for awhile much of the fruit of

the long wilderness discipline from every eye but
His.   But let a great crisis come, let the trumpet
sound for some great battle, let the giant hosts be
marshalled to hold the entrance to the promised
land, and then all earth, all heaven, shall see
how much has been gained. The soul, braced
by its obscure years of discipline, shakes off the
tatters of its desert dress, and the tricks of its
desert life, and stands erect, compact, with armour
bright and trenchant sword, the resistless heir of
the kingdom, the fell foe of the devil and his
works.   And then shall the way of God be justified by its issues—then shall the wisdom of God
be magnified in His sons.

Would to God, brethren, that I could convey
to you the earnestness of my conviction that
these obscure moments are the parents of the
ages; that when we least think it we are edifying
our eternity. These are the tiny insects which,
with constant toil, are building the structure of
the palace of the soul. The finer touches, the
higher expressions, may be impressed in the
critical moments; but the great substance out of
which the individual features grow, and of which
they are the revelation, you are fabricating day
by day in your daily marches on the common
levels of life.   I am persuaded that, were our
senses fine enough, we should see how that ex-

pression of feature which is the man's characteristic, runs through every atom of him; not otherwise is it with the expression of the higher life.

I have spoken of Israel here as a unity. I have but touched lightly on the fact that one generation perished, and another was trained in the wilderness for conquest. For the nation *is* a unity, and as a unity we are bound to treat it; it is the nation which is doctrinal to us. The nation was driven forth into the wilderness to its temptations; the nation was trained there for Canaan and rest. Each generation has those who fall and those who endure; and that means very largely, those who are reverent and those who are contemptuous of their daily lives. Despise the moments, young spirit, and the years will avenge it; and your carcase, when the wanderings are over, will lie and rot in the waste. Honour the moments, the years, the ages will reward it; and God will crown that faithfulness with the fadeless crown in the day of the manifestation of His sons.

Sermon xiv.

Pisgah: The Visions.

" And Moses went up from the plains of Moab into the mountain of Nebo, to the top of Pisgah, that is over against Jericho. And the Lord showed him all the land."—Deut. xxxiv. 1.

GOD help us, if there is to be no open vision! no glimpses of what lies above and beyond the darkness and dulness of our world! The soul can live on little, but it must have its taste of the food of angels; it can hope against hope, but it must have its vision, however rarely, to refresh its sight. A path which never rises above the dreary level of its wilderness march, ends at last in madness or paralysis. It is the mountain summits which make " the pastures " bearable. If the common hours, the monotonous daily rounds, are building life's fabric as we have seen, these moments of vision add the head-stones of beauty and the touches of grace. The solid substance of the structure is the work of the busy, undistinguished moments; but the plan was drawn in some brief hour which concentrated the

thought and emotion of a lifetime, which other
suns than that which quickens this world lighted,
and other voices than those which make the hum
of this world's business filled.

We belong to two worlds. Neither the one
nor the other completes our life. It is the action
and reaction of their influences, the intermingling
of their currents, which ministers to our vital progress. But if the one world claims us chiefly in
quantity, and ninety-nine out of every hundred
of our moments are given to undistinguished duty,
the one in which we rise into the clear celestial
atmosphere, and sweep the eagle eye of the spirit
round the horizon of a wider world, is intense in
proportion, and loads itself with some divine
nectar wherewith to sweeten the bitterness of our
common cup, or rather fills itself, like the face
of Moses, with a glory which shines on in the
glooms of the lower world. Who does not pity
the man, with a pity from which it is hard to
exclude a touch of scorn, who is content, if content be not too divine a name, to plod the mill-
round with a constant brute-like regularity of
motion ; what men call a life of " action," if
that is worthy of the name of action which is
uncheered by vision, unlit by hope.

And whence is the hope to spring ? If the
daily trudge through the monotonous pastures be

all that is open to us—if to eat, to drink, to march, to sleep, be the brief chronicle of every life—man is already at the end of all that life can offer. Worlds in fee could not help him ; oceans of pleasures, and an appetite to compass them—there is a near end to all that ; and you will soon hear a passionate cry that the end may come soon, "Let us die, and have done with this beggarly world for ever." It is, it must be, in what is lying beyond his sight and touch that the springs of hope are opened for man. In some world—is there such a world ?—where he may touch with the finer senses of his being the realities of which the shadows only mock him here ; where the bliss for which the inner organs ache, sometimes to desperation, may be tasted— full deep draughts which satisfy even a spirit ; where the soul's demands shall be met with full satisfaction, and the soul's elections shall be ratified eternally. These moments of vision are the answer. Get thee up, God-led, into thy mountain summit—it rises there close by thy wilderness path—and satiate thine eye with the vision of the glorious land. It lies there swimming in the sunlight ; the very air seems to palpitate with joy ; rivers, plains, soft mountain ranges, gleaming meadows, fair white cities, lakes that flash like gems, and mountain crests that glow like crowns

—it lies there beneath thee, softer, more lustrous, as earth is ever from mountain summits, than even thy dreams. And it is thine; thy heritage; thine for ever. Gaze, drink thy fill, stretch every sense to grasp the vision, and then rest awhile; rest, till God calls thee. Not here, not now, canst thou possess it; soon the dark rolling river shall be breasted; one struggle, one gasp, one plunge as into an unknown abyss—thou art there.

A being of two worlds! Oh! for some law of just subordination; some truth which shall strike justly the balance of their conflicting claims; some power of life, which shall extract by its potent chemistry the saps and juices with which the soil of earth can furnish us, while it lifts the divine part into diviner regions, and unfolds the beauty, and exhales the fragrance of our nobler nature in the air of its native spiritual world. The two worlds were more one in Eden than they have ever been since, or can ever be again, until the very memory of Eden is lost in the transcendent glory and bliss of heaven. Adam lived a simple life, we a double. His whole faculty exercised itself serenely on the visible around him, in calm intercourse with nature and with God. Sense, imagination, spirit, were all satisfied; at least as far as they were developed. Adam in Eden was still an undeveloped man.

22

In the second Adam, the Lord from heaven, the developed man, the complete image of God, alone appears. But to Adam it was not strange that the voice of the Lord God should be heard amidst the trees of the garden in the cool of the day: when he had fallen out of the pristine harmony by sin, then it became awful. Then, for the first time, he felt, what has been the source of the keenest suffering, but at the same time the school of the divinest discipline, to his children in all ages, that he belonged to two worlds which had lost their harmony; which would battle for the possession of his nature; whose conflicts, too, would be the torment, but also—for was not God on one side!—the hope of his life. And now there *are* two worlds, two natures: how to marry them is the one great question; how of the twain to make one flesh. The world around man has fallen out of harmony with the highest in man. He is strongly beset by the temptation to divide himself, and give himself part to one, part to the other world. To let the daily round, the common task, have the share which they claim of his time and energy, in dull submission to the inevitable; and then to live what he calls his life in another, it may be a higher, but, alas! it tends terribly to become a lower, world.

In my last discourse I spoke of these common
levels. I asked why our loving Father has bound
us thus tightly by the yoke of duties which dis-
tress and afflict us; which seem to consume our
whole life in tasks which yield us none of the
higher satisfactions, and in which it is often
impossible to find any vital interest at all. And
I asserted that there is but one answer. It is
this daily round which makes life: and God will
have us *live*. Therefore He keeps us there. He
will have us put interest into them, if we cannot
find it in them. He will have us, through these
long, weary marches, work godly principles of
action into the vital texture of our being; and
by the daily reiteration of endeavour, the daily
exercise of vigilance, the daily play of the muscles
and organs of the inner man, in the effort to
make each humble act and passion of our lives
harmonious with the will of God, dignify and
finally glorify life.

This is the meaning of our El Tih—the wanderings. The daily, hourly repetition of heavenly
acts and efforts is training us for the life of heaven.
But we are weak and dim of sight. "Who is
sufficient for these things?" we cry. Who can
realize this ideal of a daily life? Not one of us,
alas! The idea, "the glory of God," of which
we all come short in all things, is ever above us,

far, far above us; but those, methinks, realize
most of it who know most what the mountain of
vision means; who sometimes give loose to the
imagination of the spirit, and suffer God to show
them, through that organ, some glimpses of the
things unseen, unheard, unknown, which abide
with Him on high.

To Moses was entrusted the noblest, but at
the same time the weariest, life-task ever committed to the hand of man.   As a nurse with a
sick and fractious child, he had borne through the
life of a long generation the burden of that people's
follies and sins.   The same sensual cry, " What
shall we eat, what shall we drink ? " was ever,
with a few bright intervals, sounding in his ears;
and the dread foreboding, that the Lord in
righteous anger would break forth on them and
consume them, was ever weighing on his heart.
Moses had fathomed the meaning of intercession.
He had lived for years the life of an intercessor,
standing between God and a faithless and sensual
race.   " Let me alone," the Lord had said, " that
I may consume them in a moment, and I will
make of thee a greater nation."   " Nay, O my
Lord," the father of his people had answered,
" let me perish; but for the glory of thine own
name, let this nation be saved."   That man had
a right to talk of intercession.   He took the

burden of those whom he represented before God
on his own heart. We utter a slight prayer for
our fellow-men, under a passing emotion, and
call it intercession. Let us learn from this great
leader, type in many deep ways of *the* One
Intercessor, what this awful privilege and power
implies. History, I think, has few greater records
than these: "And it came to pass on the morrow,
that Moses said unto the people, Ye have sinned
a great sin : and now I will go up unto the Lord;
peradventure I shall make an atonement for your
sin. And Moses returned unto the Lord, and
said, Oh, this people have sinned a great sin, and
have made them gods of gold. Yet now, if Thou
wilt forgive their sin—; and if not, blot me, I
pray Thee, out of Thy book which Thou hast
written. And the Lord said unto Moses, Whosoever hath sinned against me, him will I blot
out of my book. Therefore now go, lead the
people unto the place of which I have spoken unto
thee : behold, mine Angel shall go before thee :
nevertheless in the day when I visit I will visit
their sin upon them. And the Lord plagued the
people, because they made the calf, which Aaron
made."—(Exod. xxxii. 30–35). "And the Lord
said unto Moses, How long will this people provoke me ? and how long will it be ere they
believe me, for all the signs which I have showed

among them ? I will smite them with the pestilence, and disinherit them, and will make of thee a greater nation and mightier than they. And Moses said unto the Lord, Then the Egyptians shall hear it, (for Thou broughtest up this people in Thy might from among them;) And they will tell it to the inhabitants of this land : for they have heard that Thou, Lord, art among this people, that Thou, Lord, art seen face to face, and that Thy cloud standeth over them, and that Thou goest before them, by day time in a pillar of a cloud, and in a pillar of fire by night. Now if Thou shalt kill all this people as one man, then the nations which have heard the fame of Thee will speak, saying, because the Lord was not able to bring this people into the land which He sware unto them, therefore He hath slain them in the wilderness. And now, I beseech Thee, let the power of my Lord be great, according as Thou hast spoken, saying, The Lord is longsuffering, and great of mercy, forgiving iniquity and transgression, and by no means clearing the guilty, visiting the iniquity of the fathers upon the children unto the third and fourth generation. Pardon, I beseech Thee, the iniquity of this people, according unto the greatness of Thy mercy, and as Thou hast forgiven this people, from Egypt even until now. And the Lord said, I have pardoned according to thy word: But as truly as I live, all the earth shall be filled with the glory of the Lord."—Numb. xiv. 11–21. Happy for the people that it was with the great Intercessor that he pleaded; that he spake with One who had the plea which Moses urged, present with overmastering force within His own heart; One who bore the whole burden of that people's sin, the whole burden of the world's sin, before the righteous Father; and was Himself, at what cost we know, surety for their future, when He yielded to the prayer of His servant, and "pardoned according to his word." The people pined for a human mediator, a human organ of communication between themselves and God. "And the people said unto Moses, Speak thou with us, and we will hear; but let not God speak with us lest we die." How little did they understand that the Lord, whom they dreaded, loved them with a tenderness and pitied them with a compassion, of which the love and pity of Moses were faint shadows— a love and compassion which would draw Him from the heart of His glory to abide with them in shame and suffering, and to pour out His soul unto death that their souls might be saved. But it is the cry of the human in all ages. How grandly does Job utter it, " For He is not a

man as I am, that I should answer Him, and
we should come together in judgment. Neither
is there any daysman betwixt us, that might lay
his hand upon us both.   Let Him take His rod
away from me, and let not His fear terrify me;
then would I speak and not fear Him ; but it is
not so with me."—Job ix. 32-35. And how finely
does Elihu conceive of the necessary conditions
of mediation, though too swift to conclude, in his
fresh, young zeal, that in himself the conditions
were fulfilled. "Behold, I am according to thy
wish in God's stead; I also am formed out of
the clay.   Behold, my terror shall not make thee
afraid, neither shall my hand be heavy upon
thee."—Job xxxiii. 6, 7.   There is but One who
can stand instead of God; who can lay His
hand upon us both.   Elihu, and all mere human
daysmen, retire before the dark, deep problem,
avowedly impotent (Job xxxvii. 19, 20); He
only can stand for us before God, and stand for
God before us, who "was in the beginning,"
" who was with God, who was God ; " and " who
became flesh," " bone of our bone, and flesh
of our flesh ; " and manifested unto us the awful
glory of the Father, full, in the human Mediator's
countenance, of grace and truth.

But Moses came as near as man could come
to the conditions. A Godlike man verily, a man

not afraid of suffering for men ; a man willing,
if he might, to save men by the sacrifice of himself, like God. The burden of that people he
bore through life ; never for one instant was he
permitted to lay it down. And to him, as to all
such, were visions vouchsafed of diviner brightness than meaner men could look upon. It was
when fresh from beholding the form of the glory
of the Lord, and with the sublime word of promise, "Doubtless I will be with thee," still ringing in his ear, that he prayed that prayer, and
prevailed to save that host from death. But for
that moment of open vision he had never faced
the drearihood of the desert ; but for that word
of ample promise he had never borne so patiently
their murmurs and cries of lust. The glooms of
his daily marches were lit by the glory which still
streamed down from that cleft of the rock on
Sinai ; and the discords that jarred around him
were lost, were blent into some grand breadth
of harmony, by the music of that everlasting promise of his Lord. He had visions such as no
other man has seen of what was behind the veil;
for he had to do, before the veil, such work as no
other man has done.

And for him, as for many a faithful pilgrim,
the brightest and most blessed vision was the
last, from the last mountain-summit which lies on

the hither side of the river of death.   The long,
long wandering of that people was over; El Tîh,
with its dreary levels, its dusty tracks, its nameless stations, was behind them.   Before them was
all of which they and their fathers for generations
had dreamed.   But one man, in all the mighty
host which stood there before the gates of Canaan,
should never press its sod—and he their prophet
leader; the man who for forty years had borne
their burdens, led their marches, and been to
them the pledge of the promised land.   The hope
of it had filled his heart through that weary pilgrimage, from the hour when he struck the first
blow of deliverance in Egypt, to that in which he
stood, with the army he had trained to order and
hardihood, before its gates.   But the word had
gone forth, "Get thee up into this Pisgah, and
die."   Why?   Because Canaan was too rich a
reward for such a life course, or because God had
awaiting him a better Canaan in heaven ?

There is something profoundly touching in this
narration of Moses : " And I besought the Lord at
that time, saying, O Lord God, Thou hast begun to
show Thy servant Thy greatness, and Thy mighty
hand : for what God is there in heaven or in earth,
that can do, according to Thy works, and according
to Thy might ?   I pray Thee, let me go over, and
see the good land that is beyond Jordan, that

goodly mountain, and Lebanon. But the Lord was wroth with me for your sakes, and would not hear me : and the Lord said unto me, Let it suffice thee ; speak no more unto me of this matter. Get thee up into the top of Pisgah, and lift up thine eyes westward, and northward, and southward, and eastward, and behold it with thine eyes : for thou shalt not go over this Jordan, But charge Joshua, and encourage him, and strengthen him : for he shall go over before this people, and he shall cause them to inherit the land which thou shalt see."—Deut. iii. 23–28.

"For your sakes," always, for your sakes ! For your sakes even I must die here, while you go over to possess the land. There is judgment here without doubt. "And Moses and Aaron went from the presence of the assembly unto the door of the tabernacle of the congregation, and they fell upon their faces : and the glory of the Lord appeared unto them. And the Lord spake unto Moses, saying, Take the rod, and gather thou the assembly together, thou, and Aaron thy brother, and speak ye unto the rock before their eyes ; and it shall give forth his water, and thou shalt bring forth to them water out of the rock : so thou shalt give the congregation and their beasts drink. And Moses took the rod from before the Lord, as He commanded him. And

Moses and Aaron gathered the congregation together before the rock, and he said unto them, Hear now, ye rebels ; must we fetch you water out of this rock ?   And Moses lifted up his hand, and with his rod he smote the rock twice : and the water came out abundantly, and the congregation drank, and their beasts also.   And the Lord spake unto Moses and Aaron, Because ye believed me not, to sanctify me in the eyes of the children of Israel, therefore ye shall not bring this congregation into the land which I have given them.   This is the water of Meribah ; because the children of Israel strove with the Lord, and He was sanctified in them."—Numb. xx. 6–13.

I say there is judgment here ; but as with all God's judgments there is mercy behind it.   There is always mercy in judgment here, if we will have it, and let God work His benignant will.   There was judgment in the expulsion from Eden, the first sentence on the human race ; but to those who review the wilderness from the battlements of the heavenly city, that very expulsion will be the theme of an outburst of praise.   In mercy to this man of God, this aged shepherd of Israel, God led him up to that summit of Pisgah, and showed him all the goodly land, but suffered not his foot to press its sods.   The people entered that land as the Lord's avengers.   As with

Pompeii, as with Sodom, the land was weary of the vice and pollution of its people, "the land itself vomiteth out its inhabitants," the Lord said, when He put the exterminating sword into the people's hand.* And what had the aged shepherd of Israel in common with scenes of struggle and slaughter? The fresh young race, hardy, daring, braced to a nobler manhood than that of their sires by the discipline of the desert, were ready for the shock. Armed for war they went up, to conquer with a red right hand their own. But that deep-thoughted, deep-hearted old man, who had found the desert silences the congenial comrades of his spirit, had caught the glow of the dawn on the mountain summits, and watched the dewy evenfall on the bosom of the parched waste for twice forty years, with an ever fresh wonder at the beauty and richness of His world who was leading Israel like a flock by His prophet's hand; whose work had been the creating of a nation, the calling of a church, the leading of a great multitude into an ever closer and deeper knowledge of the word and the ways of God—let him *see* the goodly land, with the sun-glow on it, shining through the transparent air; let him roam in imagination through the future

* It is most important to bear this in mind, when considering the exterminating character of the Jewish warfare in Canaan.

scenes of the glorious life of the people he had
loved and led; let him sweep his gaze over the
length and the breadth of the vision, from the
solemn peaks of Sinai, dim there in the distance,
to the swelling slopes of the far-off Hermon—
where one day he should leave his mountain tomb
to meet his transfigured Lord*— and away from
the many-tinted mountains of Moab, on whose
crest he stood, to the broad blue ocean sleeping
there in the distant haze; let him survey it all,
let his eye behold, let his heart clasp all the
beauty of the goodly land which had been his star
of hope through the desert; but let it be before
one blood-drop stains it, before those hills give
back one echo of the shout of infuriated foes.

In judgment, but full of deep tenderness, his
Father led him forth from the camp which he was
to guide no longer. His eye was not dim, nor
his natural force abated, as he climbed that summit—his eye ranging with a solemn joy as he
ascended, over fresh breadths of his promised land.
Was the sunset glow upon it when he reached
his resting-place? Was the land, in that splendid
transparent air, bathed in the lustrous sunset tones

---

* I am indebted for this thought to a passage in the
fourth volume of Mr. Ruskin's *Modern Painters;* in which he
describes this mountain vision, in words which are conspicuous
by their splendid eloquence even in his writings.

of which we have all had vision sometimes, and dreamed of the glories of celestial worlds? We know not: nor know we how, as the gloom settled on the vision, a darker, colder shadow fell around his spirit; but this we know, the Angel of Death who met him there had no unwilling follower; the spirits who watched for the spoils of mortality had not long to wait for their prize.

Something of that longing for rest, which seizes on the faithful servants of duty when their work is well nigh done, he bore with him up those mountain paths, where the steps of his young manhood had first learnt strength and swiftness, where his aged feet were now bearing him, how joyfully, to his rest. And some deep sense of the tenderness of His hand who had thus ordained for him, the perfect love of the Lord whom he should see at length in His glory face to face, inspired thanksgiving, as he prepared to pass from the solemn summits of that mountain world which had long been the sanctuary of his spirit, and in the sublime moment of vision, to that land of rest of which the Canaan at his feet was but the dim foreshining, the rest where all the faithful ones are at home with God, and for ever.

There was a full depth of tenderness in the counsel that led him thither; for who on earth, in this hard world, has realized his dreams?

To him Canaan could have been but a disenchantment. The Canaan of such men is to be found only on high. His land of promise was larger, fairer, more glorious, than that which lay basking in the sunlight at his feet. He had seen it through the eyes of hope, and in the light of the revelation of God. To tread its soil, abide in its cities, live with its inhabitants, whom his people with a fatal self-indulgence would spare—how fatal the narration of Bochim, in Judges ii., reveals—would have been to him no heavenly work. He had dreamt a dream of Canaan, and his God took him to a world where alone such dreams could be fulfilled. It seems like a hard sentence, but we may be assured that his spirit rejoiced when the summons came; as the mature and holy are ever glad when they catch the tread of the angel of death. To such, tempered to such fineness, purged to such pureness, earth can be but a scene of sorrowful and toilsome ministry; ever, but that it is checked by that care for others which they have learnt of Christ, they have "a desire to depart and to be with Christ, which is far better." He could not go into that land; no land of earth could be a home to such a spirit; God's judgment was a merciful angel, to conduct the worn-out soldier to his eternal rest.

Never had man so noble a lifework; never had man so grand a burial. How, where, no man knoweth. Somewhere, among those clear mountain heights, they laid him; God and the angels performed his obsequies; when earth next sees him, he is glorified with Christ. For when the Lord was transfigured, "there talked with him two men, which were Moses and Elias, who appeared in glory, and spake of his decease which he should accomplish at Jerusalem."

Brethren! am I talking idly, when I talk to you of visions? Have you never scaled the mountains that edge your wilderness, and swept your eye round a wider world than this? Israel's history, of which the life of Moses is the core, paints in visible form your life. Mountains, deserts, oases, wastes of sand, are there in solemn, if not dread, reality; but they are more dreadly real in the history of your lives. I know that the vision is not hidden from any one of you. I know that God will have you climb sometimes, and see some glimpses of what a man may be, and what, life. There is not an abandoned profligate who has not abandoned his vision to become profligate. Judas had once his vision—a vision of what a divine man might be, and a divinely governed world; perhaps, it was clearest in those days when he first joined the Lord. There are times when

23

there breaks in, on most of us at least, an awful
sense of the wealth of faculty with which God has
endowed us, and the glorious beauty and richness
of His world.   It comes to *us* but in gleams ;
there are those to whom the vision is ever
present.   "I never saw that in nature," said a
critic to Turner.   "I dare say not," was the
answer ; " but don't you wish you could, though ? "
His open eye saw what you and I can but dimly
trace in nature ; but you and I shall see it, ay,
and things infinitely more grand and fair, if the
spirit, quickened by Christ, and purged by discipline, bears up its faculty to the heavenly world.

I am not speaking here of that sense of the
Divine presence which attends the resolute and
earnest pilgrim, making his desert bright with
glory, and his night-watches glad with songs.   I
am speaking of moments when the spirit grows
intense, gathers all its force and fire, and takes a
horoscope of its powers and its destiny.   I believe
it is oftenest in sorrow that these sublime moments
come to us.   The spirit, oppressed with its burden
of cares, stirs itself to shake them off, and in
shaking them off, bounds at once to the mountain
summits of its world.   And there it ranges freely ;
it breathes a pure bright air, and sees the mists
rolling over the scene of its wanderings, while
above there is a clear heaven and God.   There is

an essential vigour in a God-sustained soul which a world's burdens could not crush to annihilation. It exults to feel that its springs of life lie deeper, and rouses itself in reaction to assert and wield a mastery over the world. "Why should a living man complain?" asks Jeremiah. A living man, one inscribed among the living in Jerusalem. Why, when he has life, God, and the future? A living soul! have you never had a vision of what a living soul may be, may do, may suffer, may know—the infinite capacity of life. I think sometimes, when I study the harmonies of this body of ours and the creation—the exquisite concords which, even through the dull menstruum of our sin-thickened senses are the springs of the intensest joys—of the rapture with which they shall one day fill the spirit, when these sensual films are shed, and the organ comes fairly into contact with its world.

I suppose that Angelo, Shakspeare, Milton, Turner, carried aching hearts about with them sometimes, when they caught the glow of a glory in the creation, which they could only partially behold. The sense of the infinite splendour, the glory of colour, tone, and form, of which God gave them vision, that they might show some part at least of what He had revealed to them to the world, saddened and oppressed them. It is

a "burden of the Lord" too, which His prophets
ever bear.   Who was it who wept much when he
beheld the vision ?   It was too high, too glorious,
for a mortal to take in.   There are moments
when the humblest of us see that the infinite
beauty, the infinite splendour, the infinite love
enfold us everywhere.   Is the finite other than the
portion of the infinite which we take in ?   And
those who have stretched out nearest to its bounds,
have the most intense sense of the boundless
beyond.   It is no human culture which affords us
this vision, which makes the soul ache and thrill,
as the senses ache with longing for their pleasures,
or the nerves thrill under the breath of love.

If I wanted to find men and women who live
much in vision, who "groan in this earthly
tabernacle being burdened," who tremble sometimes with an awful joy when God takes them
aside—takes them up into His mount, and shows
them the whole breadth of the heavenly land—I
would rather search in the homes of the weavers
of the Yorkshire valleys than in kings' palaces :
among those whose patient sinewy toil has
crowned our England with the imperial crown of
industry, and whose daily tasks and poor sur-
roundings show strange contrasts to the dreams
which haunt them, finding free utterance only in
their prayers, of what a home might be, what a

kingdom might be, what a human spirit might be, and what a world. If we want to find prophets in these days—men who live near to the Eternal, and whose vision ranges through the Infinite—I think that it is among the poor of this world that they are chiefly to be sought.

And perhaps a kindred reason may explain to us why our chief mountain of vision is on the hither side of the river of death. Death is prophetic. The seers who see most of the things unspeakable, are amongst those who are appointed to die. For those whom the Lord leads through the wilderness homewards, the last stage is a climbing of Pisgah. I have seen many such a dying, and I have rarely failed to mark, in those who were summoned, a sublime preparation for death. I have seen a light in dying eyes which was lit from no earthly fountain; I have heard broken murmurs on dying lips, whose heavenly meanings no mortal brain might know; songs gasped out by faltering tongues already tuned to concord with the hymns of angels; and smiles flitting over pallid, stiffening features, lighting up the mask of death with the likeness of the countenance which the departing spirit would wear before the Throne.

And why do the visions cluster most thickly around death? Because those who know what it

is to live must die to realize their dreams.   Like
Moses, they may see the land, but they must die
to inherit it—die with the vision before their
spirits, which fades for the moment as they die,
but when they pass, it is heaven.   To recover
Eden here is granted, thank God ! to none of us.
There is no man living who finds earth realize his
hope.   The ease-loving pilgrim never fails to find
his Goshen a bondage ;   the man of pleasure
never fails to find his Elysium a hell.   The excitement of pursuit is grand, inspiring.   " Let
me win this prize, let me clasp this treasure,
O my God, and I am satisfied ; ' Joy, joy for ever,'
shall be my song in my Paradise regained."   And
where is your Paradise ? and your Eve ?   You
have struggled hard to substantiate your vision.
" This same shall comfort us," you have said like
Lamech, of being after being, and thing after
thing.   Wealth, knowledge, power, pleasure,
friendship, love, all have been wooed to restore you
Eden, and in none of them are you at rest.   All
of them have been, according to your use of them,
either a spur, a noble stimulus to higher achievement, or a mass of corruption, which has lain,
since, lies still, rotting upon your soul.   No ! you
must die, to possess what your spirit touches in its
dreams.   We are long in learning this ; we fight
hard against the stern necessity ; and we spend

rich strength of brain and heart in realizing our
ideal. The struggle is appointed, and the failure.
The struggle, to brace and educate our spirits—
for the aspirations, which have shaped themselves
into efforts here, become the habits of eternity;
the failure, because God hath provided some
better thing for us than *our* ideal, even His own,
on high. Hope on, then, hope ever, faint pilgrim !
Strengthen the hands that hang down, and the
feeble knees, and make a straight path onward
through the desolate wastes of life. If vision
fades, get thee up into the mountain and renew
it, move to the music of heavenly choirs, work in
the brightness of heavenly sunlight, rest in the
bosom of heavenly love. Bless the hand which
breaks up thine Edens, and shows to thee visions
which earth must be purged and glorified to make
real. Be strong in patience, brave in suffering,
large, boundless, in hope. Be the pilgrim of
Canaan, led forth into the desert by the angel of
God's presence : not the exile of Eden driven out
by the cherub into the waste. Brace thy soul
for a life-long march through a desert of wanderings, for a ceaseless conflict with stern and un-
compromising foes ; but keep thine eye on that
mountain in the distance : it lifts its solemn
peak into the clear calm air, bathed in the light
of some hidden celestial sun. The day cometh

when an unseen hand shall guide you up its rugged slopes, panting, trembling, but pressing bravely on; the goodly land, unseen till then but in the mirror of hope, unfolding its breadth of beauty and glory as you climb; and when at length, from the summit, the whole stretch of the field of vision is beneath you, the angel who led you thither shall lift you to see the worlds, of which the vision is but a picture, on high.

Sermon XV.

Canaan: the Rest.

" The good land that is beyond Jordan."—Deut. iii. 25.

IT is there, a seer has seen it; and God gave him
words to paint the vision for us. A good land;
glorious in beauty, yet homelike; familiar in every
form and feature, but still a transfigured world.
It is the hope that lights the way of the wilderness—the hope that we may one day behold it,
that we may one day tread the paths and gaze
on the glories of a creation, which has been
" delivered from the bondage of corruption into
the glorious liberty of the sons of God."

If the wilderness marches of this people, which
we have traced to the edge of Jordan, be a picture of man's pilgrimage, the goodly land which
is beyond the dark rolling river must have some
pregnant suggestions of heaven. Its foreshinings
of what God has in store for the souls He loves
could be but dim, or Moses had been suffered to
go over to possess it; but they must have been
real, or the vision of it had never so gladdened

and uplifted his heart. In truth, the vision is the best part of all earthly satisfactions. To those who cannot look with the inner eye on all the prospects of this earth, and catch the glow of heaven's transfiguring sunlight upon them, that which may be seen of earth is bare as desert and black as night.

For long years this vision of Canaan had floated before his sight. It had led his marches through the wanderings, it had fed his imagination and filled his dreams. And the sight of the actual Canaan was granted. It was all of Canaan that was heaven-like. Imagination, not disenchanted by the bare and hard reality, gazed from that mountain brow over the splendid beauty and richness of the land, which spread, flooded with sunlight, at his feet. More like heaven to Moses in that hour, than even to Joshua and the heroes who won and held it; more worth the quest of a lifetime, more able to satisfy a spirit's hope.

To one only, the seer of the new Jerusalem, has a fairer vision been vouchsafed. To him heaven opened and the invisible appeared. He saw the Apocalypse of a world transfigured, as he had once seen transfigured the way-worn and tear-stained body of his Lord.

" And I saw a new heaven and a new earth: for the first heaven and the first earth were passed

away; and there was no more sea. And I John
saw the holy city, new Jerusalem, coming down
from God out of heaven, prepared as a bride
adorned for her husband. And I heard a great
voice out of heaven saying, Behold the tabernacle
of God is with men, and He will dwell with them,
and they shall be His people, and God Himself
shall be with them, and be their God. And God
shall wipe away all tears from their eyes; and
there shall be no more death, neither sorrow, nor
crying, neither shall there be any more pain : for
the former things are passed away."—Rev. xxi. 1-4.

I suppose that earth needs but the heavenly
lustre upon it to glow and shine like heaven.
Thus Moses saw the goodly land which had been
the dream of a lifetime, and had mingled its
beauty as the golden thread in the texture of the
noblest, manliest, godliest life-work ever accomplished in this world. Canaan had inspired it, if
duty had constrained it. It was the vision that
gleamed there over the dim bounds of the desert
to his prophetic sight, that lit those dreary
marches with touches of glory, such as on mists
that surge round the mountain peaks and steam
down their rugged flanks, warn night-weary
pilgrims of the advent of joyous day.

Brethren, it is the inspiration to all of us. The
dullest, darkest hearts have some dim prospect

of a better land, which makes it easier to endure.
None believe that the present is final. There is
no man's life, be his creed as atheistic as it may,
which does not, in its daily marches, toils, and
ministries, assume the existence of the God whom
it discredits, and the heaven which it denies.
Legends, golden legends, among all peoples, tell
of the heroic deeds of some divine leaders,—
Prometheus, Krishna, Beowulf, what matter their
names ?—who, by toil or suffering, have wrought
deliverances for man. The idea is there, enshrined in the heart of all the nobler peoples,
and uttered in their literature—there is a sense
in which it makes literature—and it prophesies,
with more or less explicit tones, the advent of
the righteous King. And men, dreaming of a
delivered humanity, have dreamed, too, of a
delivered world. The King who should come,
should deliver earth as well as man—should
reclaim its wastes, light up its gloom, and weave
its discords into the universal harmonies which
fill the sphere from which He came. How
grandly does the vision of a ransomed earth
cross the prophetic imagination of Isaiah, the
most regal, and, therefore, the most evangelic
of the seers. "Whereas thou hast been forsaken
and hated, so that no man went through thee,
I will make thee an eternal excellency, a joy of

many generations. Thou shalt also suck the
milk of the Gentiles, and shalt suck the breast
of kings : and thou shalt know that I the Lord
am thy Saviour and thy Redeemer, the mighty
One of Jacob. For brass I will bring gold, and
for iron I will bring silver, and for wood brass,
and for stones iron : I will also make thy officers
peace, and thine exactors righteousness. Violence
shall no more be heard in thy land, wasting nor
destruction within thy borders ; but thou shalt
call thy walls Salvation, and thy gates Praise.
The sun shall be no more thy light by day;
neither for brightness shall the moon give light
unto thee : but the Lord shall be unto thee an
everlasting light, and thy God thy glory. Thy
sun shall no more go down; neither shall thy
moon withdraw itself : for the Lord shall be thine
everlasting light, and the days of thy mourning
shall be ended. Thy people also shall be all
righteous ; they shall inherit the land for ever,
the branch of my planting, the work of my hands,
that I may be glorified. A little one shall become
a thousand, and a small one a strong nation : I the
Lord will hasten it in his time."—Isa. lx. 15–22.

A world, a home to dwell in, not cursed as this
is, with all its prophetic beauty—a world without
wastes, marshes, lava-floods, blights, famines,
plagues—a world that shall fit a redeemed, as this

fits a fallen, nature—a world whose paths shall
be the highways of angels, whose sun shall be
the face of God. "*This same shall comfort us*,"
said Lamech; "*concerning our work and the toil
of our hands, because of the ground which the Lord
hath cursed.*" The Deluge, as I have said above,
was gathering then, but he saw it not: he saw
beyond it. The cry of his heart, the cry of man's
heart, stretched out beyond the diluvial waters,
borne on the wings of an immortal dove. The
hope which he uttered, the Deluge could not bury;
the man Christ Jesus came to substantiate it; in
the "new heavens and the new earth, wherein
dwelleth righteousness," the faithful shall see it
fulfilled.

It is easy to talk sentiment or platitude about
heaven. It is less easy so to conceive of it, as to let
the vision brace the muscles of a patient, manly
life; and yet, be it what it may, this must be its
vestibule. A manly thoroughness in all occupations, toils, and duties, whether of heart, mind,
or body, must be the condition of a victorious
entrance into the land of promise, and of a session
on its throne. A vision which should make man
uneasy, unquiet here, is a child's notion of a
future, not God's. There is no uprooting, no
transplanting, essential to God's plan for us—
simply a growth through life to glory.

We will strive to climb our Pisgah, if we may, and survey the land. It will explain the past, it will justify the present, it will make the future more glorious than our dreams. It is there, close by us : behind the veil—a veil which the hand can touch ; nay, the hand of faith may lift it at any moment, may lift it now. There are not two worlds, but one, with its fore-court curtained, wherein, for the present, is our abode. But these bars of flesh are no adamantine barriers. Light permeates veils; and sound. There are those into whose hands these words may come, on whose lives the light which lights the angels to their tasks is calmly shining, and whose ears are gladdened in night-watches by the echoes of angelic hymns ; and for us all, the fact that that world is there — vivid, loving, glorious—makes this world brighter, its tasks less hard, its sorrows less intense. We may not see, nay, we may choose deliberately to ignore, the source from which our inspirations come to us; but such a world of vivid life spread round us, with only a veil to hide it, must kindle and quicken us. It makes our world other than a Hades : like the great burning African plain beyond our horizon, it modulates the atmosphere of our continent of life. There are those who could not drag themselves through their daily marches, if they did not catch some inspiration from its visions; but the great world of men, unconsciously or half-consciously, extracts or inhales from it something, which runs like an under-tone of promise through life.

A land whose physical features should be in bright contrast to Egypt's monotonous plains, was the picture which Moses held up before that people's sight: and the contrast is most instructive.

"For the land, whither thou goest in to possess it, is not as the land of Egypt, from whence ye came out, where thou sowedst thy seed, and wateredst it with thy foot, as a garden of herbs: But the land, whither ye go to possess it, is a land of hills and valleys, and drinketh water of the rain of heaven: A land which the Lord thy God careth for: the eyes of the Lord thy God are always upon it, from the beginning of the year even unto the end of the year. And it shall come to pass, if ye shall hearken diligently unto my commandments, which I command you this day, to love the Lord your God, and to serve Him with all your heart and with all your soul, that I will give you the rain of your land in his due season, the first rain and the latter rain, that thou mayest gather in thy corn, and thy wine, and thine oil. And I will send grass in thy fields for thy cattle, that thou mayest eat and be full."—Deut. xi. 10–15.

In Egypt, man's toil is the prominent feature; man made its fertility: in Canaan, God's bounty is the prominent feature; "It drinketh water of the rain of heaven." Egypt is the field in which a man, by a low form of labour, might *exist* amply; Canaan the home in which a man, by joyful concert with God, might nobly live. The eye of man was upon the one, and the flesh only was fattened by it; the eye of the Lord was upon the other, and the whole manly power was nourished there, and trained to some God-like proportion; for there were gathered up and treasured all the features which make the beauty, and all the elements which minister to the richness, of the world.

"For the Lord thy God bringeth thee into a good land, a land of brooks of water, of fountains and depths that spring out of valleys and hills; a land of wheat, and barley, and vines, and fig-trees, and pomegranates; a land of olive oil, and honey: a land wherein thou shalt eat bread without scarceness, thou shalt not lack anything in it; a land whose stones are iron, and out of whose hills thou mayest dig brass."—Deut. viii. 7–9.

No vision of a land fairer, no produce of a land richer, than that which is presented here. But

24

above all, the light of God upon it, the joy of God in blessing His people, and crowning their lives with His love, patent in all its expressions; its beauty, a constant smile of God on His beloved. Egypt is the worldly land; toil, drudge there, it will feed and fatten you. Canaan is the heavenly land; live there, it will be the noble theatre and home of your life.

In treating this subject, the rest which remaineth for the people of God, to the earthly image of which Canaan received the weary pilgrims of the desert, I shall speak in the first place of its nature, the conceptions which we are to form of the heavenly rest; and, in the second place, of the springs of its joys.

Its nature will, for the present, occupy our attention.

I. It was a *land*, a good land, the slope of that goodly mountain, even Lebanon, which Moses looked upon; it was a land of promise, which God had prepared.

I believe in the heavenly land. I believe that we are so sublimely immaterial in these days, that we are prone to conceive of things invisible so as to touch nothing more substantial than the vapours of a dream. God gives us an earth like this to tread upon, that we may have some solid notions about heaven. I suppose that earth, at

its best, must be strangely heaven-like. When
the Lord had finished the work of creation, and
left the earth with the glory of the last touch of His
hand upon it, He looked upon His handiwork,
and said, "Behold, it is very good!" There are
no comparatives of goodness with God. There is
no "yea and nay" with Him. He meant that He
had made it perfect in its beauty, perfect as His
hand could make it ; and man, in all his ages, has
caught the thought, and mused upon an image
of an Eden restored. All man's imaginings about
the world behind the veil, instinctively make an
earth like this the starting-point. It is a transfigured world which we look for—the familiar
forms, with the heavenly sunlight on them ; the
hints of beauty which earth suggests, wrought out
into broad expression ; the gleams of brightness
expanded into brilliant day!

Canaan was in a sense the heaven of Israel's
hope : the more heaven-like, perhaps, because it
was so fair a feature of our world ; because it was
a land on which a foot could be firmly and joyfully planted; a home in which a man, a family, a
nation, could nobly dwell. A *world* behind the
veil is the instinctive belief of every human spirit :
a world, with all the attributes of a world like
this, in which all the promises of this flawed and
fractured creation shall be realized ; wherein no

hope shall be frustrated, no cord of association broken, which has been consecrated by holy communion upon earth.

This is man's vision, inseparable, too, from his condition here. Imagination! we may say; blank dreams, no more! and pass it by. Imagination surely! but who inspired the imagination? Who but the Being who is the Maker of the reality, which He has kept, for ages, before the imagination of the world. I accept imagination here as a witness to reality. The imagination of the seer of Patmos was the organ by which was set before him the image of a divine reality—the "new heavens, and the new earth," wherein, saith St. Peter, "dwelleth righteousness." I cling to these words, "the new heaven and the new earth," most earnestly. They are pregnant words, pregnant with heavenly truth. St. Peter and St. John looked for a scene which should be familiar, however transfigured; a scene which should keep its home-like character, however transformed.

Heaven is a state, and not a place, we are assured by our present illuminati. Most surely: places do not constitute spirits, but spirits places. And yet one may hope that heaven is a state in which there will be firm footing, free air, and room to work. God has not double types of created things. The one for heaven, even the heaven of heavens where He abides; the other poorer, grosser, made in clay after commoner forms, for the uses of this world. God is One; His thought is one. He has but one way, and that *the* way of manifesting himself in creation— but one idea, whose realization through infinite variety He ever pursues. We speak familiarly of the boundless varieties of form in the kingdom of nature, tasking the strongest brain beyond its powers to name and catalogue them. Naturalists come home from their world-wide rambles, and bewilder us with the list of species, till then unknown to fame, which they have discovered. But as the myriad lenses in the eye of that marvellous beetle form after all but one eye, so there is a unity underlying the variety, whose image science ever pursues. For science, looking under the cloak of the visible, discourses sagely of simplicity —the few primary elements out of which all things are developed, the simplicities of form and structure, of which we have but slight modulations in all the infinite varieties of created things which surround us here. It was a poet's eye which first recovered this track of thought in the modern world. Goethe's suggestions, modern science still pursues. There is a double process at present, nay in all ages of scientific expansion:—the discovery of variety, and the discernment of unity.

The constructive minds—the builders of the future —are at work earnestly upon the last. The most instructed believe that we are on the eve of marvellous discoveries of the unity of nature, or rather disclosures—for it is a thing to be seen with the inner eye, not hunted after by the understanding—and that, ere long, the scientific world will substitute the word unity for simplicity, and discern with awe—for these unities are the awful things in nature—how one thought runs through the whole scale of the visible universe, and seems to prolong itself, as far as we can trace it, into the invisible beyond. And I mean to affirm, that St. Peter was not stooping to our weakness, and helping us by an image which we do know, to an invisible of a diverse nature, which is beyond our range ; but was describing what is, what must be, when he says, that as there are heavens and earth around us here, so there must be new heavens and a new earth around us there, struck from the same moulds, though in more heavenly substance, according to the pureness of the things and beings which abide in God's eternal heaven:—

" Seeing then that all these things shall be dissolved, what manner of persons ought ye to be in all holy conversation and godliness, looking for and hasting unto the coming of the day of God, wherein the heavens being on fire shall be dis-

solved, and the elements shall melt with fervent
heat ? Nevertheless we, according to His promise,
look for new heavens and a new earth, wherein
dwelleth righteousness. Wherefore, beloved, seeing that ye look for such things, be diligent that
ye may be found of Him in peace, without spot
and blameless."—2 Peter iii. 11–14.

One is sickened sometimes, at least I frankly
confess that I am, by the vague and vapid conceptions of a heaven with which many delight themselves, whose chief business upon earth seems
to be to rail at it, or, like priest and Levite, pass
it by, with upturned eye and hand, on the other
side. Everything which is not here, nothing
which is here, seems to be their aspiration :
as if God had made the world at random or
angrily; or as if the devil had been strong enough
to undo and remould God's constitution of things
below ! The world is a good world ; goodly as
Canaan was—beautiful, heavenly, glorious, were
but God in it as He walked in Eden. It is a
light which has gone from it, and a veil has fallen
on its beauty ; but it is just the glory that gleams
through the veil, which makes us pine and sigh for
its lifting as a revelation of heaven. Moses saw
it lifted, from Pisgah's crest. He saw in Canaan
what none who trod its sod could find. We may
well believe that there was a glory upon it to

his dying eye, such as the dying only can discern
here, for

"To death it is given
To see how this earth lies embosomed in heaven."

I often think that the removing of the tabernacle outside the camp, after the dark idolatry of
the people—that is, the moving of the visible
symbol of God's presence out from the midst of
them, not to abandon them to their fate, but, as
it were, to watch and guide them from a distance,
—is a picture of the God-forsaken, but not God-
abandoned, world of sin. Let me beg of you to
consider this passage carefully: it casts much
light on man's history, in every age and clime.
"And the Lord said unto Moses, Depart, and go
up hence, thou and the people which thou hast
brought up out of the land of Egypt, unto the
land which I sware unto Abraham, to Isaac, and
to Jacob, saying, Unto thy seed will I give it:
and I will send an angel before thee; and I
will drive out the Canaanite, the Amorite, and
the Hittite, and the Perizzite, the Hivite, and
the Jebusite: unto a land flowing with milk
and honey: for I will not go up in the midst of
thee; for thou art a stiff-necked people: lest I
consume thee in the way. And when the people
heard these evil tidings, they mourned: and no
man did put on him his ornaments. For the

Lord had said unto Moses, Say unto the children of Israel, Ye are a stiff-necked people: I will come up into the midst of thee in a moment, and consume thee: therefore now put off thy ornaments from thee, that I may know what to do unto thee. And the children of Israel stripped themselves of their ornaments by the mount Horeb. And Moses took the tabernacle, and pitched it without the camp, afar off from the camp, and called it the Tabernacle of the Congregation. And it came to pass, that every one which sought the Lord went out unto the tabernacle of the congregation, which was without the camp. And it came to pass, when Moses went out unto the tabernacle, that all the people rose up, and stood every man at his tent door, and looked after Moses, until he was gone into the tabernacle. And it came to pass, as Moses entered into the tabernacle, the cloudy pillar descended and stood at the door of the tabernacle, and the Lord talked with Moses. And all the people saw the cloudy pillar stand at the tabernacle door: and all the people rose up and worshipped, every man in his tent door."—Exod. xxxiii. 1-10.

Have we not here the relations of church and world symbolized? God's idea, a world-church— a world which should be also a church—is symbolized in this called nation: while man's sin, man's inability to dwell with God, drives the Shekinah outside the camp—the church separates itself from the world. Not forsaking it; watching it, blessing it, attracting it, consecrating it; but still as a thing apart, and to remain apart, too sadly, till the great consummation day. Here we have, in the Jewish camp, in the nation which was called to be a church, an outer circle of observers, and an inner circle of communicants with God; a sorrowful picture of what our world remains, after eighteen centuries of Diviner teaching than that which the Jews broke loose from, of more sacred Divine Presence than that which the Jews despised. The glory was gone forth from the midst of them, it shone on them from afar. All else remained in the camp as before; the organization, the supplies, the tables of the Law, the miraculous guidance, were all there still, and all unimpaired. New tables speedily replaced the old—but they were hewn this time by the hand of Moses; here too the same idea reigns. Everything which was essential to the life and progress of the nation remained untouched, but a glory had departed; a glory was gone from above them, and a joy from within them—for when the people heard these evil tidings, they mourned; and the world mourns still—which would have made their dreariest stations in the

desert as Edens, and would have forecast in the
wilderness the beauty, brightness, and blessedness of their promised land. It is just this glory,
this visible Divine Presence, which has been
driven out of our world by sin.

And I am well assured that among our visions,
when for us the veil is lifted, will be, what earth
had been, undeflowered by evil. The loving
study of the forms in which the idea of God
takes shape around us here, qualifies us to know
and to enjoy them everywhere. He who sees
most what earth is—as God makes nothing at
random, nor otherwise than according to Himself—will see most of what heaven is, when,
passing through the veil, the new heaven and the
new earth are disclosed. The men who learn
most reverently the lore of the world around
them—and none but the reverent can learn it,
Nature unveils not before those who deny her
Lord—are the elect masters of the higher school.
The wise here are the wise for ever, for to be
wise is not simply to know; wisdom takes cognizance of what is common to the two worlds.
Nothing which has been truly, reverently, learnt
will need to be unlearnt; no new education will
be necessary for the infants of the new creation
who have learnt on earth their lessons well.
Angelo's hand will not need to forget its cunning,

Newton's brain its vision of the universe, Dante's conscience its ideal of a state—he has found his "Monarchia" on high. The stars do not die when we die, nor perhaps the flowers. Strains, not unfamiliar to the ear that is versed in harmony, have streamed down on the earthly auditors of angelic choirs. The faithful students of God's hand in the visible, are learning to know His mind through the whole sphere of the invisible; they are familiar here with the things which the angels desire to look into; and pass at once from the training-school of the Spirit into the inner circle, the elect spirits which are next the throne. "A goodly land beyond Jordan." A real, substantial, homelike world.

II. The images which are employed by the sacred writers as most expressive when they are treating of heaven, are all borrowed from the higher forms of the development of man's social and national life.

This means, that the human interests and associations prolong themselves in their integrity through death, and constitute the highest sphere of interest and activity in the eternal world. A home, a city, a country, a kingdom—these are the images; on the working out of these ideas the writers of the Scripture spend all their force. Men in societies most perfectly developed, the fellow-subjects of a king who can rule them; this, to the seers, is the picture which fills the field of eternity. "Let not your heart be troubled: ye believe in God, believe also in Me. In my Father's house are many mansions: if it were not so, I would have told you. I go to prepare a place for you. And if I go to prepare a place for you, I will come again, and receive you unto Myself; that where I am, there ye may be also. And whither I go ye know, and the way ye know."—John xiv. 1-4.

"For they that say such things declare plainly, that they seek a country. And truly, if they had been mindful of that country from whence they came out, they might have had opportunity to have returned. But now they desire a better country, that is, an heavenly: wherefore God is not ashamed to be called their God: for He hath prepared for them a city."—Heb. xi. 14-16.

"For He looked for a city which hath foundations, whose builder and maker is God."—Heb. xi. 10.

It is not too much to say, that God's great universe has been built as a theatre for the development of man's life. The creation teems with life, beings rational and irrational, of infinite ranks and orders; but in the centre of them all, the earth around which they arrange themselves as moons, stands man, himself the moon of a more central sun. We know little of the angels; nothing but that they are, and that they are ministers. We are intended to know but little; yet this we know full surely, the human and not the angelic is the dominant tone through all the spheres of the invisible world. That nature which He bore as His own who is the Lord of Angels, is the key to all the concords of the universe; the human through Christ underlies the universal developments of life. The angelic is ministrant to the human, attends it, and will attend it, through eternity. The man who has been trained under the Word and by the Spirit in the wilderness of life, passes through the veil to play the chief part on a wider stage, to live a life which is the next thing in the universe to God.

A rest from trouble is the heavenly dream of some of us; to lie in the bosom of the celestial sereneness, as on a downy sleeping bed, whose softness may soothe the strain of an overworn spirit, and lull, as an anodyne, the agony of a sorely stricken heart. But for man to rest, is to live. To rest in God, is to enter into life. All images of heaven present life and its motions; life in its highest strain, under its heaviest obliga-

tions, in its most earnest activity, its most unselfish and, therefore, most satisfying joys. It is
the organization of men which is the leading feature of the life of the city or the kingdom; the
discovery of the relations and duties which man
sustains and owes; the stimulating his loftiest
powers by the magnet of association; the concert of developed intellects, the emulation of
noble and fertile hearts. The life of men in their
societies is like a hotbed to their natures; the
virtues and the vices start under its heat. But
there, where vice, if rampant, is most corrupting,
where wrong, if unchecked, is most destructive,
where selfishness, if untamed, is most blighting,
where the devil, if unconquered, reigns most
deadly unto death, there, in the thick and throng
of life, is the field of man's noblest and purest
activities: in killing that vice, in righting that
wrong, in curbing that selfishness, in mastering
that devil there, he finds the field of his grandest
victories; and there, where the throng is densest,
where the fight is hottest, he is most completely
in training for the ruling of his Father's kingdom
on high.

Hearts weary of the woe and wrong of the life
of great cities, and of the vice and selfishness
which breed fast in all throngs of men, look
longingly to heaven, with a sentiment not much

higher than that which moved a world-sick poet
to cry for a desert,

> " Where he might all forget the human race ! "

"A lodge in some vast wilderness!" cried another
heart-weary one. Anywhere, away from man.
Heaven! The world where earth, with all its
storm and strife may be forgotten; alone with
the quiet angels, within the tranquil sphere of
the serene activity of God.

Nothing like this was Canaan; nothing like
this will be heaven. It is the sphere in which
the elect spirits who have won the prizes in life's
battles, who have come forth from the chaos of
strife, trained, inured, yet pure, shall play out
their parts on a grander scale, in a wider theatre,
under the eye of a more absolute and exigent
King. All that society on earth aims at and
misses, the grand order of human relations, the
majestic procession of human activities, of which,
marred and crippled as they are on earth, the
wisest and noblest have not ceased to dream,
shall there be realized; with Christ the King
visibly in the centre of it, and the angels atten-
dant to watch the actors and applaud the results.

I know not why we should hesitate to believe
that man, and the life of his world, lies on the
threshold of the higher developments of being;

that God's universe has to be peopled with God-like beings through us. All that we know of the universe shows man the chief actor in its higher occupations. The angels come, manlike, to talk with us about man's interests. Gabriel, Michael, stand for the ward and government of provinces of the human world. The veil has been lifted, and out of the ineffable splendour, which no unpurged human eye could look upon, this form appeared as the fountain of all power, the seat of all dominion, through all the spiritual spheres.

"And I turned to see the voice that spake with me. And being turned, I saw seven golden candlesticks; and in the midst of the seven candlesticks one like unto the Son of man, clothed with a garment down to the foot, and girt about the paps with a golden girdle. His head and His hairs were white like wool, as white as snow; and His eyes were as a flame of fire; and His feet like unto fine brass, as if they burned in a furnace; and His voice as the sound of many waters."— Rev. i. 12–15.

And lest it should be thought that the human is here accidental, a dress assumed for a time and for a purpose, to be laid aside as soon as the end was gained, a fuller vision was disclosed.

"And I beheld, and, lo, in the midst of the throne and of the four beasts, and in the midst of

25

the elders, stood a lamb as it had been slain, having seven horns and seven eyes, which are the seven Spirits of God sent forth into all the earth. And He came and took the book out of the right hand of Him that sat upon the throne. And when He had taken the book, the four beasts and four and twenty elders fell down before the Lamb, having every one of them harps, and golden vials full of odours, which are the prayers of saints." —Rev. v. 6–8. [*Read to the end of the chapter.*]

There the very form of the human sufferer was shown in the very heart of the glory of the central throne; and the love which wrestled on Calvary for a world's redemption, and triumphed through death, becomes the chosen theme of celebration, not to ransomed humanity, but to the myriad angelic hosts " for ever and ever."

It is easy to talk idly on themes of such magnitude and distance; but thus much, surely, the Scriptures seek to express to us, that heaven and earth are related much as the theatre of life, the great world, is to the little world of the schoolboy, where he has to practise the part and train himself for the station, which he is to fill in the day of his developed life. The faculty educated, the energy disciplined, the wisdom acquired, the patience exercised, the charity touched to its finest issues, in that life of man on earth in which man is in closest contact with man, under the heaviest obligations of duty, with the largest vocation to ministry, and the keenest stimulus to energy; these are the qualities which Heaven welcomes to its theatre—this is the life which is the training-school for the thrones of God's kingdom on high. All which makes schism between your most active and energetic life as men here, and your vision of what awaits you there, dishonours earth and heaven equally. The Lord, the King there, is King of both worlds. He sets you your tasks in this, your commonest as well as your highest; not that He may disgust you with earth to make heaven sweeter, but that he may so train your faculty as to make heaven richer, its life more fruitful, more noble, more glorious, through eternity. And I dare to say, of some of your dreariest wanderings, the years which you have spent over your commonest and weariest tasks, you will never understand them, you will never see how precious their ministry has been to you, till you have grown familiar with the life and occupation of God's eternal Kingdom of Heaven.

III. That good land beyond Jordan had some heaven-like feature herein; it was to be the theatre of the highest and holiest human association, under conditions most favourable to the most perfect development ; and in an atmosphere of life which God's benediction should make an atmosphere of bliss.

Canaan was nothing like this, you will be ready to answer. Alas ! no. For the most part the very reverse of all this. And yet the picture of what a life in Canaan might be, is not a man's dream, but God's. His Spirit dictated these words. " If ye walk in my statutes, and keep my commandments, and do them ; then I will give you rain in due season, and the land shall yield her increase, and the trees of the field shall yield their fruit. And your threshing shall reach unto the vintage, and the vintage shall reach unto the sowing time : and ye shall eat your bread to the full, and dwell in your land safely. And I will give peace in the land, and ye shall lie down, and none shall make you afraid : and I will rid evil beasts out of the land, neither shall the sword go through your land. And ye shall chase your enemies, and they shall fall before you by the sword. And five of you shall chase an hundred, and an hundred of you shall put ten thousand to flight : and your enemies shall fall before you by the sword. For I will have respect unto you, and make you fruitful, and multiply you, and establish my covenant with you. And ye shall eat old store, and bring forth the old because of the new. And I will set my tabernacle among you: and my soul shall not abhor you. And I will walk among you, and will be your God, and ye shall be my people. I am the Lord your God, which brought you forth out of the land of Egypt, that ye should not be their bondmen; and I have broken the bands of your yoke, and made you go upright."—Levit. xxvi. 3–13.

A model human society we have here; not reduced to its simplest elements, as in Abraham's patriarchal tent, but developed into its highest form as a nation and a church, and dwelling in a model earthly home. This was the vision which was before the mind of the great leader, the mind of the people in a measure, and the mind of God; who alone saw when and how it should be real. In the rich variety of the physical features of the land, they had all which could educate the eye and charm the imagination, all that could draw out the patriotic passion, and add richness and compass to their hymns; all that could make life rich as life could be in variety and interest was around them there —how the eye of their seer flashed as he gazed on it all from his mount of vision—faint image, with all its splendour, of the infinite variety and richness of the homes that await us in heaven.

While within the bosom of the community was all out of which could spring a national life of conspicuous glory and entrancing joy. This is joy, this is glory, to dwell nobly, purely, faithfully with men, under the smile of God. A called nation, known to the great God by name, each one of them, and marked by Him with a seal which, while they overlaid it not, nature reverenced and the angels; with homes guarded by the most sacred sanctions, and enriched by the most ample benedictions; a government on the one heavenly model, the rule of the wisest and ablest, the secret of finding whom earth has not discovered yet; and worship which, while it exercised, expanded quite infinitely the highest powers of their being—here is the material and home of a life which that people by faithlessness brought down to shameful beggary and pitiful straits, but which the children of the kingdom, who have succeeded to their lost inheritance, are trained here to live out under the shadow of the sceptre of the Son of David, the Divine Man, in heaven.

Expansion, development, in purer and yet purer forms, of the manifold sympathies, affections, intelligences of man, the faculty of his body, brain, and heart, is the key to the preparations of this training school of the Spirit, who is the one Purifier and Educator of men.   While life, large, free, royal life—life that can manifest what is most divine in God, after the image of Him who is His image—life is the key to the rest of heaven.

Sermon xvi.

The Everlasting Joy.

" Everlasting joy shall be unto them."—Isaiah lxi. 7.

IN my last discourse I considered the nature and conditions of the heavenly rest—the rest of the human spirit in a world which is capable of being the theatre of its developed life. A spirit rests only in the full sweep of its orbit around the Being who is its sun. In order to complete the subject which I have treated in these pages, I must speak now of the springs of its everlasting joy. The advent of the Lord opened these springs of everlasting joy for man. To share His life is to share His eternal joy. But here we taste that joy but sparingly. The Christian life is less a being than a becoming; we are growing up into Christ; we are learning to live in Him. The world and the flesh have their springs of pleasure, and tempt us to their Marahs. Who can say with the Psalmist, " All my springs are in Thee ? " We find bitter waters where we looked for joys unspeakable ; warned, we seek the true fountain, and some foretaste of the everlasting joy of the blessed uplifts our hearts. But we pore with intense earnestness over the words which picture the joys of the future ; we pant with passionate longing for the fruit of the tree and the draught of the river which were shown to the seer of the Apocalypse—the vision of which, in all ages, has lit with hope man's wilderness life. The joy is there. "Everlasting joy unto them." Let us consider what are its springs. I shall dwell on three—the three chief satisfactions—the purest springs of joy for the human spirit, intellect, and heart.

I. The inward harmony, the perfect order of the being, the concert of every faculty and every force in the fulfilment of the will of God. That is the peace of God—the perfect peace. More exquisite is it to the imagination of the racked and tormented spirit which is in arms "against a sea of troubles," and a host of rebellious powers, than is the haven to the mariner storm-tossed on the dark rough ocean, or—

> " To those wild eyes that watch the wave
>   In roarings round the coral reef,"

the vision of peaceful and blessed home.

God, my Redeemer! There is but one redemption possible for man—restoration to the rule of his rightful King. The redeemed man is the governed man ; the man who has re-found the

King who can evoke his loyal passions, and control and direct his manifold powers. This rule, the rule of his true King, has been lost to him through sin. This supreme, complete control of his being heaven will restore. The inward strife is the real agony of the spirit. Let a man be at peace within, at one with himself and God, and worlds have no power to harm or torment him. He may slumber calmly—as the Lord on that pillow, drenched with the spray of the storm—through the fiercest shocks of the wildest tempests; give him inward unity, he is at rest; God's rest, God's peace, reigns within. "Who is he that shall harm you if ye be the followers of the good One?" But who is at one with himself? Who that is in earnest about the Divine life does not utter and re-echo that most profound and pregnant of prayers, "Unite my heart to fear Thy name?" Now it is all at war. There are hostile camps within me, and deadly strifes. Flesh and spirit, mind and conscience, heart and reason, all jangled and at discord; each contending fiercely for the supreme rule of my spirit, and rending my very being in sunder by their mad war. They have broken loose from their true monarch, and have fallen under a tyrant, who exaggerates their discords and inflames their hate.

The tyrant is simply the wrong king; the king

who commands no reverence, kindles no loyalty, constrains no obedience, quickens no love; the king whom the revolted powers have accepted as lord in the tumult of passion, but who wields no authority, and makes no order in the distracted state. The wildest and most desperate endeavours have been made by the earnest in all ages to reduce the confusion to order, the discord to concord, or even the semblance of it. Simeon Stylites was at work on the problem up there upon his pillar; St. Bernard there, fainting with exhaustion and vigil in his cell: they said, as myriads of brave hearts have said, it is worth while to endure all this, which would drive the dullest and most patient of brutes to seek the exodus of suicide, ay, and far more than this, if by the maceration of the flesh the seeming even of unity may be realized within: it is worth while to torture the flesh as no demon of cruelty ever ventured to torture a fellow, if it can be tamed into submission; if the spirit may be restored to its rightful supremacy, even by the murder of that flesh which was given into its bosom to live with it as its bride.

But no force of will ever compacted this unity: nor can the maiming or crippling of our being in any province or organ, be the way into the peace of God. To find the king of the whole being is the one secret of unity; to find the centre of its system, the lord of its life. An unsphered planet could be won back to the harmony of its sister planets, only by the attraction of their common sun. The King has appeared and claims His own. To feel that He has His own, that we are His, His wholly, His for ever, will be the deepest spring of the bliss of heaven. He has laid His touch upon us, and the disorderly troop of rebel and vagrant powers see the eye and feel the hand of a master, and tremble. There is a stir and mutual motion, as in the valley of dry bones in the prophet's vision; Chaos is growing into Cosmos; the inward world is settling into peace.

But just as the recovery of the body from a torpor of faintness is an exquisite agony, so there is fearful heartache over this reorganizing process in the soul. Men who have been half killed tell us that the coming to life again is the keenest suffering. It is this coming to life which is the pain of the present; the sensation of life will be the bliss of the future. But for the present it is a daily dying. "Always bearing about in the body the dying of the Lord Jesus." And at times we are tempted to cry, "My God, the pain is too sharp, let us alone, let us back, let us die in torpor, anything better than this agony of nascent life." And it is life-long. It is the work of the child of God in this life to recover the possession of his faculty through the vital attraction of his Saviour, and yield it to His service; when the recovery is complete, when the flood of life flows freely through every pulse and channel, earth becomes too dark a prison-house, it is time to arise and to go home. Hence the experience which the Apostle Paul unfolds so richly in the fourth chapter of his Second Epistle to the Corinthians, in which he sets forth his life as a daily death; that death being the birth-throe of an inner life into the sphere for which it was born, and in which it shall abide for ever.

Oh! the anguish of the weary struggle against the lusts which we have learnt to hate, the follies which we have learnt to scorn, the habits which we have disowned, the longings which we would strangle to death. Oh! the heart-ache of the pining for the state, in which what the soul loves and honours in its sanctuary shall win the love and homage of the whole being, and lead captive the troop of its appetites and lusts; in which the vision of life which we see from our Pisgahs, shall be fouled no more by the stains of the flesh and the dirt of the world when we descend to its arena, but shall draw the whole being with its sweet attractions, and harmonize every power and passion in the work of making it real. Oh

God! unite us! unite our hearts in this blest concert of powers! unite them indissolubly to all that is good, and fair, and of Thee!

The vision of the beauty of the Lord when we pass through the veil, will be God's answer. We shall see Jesus, and, as with Paul, the unity will be completed, the arch will be keyed. We know little of heaven's occupations, the aspect of its homes, the modes of its speech, the forms of its life. We know only that the God-man is there, and reigns. That He whom we can love with intensest passion, and serve with exulting joy, will meet us on its threshold, will sweep the flood of His attractions round every limb and organ of our being, and thrill us in one intense moment with the sense that we are one, that we are blessed. To see Him, as they see Him who prevail to pass through death as conquerors, is to put off the stains and weaknesses of flesh. As Elijah dropped in one blest moment the garment of mortality, the vision of Jesus shall complete the enfranchisement of our souls in death. A flood of divine strength shall pour through the languid ducts and pulses of the being. Our hearts shall be uplifted for ever by the sense that there is the power in us now to realize our aspirations, that we have mastered the art of substantiating our dreams. That clinging sense

of infirmity, which never ceased to oppress us,
shall drop off like the bands of slumber, at the
first flash of that heavenly sun. Power to become
sons, power to live like sons—this is what we
have been pining, panting, praying for ; and
when we see Jesus, it shall flow into us, as daylight floods the darkness, exhilarating the spirit
with that most intense of all joys—the joy of
vivid, glowing, victorious life. "The goodly land
beyond Jordan " is good to us, because the Lord
is there ; the Lord, whose suffering presence here
reclaimed this earth as God's dominion ; whose
glorious appearing, in the day of the manifestation of the sons of God, shall be the proclamation,
that the reconquest of man and of all things unto
Himself is complete. One vision of the glorified
Man, as we pass the Jordan, shall fill us with
that joy of hope which is unspeakable and full of
glory. What if we wait and watch awhile, that
those who follow may pass with us into the
perfect bliss; the hope which the Lord sustains
shall sustain our spirits, and fill them with a
rapture which the heaven of heavens alone can
complete. The very vision of His form shall be
the assurance and the prophecy that the largest
and deepest purposes of His love shall have complete accomplishment; the full revelation must
await the day when the whole company of the

redeemed shall throng the plains of the restored
creation, and range themselves in their heavenly
ranks and orders, not around the symbol of a
Divine Presence, but around the glorious Person
of Christ, the King.

II. The full vision of the glory of God in the creation, the beholding of all that God has meant, and
sin has marred, in the constitution of the worlds.

The spirit demands, as we have seen, the restoration of its lost supremacy, to be blessed;
to rule, ruled by Christ, its subject powers. There
is that faculty in man which claims further, for
its satisfaction, to behold the glory of God's
universe unveiled, face to face, as a man looks
into the face of his beloved. Of all the deadly
legacies which theological strife has handed down
to us, there is none deadlier than that dread of
the study of the revelation of the mind of God
in the creation, which infects so strangely a large
and influential section of the Church. There is
an infidel dread of inquiry into the visible things,
"by which, from the creation of the world, the
invisible things of God are clearly seen, being
understood by the things that are made, even His
eternal power and Godhead," which has tended
very largely to create a miserable, mutually detri-
mental, schism, between the Christian belief and
activity and the intellectual life of our time. This

fear of the study of Nature, and the observation of all that she can reveal to us about God, palsies the manhood of the godly in the Church, and widens continually the breach between it, and the world it was set to enlighten and to guide to salvation.

And yet how much of the joy of life for all of us springs unconsciously from this pure fountain, the beauty, the tenderness, the glory, which spread their revelations round us as we tread—how often with careless eye and heart!—the pathways of this wonderful world. " Fearfully and wonderfully made " is creation, as well as man. Who does not pity from his very heart the plodder who has never, when beholding the morning's pomp, or the evening's glow, the gleaming of the dew in the eye of the summer dawn, or the solemn host of stars on a clear winter's night, poured forth a rapturous gush of praise, that God had led him forth into a world like this ? We fume and fret over our human collisions and mischances. This one refuses us a glance of love, that one bends on us a sneer or frown : but how calmly Orion looks down upon it all, and rebukes our petulance ! how tenderly the moonbeams kiss our flushed brows, and tell us, as a dumb creature might tell its thoughts, that the troubles of life are not infinite nor eternal, that there are fountains of pure joy

26

for man which flow on, despite the "slings and arrows" of his fellows, the same yesterday, to-day, and for ever.

But none can find a full response in nature. Nature is most to him who sees the limits of her ministry. Indeed her truest lovers find a strange sadness in her tones. There is a profound depth of truth in the apostle's thought about the groaning of the whole creation, its travailing in pain until the day of the manifestation of the sons of God. The veil has been dropped over the pristine splendour of creation, or at least over our vision of it, by sin. The world around us has been set in tune with our state of toil and discipline by the Lord. There are flashings through the veil, and a glow behind it, which tints its pallor; but it is there, most palpable to the finer spirits who search out, through the creation, the thoughts of the Creator, God. There runs a deep, sad undertone of aspiration through the universe. Each order of creatures has a propulsive movement to a higher order—some rudiment of an organ or a use which can only be justified and explained by that which *is to come* next above it in the scale of life. The whole looks on to man and sees itself completed in him; that is, in his completeness, which is not realized yet. This explains the groaning of

creation. It is the groan of man prolonged
through the orders of which he is the head.
The cry of the creation is as it were the cry
of a soul in bonds. Is it Goethe or Bettina
who says, that "nature seems ever like a captive
sighing to be delivered?" It aims at an ideal
beauty and harmony which art interprets, which
is never realised here, which never will be realised
on this side of the flood of death. We see these
things but dimly—we, whose organization is less
fine and keen. But we are bound to take note of
them; what touches consciously the finer spirits,
touches unconsciously, let us be sure, and influences the destinies of the common millions of
our race. The sick, with their sharper senses,
are conscious of atmospheric influences which the
multitude take no note of, but which are raising
or depressing the vital spirits of the inhabitants
of a whole land. Again, the people use a speech
in their commonest talk, whose ample and elaborate forms have been wrought to that amplitude
and completeness, by the subtle discussions, and
consequent distinctions, of schoolmen, whose
theses the multitude would have laughed out of
the schools. And if the mass, occupied with the
weary task of life, with but rare and partial
vision of Nature, find her quite fair and good
enough for their satisfaction, let them not despise

26—2

the wisdom of the wise who see a veil upon her glory—the Pauls, whose "whole creation groaneth and travaileth in pain together until now."

But, veiled as she is, like the elder dispensation, like the elder dispensation she is glorious still; though that glory shall be done away, not abolished, but absorbed, "by that glory which excelleth," when the apocalypse of the new heaven and the new earth shall be revealed. Behind the veil are marvels of God's handiwork, and glories of his art, which it were worth "the wanderings" of a life to look upon. I sometimes think that did we know, as we seem to draw near the dark cold river, what splendours lie beyond it, we should rush to the margin, plunge headlong, breast it, and be there.

To the pure-hearted alone is the vision open. There is no veil which can be drawn over Nature so thick, as the crust which the sensual gather around the organs and the very senses of their being. "The graves of lust" bury not the soul only, but its world—nay, two worlds. To the child and to the child-like, the wonder is ever fresh, the glory is ever glowing; and to such a vision is opened, which exalts their joy to rapture when they look, according to His promise, for the new heaven and the new earth; that is, for the true revelation of the world. Ezekiel saw the vision,

and John, and fell entranced as dead. To see
the face of that glorious world and live, is as hard
as to see the face of God. To them it had an
awful splendour and majesty, as the face of day to
him who has been long mewed in darkness, or
life to that risen man who had been bound by
the bands of death. What radiant colour, what
ravishing tones, what resplendent and exquisite
forms shall burst upon us when the veils are
parted, they who have passed through alone could
tell us; though methinks those can guess somewhat who have looked into the dying eyes of such
as are "departing to be with Christ, which is
far better." What boundless riches of Divine
wisdom the creation, which becomes visible to the
eye that is purged by death, can unfold! What
books of Divine thoughts for the disciplined and
reverent intellect to explore! To roam with the
eagle sight and the tireless strength of the immortal body through the fields of the redeemed
creation; to range through the depths, in which
we grope, as through a glass darkly, by the ministry of science, but where we shall then see all
that God can manifest of glory face to face, and
know even as also we are known! We have but
here the grammar of the speech of celestial form,
the manual of its music. Pray God that we learn
it lovingly, and practise it tunefully, that we may

be fit to talk of God's handiwork with the angels, and to bear the part that beseems us, in their hymns of praise !

III. The heart claims its satisfaction, in the communion of the blessed—the joy of fellowship when the struggle and toil are ended for ever—the companionship of the elect and beloved—intercourse with the elder spirits who are before the throne.

It is hard, in this world, not to dread meetings because of partings, greetings because of farewells. The purest joys are dashed by the foretaste of sorrow, the closest and dearest bonds have no assurance against the rude violence of death. And it is well. We would not live always : we would not take our fill of joy in such a world as this. Our hope stretches into brighter and more blessed regions, where those who meet have met for ever ; where those who love need no dark warnings, lest love should grow idolatrous and write its epitaph. For those who meet, meet before the face of God, and those who love, love in Him. Our highest fellowships here are a portion of God's fellowship. We must love that which is of Him in our dear ones, if we would not love to our loss. There, our whole society shall be but the organ of His communion. We can loose the bands, spread wide the tendrils of our affection, they will but maintain

the vivid circulation of His life. Which of us has
not wept bitterly over the desecrations of the holiness of love, the poisonings of the sweetness of
friendship, by sin ? Which of us has not longed,
in some hour of blest communion, to pass up ere
sin could stain it, and present it for consecration
before the face of Christ ?

But our friendships as well as ourselves must
"wander." By the way of the wilderness they, too,
are led to their glorious rest. Happy if they early
drop their plaints and lusts as they travel, and
stand pure and earnest, loyal and submissive,
before the river which guards the borders of the
celestial land. Oh ! the bliss of the long-tried
friendships and loves that shall reach it, the way-
worn comrades who shall renew their pledges on
the farther side of the river of death. Not a pang,
not a parting, not a self-denial, not a self-sacrifice,
but shall then be fondly remembered ; acts and
sufferings which could not be spoken of here—too
sacred, too solemn—will reveal there their depths
of love. On earth love must go cross-bearing,
like Him from whose essential Being it springs.
Many an agony of suffering and sacrifice, known
only to Christ, it must endure. But it shall be
known then : the thorn scars shall glow with
lustre, and be the gems in the Crown of Life.
Bear bravely, silently, the strain of unselfish, self-

sacrificing, ministering tenderness; it is making love immortal; it is making the bliss of Heaven intense and complete.

I think, too, of long-sundered ones, whose love cannot forget: who have laid up its hope in trust with Christ, and shall find it again on the eternal shore. Mothers, who, in their death-agony, have committed their orphans with sublime confidence to the Father of the fatherless, and will claim them at His hand in their glorious forms on high. The lovers, too, who have loved with an immortal passion; the twin souls that but *exist* asunder, that strain through the veil of death, to be locked in the bands of an immortal fellowship, and burn with a life intenser than the seraphim, before the throne of Him who made them one. There are long life-agonies, too, which make no moan on earth; hearts breaking for years in unlovely or hateful bonds of fellowship, from which there is no extrication, whose only utterance is through weary wasted features and eyes dim with ceaseless tears, or it may be in those nobler ministerings to misery which the stricken only can yield. For such, heaven has compensations which shall explain and justify even sorrow like theirs. There are kindred spirits in those heavenly mansions ready to receive them to an immortal fellowship, and make them rich

in the bliss of communion and love through
eternity. He, who for one dread moment was
alone on earth, as even the loneliest has never
been, is there the centre of all observation, and
the object of all adoration and love. Perhaps,
the loneliest here are training to be the centres
of spheres of attraction, of homes of love, in the
many mansions of the Father's kingdom on high.

Nor is it forbidden to sit beneath the footstool
of the masters, and gather wisdom from the most
eloquent lips. The things once unspeakable have
now found their expression; the unsearchable
mysteries have found their interpreters. It shall
be permitted to us to fathom the depth of the
wisdom and the love of God in Christ, with a
Paul for an expositor, or, mingling with the
wise and the great of old, lift ourselves to their
levels, while they press on to higher achievements,
and pass up to a nearer vision of God. No
dreary average of endowment, no weary same-
nesses of glory, shall repeat the monotone of
Egypt above. "One star differeth from another
star in glory." "So also is it in the resurrection
of the dead." A grand and free variety, more
richly multiform, more profoundly one, than that
which accomplished the soul's education, shall
minister to its life in the realm of life, in
heaven.

Nor is the passage a long one ; nor is the home far. The analogues of death are all round us in the creation, and nowhere are they terrible but in the apprehension of the sinner—man. There is no death which man knows which is not the germ of a higher, finer, braver life. Nothing dies but to minister to progress. No order of creation perishes but a more perfect one appears. Wherever we see decay and dissolution, be sure that the stuff is wanted for a finer manufacture ; God breaks up nothing but to improve. It is true in nature ; it is true in history. The same great thought runs through the whole scale of being, and finds its highest expression in God's ordinance of death and resurrection for man. Sin made it a terror ; Christ makes it an angel. It is to inherit the kingdom, that flesh and blood must be put off. Man, too, is to be purged and refined in common with the creation, to put off his coarser and grosser habiliments, and be clothed in flesh of finer texture, and fit for more subtle and delicate use : of this, death is but the minister. Our best angel, could we see it, is Christ's angel of death. And the home to which he leads us, as we have said, may not be so far away. We talk and muse on it as distant, but were the veils lifted we might see with wonder that it is here. There are strange comminglings of the two worlds even in our daily marches; and sometimes the thought haunts us that the dearest, who have passed through the veil, are not far away. The idea that the two worlds interpenetrate and intermingle, is fast growing familiar. We may shrink, even with loathing, from the thought that the great dead are ready to obey our idle biddings, and that they have no better occupation than to make an evening's entertainment for a " circle " of empty hearts; and yet we may believe that they may touch us in our solemn moments, foil our tempters, hush our passions, soothe our frets, and inspire our hopes. All that makes the future home-like; all that casts out fear and opens vision to those who believe; all that makes the apparitor of death angelic, and brings life and immortality into the broad daylight of our common world, is God's truth about heaven.

But why has God made death so dread, if He would have us so familiar with it? If death is to be our benignant angel, why has He clothed him with a presence so awful; why has He taught the flesh—yea, and something deeper than the flesh—to shudder at his advancing tread? Is life so blessed, then, brethren, that we should be content to await the summons, if all the benignant beauty of death were unveiled? Should we not rush up life's pathways to meet him, shout to him as our deliverer, and pray him to bear us swiftly home? And is it not right that the doomsman should still wear his terror, though Christ has transmuted the doom to benediction—the darkness to glory? Is it not well that sin should have amongst us still a stern expositor; that we should, while evil still tempts us, haunts us, and is inwoven with the very texture of our being, tremble and shudder at death? Death remains awful; for the sin remains awful from which it sprang, and the cost of that Redemption is awful by which it shall be destroyed. I say that death is terrible still. Nothing can fully cast out its terror. Conquer every enemy, there is a last enemy who still remains to be mastered; before whose advent the flesh will quiver, the heart will flutter, the soul will agonize still. And yet I think that the terror, to those who pass through it, is less terrible than appears. Who has not marked that beautiful preparedness for death in those who are manifestly appointed to die? I suppose that, as they draw near the veil, it becomes more fully transparent; the soul gets absorbed in vision; and the agonized quiverings of the perishing flesh, which is all that we can look upon, are to the dying not worthy to be compared with the glory which is being revealed. Who feels the pain of a wound amid the high excitements of battle ? Fear not, trembler ! to whom death is the great terror still, fear not : there are visions to be seen in that dark valley, and bliss to be tasted, which purge all the pain of the dying away.

Oh ! could we but at this moment lift the veil, and sweep one earnest glance over the heavenly plains, our life would become a longing for the moment of emancipation ; and of all God's angels, the brightest and most welcome would be His Angel of Death ! Who would not rather depart, and be with Christ, which is far better, if he were as sure as the Apostle was at length, that his life-work was accomplished, his battle fought out, his victory for ever won ? What here should keep us from the white-robed throng, the palm, the crown, the vision of the Saviour, the rest of the blessed and glorified with Him ? " I would not live alway," is the cry of all earnest and faithful hearts ; " here I can but guess what life means." " Oh, that I now might die ! " were we more often on Pisgah, would be more often our prayer ; not in desperate mood, as the bankrupts of life, but in hopeful, and therefore patient mood, as the heirs of eternity.

And how many of the heirs may read these lines ? Sons of God, still hanging round the flesh-pots, still haunting, though weeping and groaning, the Goshens of life! Methinks, at this moment, the summons of a Divine leader is again ringing through the air. A Divine hand is again leading you out one step towards the free broad desert, from the prison-house of sin. Again there is stormy strife within the innermost recesses of your being. "Go forward," saith the Divine guide; "Come back," cries the clinging world, and wantons round you lest you should burst her spells. The Divine call and the earthly passions are warring; and devils, and angels, and some dearer than dear life, are watching—how eagerly! —the path which you elect to take. What dear associations for some of you, for all of you, if you knew where your true kindred dwell, surround the path of Divine duty. How sacred the tracks of the desert grow by the footsteps that have trodden them! The great cloud of witnesses is above and around you, but they have left their foot-tracks in the desert; and there are the stains of the tears and the blood of those, who were not afraid of the fellowship of the sufferings of the Saviour, and who passed up to glory, by being conformed even unto His death. How many of them are there on the far side of Jordan, straining back their gaze to watch your steps! They rest not yet in glory, they wait that you may pass with them; they watch while you are struggling, sustained by the hope that you will rest with them at last. Come, then, and join the beloved company; the way will be bright in their companionship, the rest will be blessed in their arms. Listen to the voice of the Divine Captain : " Mine angel shall go before thee, and shall bring thee into the place which I have prepared." See here before you, at this moment, His bright, flaming pillar, casting forth its lustre over the desert, and marking through its desolate wilds, your heavenward way : and see there, in the far distance, the brightening splendour, the full unfolding of celestial glories, in the midst of which the angels, in blest anticipation, are hymning your triumphs and weaving your crowns.

" EXCEPT THY PRESENCE GO WITH ME, CARRY ME NOT UP HENCE."

" AND GOD SAID, MY PRESENCE SHALL GO WITH THEE, I WILL GIVE THEE REST."

THE END.

London: SMITH, ELDER and Co., Little Green Arbour Court, Old Bailey, E.C.

65, *Cornhill, London,*
November, 1862.

NEW AND STANDARD WORKS

PUBLISHED BY

SMITH, ELDER AND CO.

ELEGANT GIFT BOOK.

The New Forest; Its History and Scenery.
By JOHN R. WISE. With Sixty Views, and other Illustrations, by
WALTER CRANE. A New Map of the Forest, and Sections. Small 4to.
Printed on Toned Paper, and Superbly Bound. Price One Guinea.

Shakespeare Commentaries. By Professor GERVINUS.
Translated under the Author's superintendence, by F. E. BUNNETT.
Two Volumes. Demy 8vo. Price 24s. cloth.

Journal of a Political Mission to Afghanistan,
With an Account of the Country and People. By H. W. BELLEW,
Surgeon to the Mission. With 8 Plates. Demy 8vo. Price 16s. cloth.

Waterloo : The Downfall of the First Napoleon.
A History of the Campaign of 1815. By GEORGE HOOPER. With
Maps and Plans. Demy 8vo. Price 15s. cloth.

Life in Nature. By JAMES HINTON. Author of "Man and
his Dwelling Place." Crown 8vo. Price 6s. cloth.

Ten Years in the United States; Being an
Englishman's Views of Men and Things in the North and South. By
D. W. MITCHELL. Post 8vo. Price 9s. cloth.

Adventures of a Boy Lost Among the Affghans.
Related by Himself. Post 8vo. With Portrait. Price 7s. 6d. cloth.

Sisterhoods in the Church of England. By
MARGARET GOODMAN. Author of "Experiences of an English Sister
of Mercy." Post 8vo. Price 6s. cloth.

A New Volume of Sermons. By the late Rev.
FREDERICK W. ROBERTSON, M.A., of Brighton. Post 8vo.

An Analysis of Mr. Tennyson's "In Me-
moriam." By the late Rev. FREDERICK W. ROBERTSON, M.A. Fcap.
8vo. Cloth.

England Under God. By the VENERABLE ARCHDEACON EVANS. Author of "The Rectory of Valehead." Crown 8vo. 7s. 6d. cl.

After Dark. BY WILKIE COLLINS. Author of "The Woman in White," &c. A new Edition. With Four Illustrations. Crown 8vo. Price 5s. cloth.

London People: Sketched from Life. By CHARLES BENNETT. With Numerous Illustrations. Fcap. 4to, elegantly bound.

Roundabout Papers. (Reprinted from the *Cornhill Magazine*.) By W. M. THACKERAY. With Illustrations. Crown 8vo.

Life in the Forests of the Far East; or Travels in Northern Borneo. By SPENSER ST. JOHN, F.R.G.S., F.E.S. Late H.M.'s Consul-General in Borneo, now H.M.'s Chargé d'Affaires to Hayti. Second Edition, Revised. Illustrated with Sixteen Coloured and Tinted Lithographs, and Three Maps. Two Volumes. Demy 8vo. 32s.

Cochin, its Past and its Present; including an Account of the History, Ethnology, Zoology, and Botany of Cochin : with Remarks on the Religion, Manners, and Customs of its various Castes and Sects. By FRANCIS DAY, Esq., F.L.S., Civil Surgeon of Cochin. In One Volume, 8vo.

NEW JUVENILE WORKS.

Tuflongbo's Journey in Search of Ogres. With an Account of his Early Life, and how his Shoes got worn out. By HOLME LEE, Author of "Legends of Fairy Land," &c. Fcap. 8vo. With Seven Illustrations. Price 3s. 6d. cloth.

Stories of Old; or Bible Narratives suited to the Capacity of Young Children. By CAROLINE HADLEY. 1st Series.—Old Testament. With Seven Illustrations, by WALTER CRANE. Fcap 8vo. Price 3s. 6d. cloth. 2nd Series.—New Testament. With Seven Illustrations, by WALTER CRANE. Fcap 8vo. Price 3s. 6d. cloth.
** The Volumes are sold separately.
By the same Author.

Children's Sayings : or, Early Life at Home. Four Illustrations, by WALTER CRANE. Square 16mo. 2s. 6d. cloth.

NEW NOVELS.

Entanglements. By the Author of "Mr. Arle," "Caste," &c. Two Vols.

Normanton. By A. J. BARROWCLIFFE, Author of "Amberhill," and "Trust for Trust." One Vol.

Skirmishing. By the Author of "Who Breaks, Pays," and "Cousin Stella." One Vol.

HISTORY AND BIOGRAPHY.

Vancouver Island and British Columbia: Where they are; What they are; and What they may become.

By Dr. Alexander Rattray,
of the Royal Navy. Post 8vo. Four Plates and Two Maps. 5s. cloth.

History of the Four Conquests of England.

By James Augustus St. John, Esq.
Two Vols. 8vo. Price 28s. cloth.

History of the Venetian Republic:

By W. Carew Hazlitt.
Complete in 4 vols. 8vo, with Illustrations, price 2l. 16s., cloth.
*** Volumes III. and IV. may be had separately.

The Life and Letters of Captain John Brown.

Edited by Richard D. Webb.
With Portrait. Fcap 8vo. Price 4s. 6d. cloth.

Life of Schleiermacher,

As unfolded in his Autobiography and Letters.
Translated by Frederica Rowan.
Two vols. post 8vo, with Portrait. Price One Guinea, cloth.

The Life of Charlotte Brontë (Currer Bell).

By Mrs. Gaskell.
Fourth Library Edition, revised, one vol., with a Portrait of Miss Brontë and a View of Haworth Parsonage. Price 7s. 6d.; morocco elegant, 14s.

Life of Edmond Malone,

Editor of Shakspeare's Works. With Selections from his MS. Anecdotes.
By Sir James Prior.
Demy 8vo, with Portrait, 14s. cloth.

The Autobiography of Leigh Hunt.

One vol., post 8vo, with Portrait. Library edition. Price 7s. 6d. cloth.

Life of Lord Metcalfe.

By John William Kaye.
New Edition, in Two Vols., post 8vo, with Portrait. Price 12s. cloth.

Life of Sir John Malcolm, G.C.B.

By John William Kaye.
Two Vols. 8vo, with Portrait. Price 36s. cloth.

The Autobiography of Lutfullah.

A Mohamedan Gentleman; with an Account of his Visit to England.
Edited by E. B. Eastwick, Esq.
Third Edition, Fcap 8vo. Price 5s. cloth.

The Life of Mahomet.

With Introductory Chapters on the Original Sources for the Biography of Mahomet, and on the Pre-Islamite History of Arabia.
By W. Muir, Esq., Bengal C.S.
Complete in Four Vols. Demy 8vo. Price 2l. 2s. cloth.
*** Vols. III. and IV. may be had separately, price 21s.

Women of Christianity

Exemplary for Piety and Charity.
By Julia Kavanagh.
Post 8vo, with Portraits. Price 5s. in embossed cloth.

VOYAGES AND TRAVELS.

Robert O'Hara Burke and
the Australian Exploring Expedition of 1860.

By Andrew Jackson.

With Map and Portrait. Post 8vo. Price 6s. cloth.

The Rifle in Cashmere.

A Narrative of Shooting Expeditions in Ladak, Cashmere, &c. With Advice on Travelling, Shooting, and Stalking. To which are added notes on Army Reform and Indian Politics.

By Arthur Brinckman.

Late of H.M.'s 94th Regiment. With Two Illustrations. Post 8vo. Price 8s. 6d. cloth.

Scripture Lands

In connection with their History: With an Appendix: and Extracts from a Journal kept during an Eastern Tour in 1856-7.

By the Rev. G. S. Drew,

Author of "Scripture Studies," &c. Second Edition, post 8vo, with a Map, price 10s. 6d. cloth.

A Visit to the Philippine Isles in 1858–59.

By Sir John Bowring,

Demy 8vo, with numerous Illustrations, price 18s. cloth.

Narrative of the Mission to Ava.

By Captain Henry Yule, Bengal Engineers.

Imperial 8vo, with Twenty-four Plates (Twelve coloured), Fifty Woodcuts, and Four Maps. Elegantly bound in cloth, with gilt edges, price 2l. 12s. 6d.

Egypt in its Biblical Relations.

By the Rev. J. Foulkes Jones.

Post 8vo, price 7s. 6d. cloth.

Japan, the Amoor, and the Pacific.

A Voyage of Circumnavigation in the Imperial Russian Corvette "Rynda," in 1858-59-60.

By Henry Arthur Tilley.

8vo, with illustrations, 16s. cloth.

Through Norway with a Knapsack.

By W. M. Williams.

With Six Coloured Views. Third Edition, post 8vo, price 12s. cloth.

Turkish Life and Character.

By Walter Thornbury.

Author of "Life in Spain," &c. &c. Two Vols., with Eight Tinted Illustrations, price 21s. cloth.

Voyage to Japan,

Kamtschatka, Siberia, Tartary, and the Coast of China, in H.M.S. *Barracouta.*

By J. M. Tronson, R.N.

8vo, with Charts and Views. 18s. cloth.

To Cuba and Back.

By R. H. Dana,

Author of "Two Years before the Mast," &c.

Post 8vo, price 7s. cloth.

Life and Liberty in America.

By Dr. C. Mackay.

Second Edition, 2 vols., post 8vo, with Ten Tinted Illustrations, price 21s.

WORKS OF MR. RUSKIN.

Modern Painters.

Now complete in five vols., Imperial 8vo, with 87 Engravings on Steel, and 216 on Wood, chiefly from Drawings by the Author. With Index to the whole Work.   Price 8*l.* 6*s.* 6*d.*, in cloth.

EACH VOLUME MAY BE HAD SEPARATELY.

Vol. I.   6th Edition.   OF GENERAL PRINCIPLES AND OF TRUTH. Price 18*s.* cloth.

Vol. II.   4th Edition.   OF THE IMAGINATIVE AND THEORETIC FACULTIES.   Price 10*s.* 6*d.* cloth.

Vol. III. OF MANY THINGS. With Eighteen Illustrations drawn by the Author, and engraved on Steel.   Price 38*s.* cloth.

Vol. IV. ON MOUNTAIN BEAUTY.   With Thirty-five Illustrations engraved on Steel, and 116 Woodcuts, drawn by the Author. Price 2*l.* 10*s.* cloth.

Vol. V.   OF LEAF BEAUTY; OF CLOUD BEAUTY; OF IDEAS OF RELATION.   With Thirty-four Engravings on Steel, and 100 on Wood.   Price 2*l.* 10*s.*   With Index to the five volumes.

The Stones of Venice.

Complete in Three Volumes, Imperial 8vo, with Fifty-three Plates and numerous Woodcuts, drawn by the Author.   Price 5*l.* 15*s.* 6*d.* cloth.

EACH VOLUME MAY BE HAD SEPARATELY.
Vol. I. The FOUNDATIONS, with 21 Plates. Price 2*l.* 2*s.*   2nd Edition.
Vol. II. THE SEA STORIES, with 20 Plates. Price 2*l.* 2*s.*
Vol. III. THE FALL, with 12 Plates.   Price 1*l.* 11*s.* 6*d.*

The Seven Lamps of Architecture.

Second Edition, with Fourteen Plates drawn by the Author.   Imp. 8vo. Price 1*l.* 1*s.* cloth.

Lectures on Architecture and Painting.

"Unto this Last."

Four Essays on the First Principles of Political Economy.
With Preface. Fcap 8vo.   3*s.* 6*d.* cloth.

Pre-Raphaelitism.

A New Edition.   Demy 8vo.   Price 2*s.*

The Two Paths:

Being Lectures on Art, and its relation to Manufactures and Decoration.
One vol., crown 8vo, with Two Steel Engravings.   Price 7*s.* 6*d.* cloth.

The Elements of Drawing

Sixth Thousand, crown 8vo, with Illustrations drawn by the Author.   Price 7*s.* 6*d.* cloth.

The Elements of

RELIGIOUS.

Sermons:
By the late Rev. Fred. W. Robertson,
Incumbent of Trinity Chapel, Brighton.
FIRST SERIES.— Ninth Edition, post
8vo. Price 9s. cloth.
SECOND SERIES. — Eighth Edition.
Price 9s. cloth.
THIRD SERIES.—Seventh Edition, post
8vo, with Portrait. Price 9s. cloth.

Expositions of St. Paul's Epistles to the Corinthians.
By the late Rev. Fred. W. Robertson.
Second Edition. One thick Volume,
post 8vo. Price 10s. 6d. cloth.

Lectures and Addresses.
By the late Fredk. W. Robertson,
A New Edition. Fcap 8vo. 5s. cloth.

The Gospel in the Miracles of Christ.
By Rev. Richd. Travers Smith, M.A.
Chaplain of St. Stephen's, Dublin.
Fcap 8vo, price 5s. cloth.

Sermons:
Preached at Lincoln's Inn Chapel.
By the Rev. F. D. Maurice, M.A.
FIRST SERIES, 2 vols., post 8vo, price
21s. cloth.
SECOND SERIES, 2 vols., post 8vo,
price 21s. cloth.
THIRD SERIES, 2 vols., post 8vo,
price 21s. cloth.

Experiences of an English Sister of Mercy.
By Margaret Goodman.
3rd edit. revised, Fcap 8vo. 3s. 6d. cloth.

Tauler's Life and Sermons.
Translated by Miss Susanna Winkworth.
With Preface by Rev. C. KINGSLEY.
Small 4to, price 7s. 6d. cloth.

The Soul's Exodus and Pilgrimage.
By the Rev. J. Baldwin Brown,
Author of "The Divine Life in Man."
Second Edition. Crown 8vo. 7s. 6d.
cloth. Morocco elegant, 12s.

"Is it not Written?"
Being the Testimony of Scripture
against the Errors of Romanism.
By Edward S. Pryce, A.B.
Post 8vo. Price 6s. cloth.

Quakerism, Past and Present:
Being an Inquiry into the Causes of
its Decline.
By John S. Rowntree.
Post 8vo. Price 5s. cloth.
*** This Essay gained the First Prize
of One Hundred Guineas offered for
the best Essay on the subject.

The Peculium;
An Essay on the Causes of the Decline
of the Society of Friends.
By Thomas Hancock.
Post 8vo. Price 5s. cloth.
*** This Essay gained the Second
Prize of Fifty Guineas, which was
afterwards increased to One Hundred.

THE BISHOP OF SALISBURY v. DR. WILLIAMS.

The Defence of Dr. Rowland Williams;
Being a Report of the Speech delivered
in the Court of Arches, by JAMES
FITZJAMES STEPHEN, M.A., Recorder
of Newark-on-Trent. Published
from the Shorthand Writer's Notes,
Revised and Corrected. Post 8vo.
Price 10s 6d. cloth.

MISCELLANEOUS.

Lectures on Horses and Stables.

By *Lieut.-Col. Fitzwygram*,
15th (the King's) Hussars.
First and Second Series (to be continued). Demy 8vo. Price 4s. 6d. cloth.

Reminiscences of Captain

Gronow. With Four Illustrations. Second Edition, Revised. Crown 8vo. 9s. cloth.

Essays by a Barrister.

(Reprinted from the *Saturday Review*.)
Post 8vo. Price 9s. cloth.

Studies in Animal Life.

By *George Henry Lewes*.
Author of "The Life of Goethe," "Sea-Side Studies," "Physiology of Common Life," &c. With Illustrations. Post 8vo. Price 5s. cloth.

Education in Oxford :

Its Method, its Aids, and its Rewards.
By *James E. Thorold Rogers, M.A.*
Post 8vo, price 6s. cloth.

Manuals for Ladies.

Flowers for Ornament and

Decoration ; and How to Arrange Them. With Coloured Frontispiece. Price 2s. 6d. cloth.

By the same Author.

In-Door Plants ; and How

to Grow Them for the Drawing-Room, Balcony, and Green-House. 5th Thousand. With Coloured Frontispiece. Price 2s. 6d. cloth.

Song Birds ; and How to

Keep Them. With Coloured Frontispiece. Fcap 8vo. Price 2s. 6d. cloth.

The Correspondence of Leigh Hunt.

Edited by his Eldest Son.

Two Vols. Post 8vo, with Portrait. Price 24s. cloth.

Intellectual Education,

and its Influence on the Character and Happiness of Women.
By *Emily Shirreff*.
2nd Ed. Crown 8vo. Price 6s. cloth.

Household Medicine ;

and Sick-Room Guide.

Describing Diseases, their Nature, Causes, and Symptoms, with the most approved Methods of Treatment, and the Properties and Uses of many new Remedies.

By *John Gardner, M.D.*

8vo, with numerous Illustrations.
Price 10s. 6d. cloth.

The Four Georges :

Sketches of Manners, Morals, Court and Town Life.

By *W. M. Thackeray*.

With Illustrations. Crown 8vo. Price 5s. cloth.

Shakspere and his Birthplace.

By *John R. Wise*.

With 22 Illustrations by W. J. Linton. Crown 8vo. Printed on Toned Paper, and handsomely bound in ornamental cloth, gilt edges, price 7s. 6d.

*** Also a cheap edition, 2s. 6d. cloth.

Port and Trade of London :

Historical, Statistical, Local, and General. *By Charles Capper,* Manager of the Victoria (London) Docks. Price 15s. cloth. 8vo.

New Zealand and the War.

By William Swainson, Esq.

Author of " New Zealand and its Colozation." Post 8vo. 5s. cloth.

The Lady's Guide to the

Ordering of her Household, and the Economy of the Dinner Table. *By a Lady.*

Crown 8vo. Price 10s. 6d. cloth.

The Early Italian Poets.

Translated by D. G. Rossetti.

Part I.—Poets chiefly before Dante. Part II. — Dante and his Circle. Price 12s. cloth. Post 8vo.

Book of Good Counsels :

An Abridged Translation of the Sanscrit Classic, the "Hitopadesa."

By Edwin Arnold, M.A., Oxon.

Author of " Education in India,". &c. With Illustrations by Harrison Weir. Crown 8vo, 5s. cloth.

Ragged London.

By John Hollingshead.

Post 8vo, 7s. 6d. cloth.

Man and his Dwelling Place.

An Essay towards the Interpretation of Nature.

Second Edition. With a New Preface. Crown 8vo, 6s. cloth.

Household Education.

By Harriet Martineau.

A New Edition. Post 8vo. Price 5s. cloth.

The Conduct of Life.

By Ralph Waldo Emerson,

Author of " Essays," " Representative Men," &c. Post 8vo, price 6s. cloth. *** Also a Cheap Edition, 1s. cloth.

Annals of British Legislation :

A Classified Summary of Parliamentary Papers.

Edited by Dr. Leone Levi.

The yearly issue consists of 1,000 pages, super-royal 8vo, and the Subscription is Two Guineas, payable in advance. Vols. I. to X. may now be had. Price 10l. 10s. cloth.

A Handbook of Average.

With a Chapter on Arbitration.

By Manley Hopkins.

Second Edition, Revised and brought down to the present time.

8vo. Price 15s. cloth; 17s. 6d. halfbound law calf.

Sea Officer's Manual.

Being a Compendium of the Duties of Commander and Officers in the Mercantile Navy.

By Captain Alfred Parish.

Second Edition. Small post 8vo. Price 5s. cloth.

Manual of the Mercantile Law

Of Great Britain and Ireland.

By Dr. Leone Levi.

8vo. Price 12s. cloth.

Commercial Law of the World.
By Dr. Leone Levi.
Two vols. royal 4to. Price 6*l.* cloth.

Victoria,
Or the Australian Gold Mines in 1857.
By William Westgarth.
Post 8vo, with Maps. 10*s.* 6*d.* cloth.

New Zealand and its Colonization.
By William Swainson, Esq.
Demy 8vo. Price 14*s.* cloth.

Life in Spain.
By Walter Thornbury.
Two Vols. post 8vo, with Eight Tinted Illustrations, price 21*s.*

A Treatise on Rifles, Cannon, and Sporting Arms.
Gunnery:
By William Greener,
Author of "The Gun."
Demy 8vo, with Illustrations.
Price 14*s.* cloth.

On the Strength of Nations.
By Andrew Bisset, M.A.
Post 8vo. Price 9*s.* cloth.

Results of Astronomical Observations
Made at the Cape of Good Hope.
By Sir John Herschel.
4to, with Plates. Price 4*l.* 4*s.* cloth.

Astronomical Observations.
Made at the Sydney Observatory in the year 1859.
By W. Scott, M.A.
8vo. 6*s.*

On the Treatment of the Insane,
Without Mechanical Restraints,
By John Conolly, M.D.
Demy 8vo. Price 14*s.* cloth.

England and her Soldiers.
By Harriet Martineau.
With Three Plates of Illustrative Diagrams. 1 vol. crown 8vo, price 9*s.* cloth.

Tea Planting in the Himalaya.
By A. T. McGowan.
8vo, with Frontispiece, price 5*s.* cloth.

Signs of the Times;
Or, The Dangers to Religious Liberty in the Present Day.
By Chevalier Bunsen.
Translated by Miss S. WINKWORTH.
One vol. 8vo. Price 5*s.* cloth.

Wit and Humour.
By Leigh Hunt.
Price 5*s.* cloth.

Jar of Honey from Hybla.
By Leigh Hunt.
Price 5*s.* cloth.

Men, Women, and Books.
By Leigh Hunt.
Two vols.   Price 10*s.* cloth.

Zoology of South Africa.
By Dr. Andrew Smith.
Royal 4to, cloth, with Coloured Plates.

MAMMALIA	£3
AVES	7
REPTILIA	5
PISCES	2
INVERTEBRATÆ	1

Religion in Common Life.
By William Ellis.
Post 8vo.   Price 7*s.* 6*d.* cloth.

Life of Sir Robert Peel.
By Thomas Doubleday.
Two vols. 8vo.   Price 18*s.* cloth.

Principles of Agriculture;
Especially Tropical.
By B. Lovell Phillips, M.D.
Demy 8vo.   Price 7*s.* 6*d.* cloth.

Books for the Blind.
Printed in raised Roman letters, at
the Glasgow Asylum.

SMITH, ELDER AND CO.'S SHILLING SERIES
OF

STANDARD WORKS OF FICTION.

Well printed, on good paper, and tastefully bound.
Price ONE SHILLING each Volume,

THIRD ISSUE.

WHEAT AND TARES. Reprinted from "Fraser's Magazine."
AMBERHILL. By A. J. BARROW-CLIFFE.

YOUNG SINGLETON. By TALBOT GWYNNE.
A LOST LOVE. By ASHFORD OWEN.

SECOND ISSUE.

LOST AND WON. By GEORGIANA M. CRAIK.
HAWKSVIEW. By HOLME LEE.
FLORENCE TEMPLAR. By Mrs. F. VIDAL.

COUSIN STELLA; OR, CONFLICT. By the Author of "Who Breaks—Pays."
HIGHLAND LASSIES; OR, THE ROUA PASS.

FIRST ISSUE.

CONFIDENCES. By the author of "Rita."
ERLESMERE; OR, CONTRASTS OF CHARACTER. By L. S. LAVENU.
NANETTE AND HER LOVERS. By TALBOT GWYNNE.
THE LIFE AND DEATH OF SILAS BARNSTARKE. By TALBOT GWYNNE.
TENDER AND TRUE. By the Author of "Claran."

ROSE DOUGLAS; THE AUTOBIOGRAPHY OF A SCOTCH MINISTER'S DAUGHTER.

GILBERT MASSENGER. By HOLME LEE.

THORNEY HALL: A STORY OF AN OLD FAMILY. By HOLME LEE.

MY LADY: A TALE OF MODERN LIFE.

THE CRUELEST WRONG OF ALL.

WORKS ON INDIA AND THE EAST.

Our Last Years in India.
By Mrs. John B. Speid.
Post 8vo.　Price 9s. cloth.

The Wild Sports of India,
With detailed Instructions for the Sportsman; to which are added Remarks on the Breeding and Rearing of Horses, and the Formation of Light Irregular Cavalry
By Major Henry Shakespear,
late Commandant Nagpore Irregular Force. With Portrait of the Author. Second Edition, much Enlarged. Post 8vo.　Price 10s. cloth.

Cotton; an Account of its Culture in the Bombay Presidency.
By Walter Cassels.
8vo, price 16s. cloth.

Narrative of the North China Campaign of 1860.
By Robert Swinhoe.
Staff Interpreter to Sir Hope Grant. 8vo, with Illustrations.　12s. cloth.

PRIZE ESSAY.
Caste:
Considered under its Moral, Social, and Religious Aspects.
By Arthur J. Patterson, B.A., of Trinity College.
Post 8vo.　Price 4s. 6d. cloth.

The Sanitary Condition of Indian Jails.
By Joseph Ewart, M.D.,
Bengal Medical Service.
With Plans, 8vo.　Price 16s. cloth.

Egypt, Nubia, and Ethiopia.
Illustrated by 100 Stereoscopic Photographs, taken by Francis Frith, for Messrs. Negretti and Zambra; with Descriptions and numerous Wood Engravings, by Joseph Bonomi, F.R.S.L., and Notes by Samuel Sharpe. In One Vol. small 4to. Elegantly bound.　Price 3l. 3s.

Campaigning Experiences
In Rajpootana and Central India during the Mutiny in 1857–8.
By Mrs. Henry Duberly.
Post 8vo, with Map.　Price 10s. 6d. cloth.

Narrative of the Mutinies in Oude.
By Captain G. Hutchinson,
Military Secretary, Oude.
Post 8vo.　Price 10s. cloth.

A Lady's Escape from Gwalior
During the Mutinies of 1857.
By Mrs. Coopland.
Post 8vo.　Price 10s. 6d.

Views and Opinions of Gen. Jacob, C.B.
Edited by Captain Lewis Pelly.
Demy 8vo.　Price 12s. cloth.

Papers of the late Lord Metcalfe.
By John William Kaye.
Demy 8vo.　Price 16s. cloth.

The English in India.
By Philip Anderson, A.M.
Second Edition, 8vo.　Price 14s. cloth.

Indian Exchange Tables.
By J. H. Roberts.
8vo. Second Edition, enlarged.
Price 10s. 6d. cloth.

Christianity in India.
A Historical Narrative.
By John William Kaye.
8vo. Price 16s. cloth.

The Parsees:
Their History, Religion, Manners, and Customs.
By Dosabhoy Framjee.
Post 8vo. Price 10s. cloth.

The Vital Statistics
Of the European and Native Armies in India.
By Joseph Ewart, M.D.
Demy 8vo. Price 9s. cloth.

The Bhilsa Topes;
Or, Buddhist Monuments of Central India.
By Major Cunningham.
One vol. 8vo, with Thirty-three Plates.
Price 30s. cloth.

The Chinese and their Rebellions.
By Thomas Taylor Meadows.
One thick volume, 8vo, with Maps.
Price 18s. cloth.

Hong Kong to Manilla.
By Henry T. Ellis, R.N.
Post 8vo, with Fourteen Illustrations.
Price 12s. cloth.

The Botany of the Himalaya.
By Dr. Forbes Royle.
Two vols. roy. 4to, cloth, with Coloured Plates. Reduced to 5l. 5s.

A Visit to the Suez Canal Works.
By George Percy Badger.
Demy 8vo. With Map. Price 2s. 6d.

The Defence of Lucknow.
By Captain Thomas F. Wilson.
Sixth Thousand. With Plan. Small post 8vo. Price 2s. 6d.

PRIZE ESSAYS.
By B. A. Irving.

The Theory of Caste,
8vo. 5s. cloth.

The Commerce of India with Europe.
Post 8vo. Price 7s. 6d. cloth.

Moohummudan Law of Sale.
By N. B. E. Baillie, Esq.
8vo. Price 14s. cloth.

Moohummudan Law of Inheritance.
By N. B. E. Baillie, Esq.
8vo. Price 8s. cloth.

The Cauvery, Kistnah, and Godavery:
Being a Report on the Works constructed on those Rivers, for the Irrigation of Provinces in the Presidency of Madras.
By Col. R. Baird Smith, F.G.S.
Demy 8vo, with 19 Plans. 28s. cloth.

Land Tax of India.
According to the Moohummudan Law.
By N. B. E. Baillie, Esq.
8vo. Price 6s. cloth.

FICTION.

Winifred's Wooing.
By Georgiana M. Craik. One Vol.

A Bad Beginning : A Story
of a French Marriage. Two Vols.

A Loss Gained.
By Philip Cresswell. One Vol.

Carr of Carrlyon.
By Hamilton Aïdé.
Author of " Rita," &c. 3 vols.

Warp and Woof.
By Holme Lee. Three Vols.

Who Breaks—Pays.
In Two Vols.
By the Author of " Cousin Stella."

The Wortlebank Diary :
With Stories from Kathie Brande's
Portfolio.
By Holme Lee. Three Vols.

Over the Cliffs.
By Mrs. Chanter,
Author of " Ferny Combes." 2 vols.

Lovel the Widower.
By W. M. Thackeray.
With six Illustrations. Post 8vo.
Price 6s. cloth.

Esmond.
By W. M. Thackeray.
Third Edition, crown 8vo. 6s. cloth.

The Adventures of Philip
on his Way through the World;
shewing who Robbed him, who
Helped him, and who Passed him by.
By W. M. Thackeray.
Author of " Esmond," Vanity Fair,"
" Virginians," &c. Three Volumes.
Post 8vo.

The Cotton Lord.
By Herbert Glyn. Two Vols.

Said and Done. One Vol.

Scarsdale ;
Or, Life on the Lancashire and Yorkshire Border Thirty Years ago. 3 vols.

Agnes of Sorrento.
By Mrs. Harriet Beecher Stowe.
Post 8vo. Price 7s. 6d. cloth.

Herbert Chauncey :
A Man more Sinned against than
Sinning.
By Sir Arthur Hallam Elton, Bart.
In 3 vols.

Hills and Plains. Two Vols.

The Firstborn.
By the Author of " My Lady."
Three volumes.

The Tragedy of Life.
By John H. Brenten. Two Vols.

Framley Parsonage.
By Anthony Trollope,
Illustrated by J. E. Millais, R.A.
Three Vols. Post 8vo, 21s. cloth.
Also a cheap Edition. 1 vol., post 8vo.
Price 5s. cloth.

Phantastes :
A Faerie Romance for Men and
Women.
By George Macdonald.
Post 8vo. Price 10s. 6d. cloth.

The Fool of Quality.
By Henry Brooke.
New and Revised Edition, with Biogra-
phical Preface by the Rev. Chas.
Kingsley, Rector of Eversley.
Two vols., post 8vo, with Portrait of
the Author, price 21s.

CHEAP EDITIONS OF POPULAR WORKS.

Against Wind and Tide.
By Holme Lee.
Author of " Sylvan Holt's Daughter," "Kathie Brande," &c. A New and Cheaper Edition. Fcap 8vo. Price 2s. 6d. cloth.

Lavinia. Price 2s. 6d. cloth.

Sylvan Holt's Daughter.
By Holme Lee. Price 2s. 6d. cloth.

The Autobiography of Leigh Hunt.
Price 2s. 6d. cloth.

WORKS OF THE BRONTE SISTERS.
Price 2s. 6d. each vol.
By Currer Bell.

The Professor.
To which are added the POEMS of Currer, Ellis, and Acton Bell. Now first collected.

Jane Eyre.
Shirley.
Villette.
Wuthering Heights and Agnes Grey.
By Ellis and Acton Bell.
With Memoir by CURRER BELL.

Tenant of Wildfell Hall.
By Acton Bell.

Life of Charlotte Brontë
(Currer Bell).
By Mrs. Gaskell.
Cheap edition. 2s. 6d. cloth.

Lectures on the English Humourists
Of the Eighteenth Century.
By W. M. Thackeray.
Price 2s. 6d. cloth.

The Town. *By Leigh Hunt.*
With 45 Engravings. 2s. 6d. cloth.

Transformation.
By Nathaniel Hawthorne.
Price 2s. 6d. cloth.

Kathie Brande:
The Fireside History of a Quiet Life.
By Holme Lee. Price 2s. 6d. cloth.

Below the Surface.
By Sir A. H. Elton, Bart., M.P.
Price 2s. 6d. cloth.

British India.
By Harriet Martineau. 2s. 6d. cloth.

Italian Campaigns of General Bonaparte.
By George Hooper.
With a Map. Price 2s. 6d. cloth.

Deerbrook.
By Harriet Martineau. 2s. 6d. cloth.

Tales of the Colonies.
By Charles Rowcroft. 2s. 6d. cloth.

A Lost Love.
By Ashford Owen. 2s. cloth.

Romantic Tales
(Including "Avillion").
By the Author of " John Halifax, Gentleman." 2s. 6d. cloth.

Domestic Stories.
By the same Author. 2s. 6d. cloth.

After Dark.
By Wilkie Collins. 2s. 6d. cloth.

School for Fathers.
By Talbot Gwynne. 2s. cloth.

Paul Ferroll.
Price 2s. cloth.

JUVENILE AND EDUCATIONAL.

The Parents' Cabinet

Of Amusement and Instruction for Young Persons.

New Edition, revised, in Twelve Shilling Volumes, with numerous Illustrations.

** The work is now complete in 4 vols. extra cloth, gilt edges, at 3*s.* 6*d.* each ; or in 6 vols. extra cloth, gilt edges, at 2*s.* 6*d.* each.

Every volume is complete in itself, and sold separately.

By the Author of "Round the Fire," &c.

Round the Fire :

Six Stories for Young Readers.
Square 16mo, with Four Illustrations.
Price 2*s.* 6*d.* cloth.

Unica :

A Story for a Sunday Afternoon.
With Four Illustrations. 2*s.* 6*d.* cloth.

Old Gingerbread and the Schoolboys.

With Four Coloured Plates. 2*s.* 6*d.* cl.

Willie's Birthday :

Showing how a Little Boy did what he Liked, and how he Enjoyed it.
With Four Illustrations. 2*s.* cloth.

Willie's Rest :

A Sunday Story.
With Four Illustrations. 2*s.* cloth.

Uncle Jack, the Fault Killer.

With Four Illustrations. 2*s.* 6*d.* cloth.

Philo-Socrates.

Parts I. & II. " Among the Boys."
Part III., IV.—"Among the Teachers."
By William Ellis.
Post 8vo. Price 1*s.* each.

Legends from Fairy Land.

By Holme Lee,
Author of " Kathie Brande," "Sylvan Holt's Daughter," &c.
With Eight Illustrations. 3*s.* 6*d.* cloth.

The Wonderful Adventures of Tuflongbo and his Elfin Company in their Journey with Little Content, through the Enchanted Forest.

By Holme Lee,
Author of " Legends from Fairy Land," &c.
With Eight Illustrations. Fcap 8vo.
Price 3*s.* 6*d.* cloth.

The King of the Golden River ;

Or, the Black Brothers.
By John Ruskin, M.A.
Fourth Edition, with 22 Illustrations
Richard Doyle. Price 2*s.* 6*d.*

Elementary Works on Social Economy.

By William Ellis.
Uniform in foolscap 8vo, half-bound.
I.—OUTLINES OF SOCIAL ECONOMY. 1*s.*6*d.*
II.—PROGRESSIVE LESSONS IN SOCIAL SCIENCE.
III.—INTRODUCTION TO THE SOCIAL SCIENCES. 2*s.*
IV.—OUTLINES OF THE UNDERSTANDING. 2*s.*
V.—WHAT AM I? WHERE AM I? WHAT OUGHT I TO DO? &c. 1*s.* sewed.

Rhymes for Little Ones.

16 Illustrations. 1*s.* 6*d.* cl., gilt edges.

Stories from the Parlour Printing Press.

By the Authors of the " Parent's Cabinet."
Fcap 8vo. Price 2*s.* cloth.

Juvenile Miscellany.

Six Engravings. Price 2*s.* 6*d.* cloth.